RIP VAN WINKLE'S REPUBLIC

Washington Irving, 1824, by William Brockedon. Pencil and chalk, 14 ⅞ × 10 ⅝. Courtesy National Portrait Gallery, London.

RIP VAN WINKLE'S REPUBLIC

Washington Irving in History and Memory

EDITED BY **ANDREW BURSTEIN**
AND **NANCY ISENBERG**

LOUISIANA STATE UNIVERSITY PRESS
BATON ROUGE

Published with the assistance of the Charles P. Manship Chair Endowment
at Louisiana State University

Published by Louisiana State University Press
lsupress.org

Copyright © 2022 by Louisiana State University Press
All rights reserved. Except in the case of brief quotations used in articles or reviews,
no part of this publication may be reproduced or transmitted in any format or by
any means without written permission of Louisiana State University Press.

Louisiana Paperback Edition, 2025

DESIGNER: Michelle A. Neustrom
TYPEFACE: Source Serif

Excerpt from "A Book in the Ruins" from *New and Collected Poems: 1931–2001*
by Czeslaw Milosz. Copyright (c) 1988, 1991, 1995, 2001 by Czeslaw Milosz Royalties, Inc.
Used by permission of HarperCollins Publishers.

A portion of "Rites and Times of the Grand Tour," by Michelle Sizemore, first appeared
in her book *American Enchantment: Rituals of the People in the Post-Revolutionary World* (2018)
and is reproduced by permission of Oxford University Press.

Cover illustration: *Joseph Jefferson as Rip Van Winkle*, 1871, by George Waters. Oil on canvas.
Courtesy Historic Hudson Valley, Pocantico Hills, NY (SS.79.7).

LIBRARY OF CONGRESS CATALOGING-IN-PUBLICATION DATA

Names: Burstein, Andrew, editor. | Isenberg, Nancy, editor.
Title: Rip Van Winkle's republic : Washington Irving in history and memory / edited by Andrew Burstein and Nancy Isenberg.
Description: Baton Rouge : Louisiana State University Press, [2022] | Includes bibliographic references and index.
Identifiers: LCCN 2021055029 (print) | LCCN 2021055030 (ebook) | ISBN 978-0-8071-7759-4 (cloth) | ISBN 978-0-8071-7803-4 (pdf) | ISBN 978-0-8071-7804-1 (epub) | ISBN 978-0-8071-8493-6 (paperback)
Subjects: LCSH: Irving, Washington, 1783–1859—Criticism and interpretation. | Irving, Washington, 1783–1859. Sketch-book of Geoffrey Crayon, gent. | Van Winkle, Rip (Fictitious character) | American literature—1783–1850—History and criticism. | Authors, American—19th century—Biography. | United States—In literature. | United States—History—1783–1865.
Classification: LCC PS2088 .R57 2022 (print) | LCC PS2088 (ebook) | DDC 813/.2—dc23/eng/20220721
LC record available at https://lccn.loc.gov/2021055029
LC ebook record available at https://lccn.loc.gov/2021055030

> . . . Pages of books lying
> Scattered at your feet are like fern-leaves hiding
> A moldy skeleton, or else fossils
> Whitened by the secrets of Jurassic shells.
> A remnant life so ancient and unknown
> Compels a scientist, tilting a stone
> Into the light, to wonder. He can't know
> Whether it is some dead epoch's shadow
> Or a living form. . .
> —CZESLAW MILOSZ,
> "A Book in the Ruins" (1941)

CONTENTS

Preface: Why Washington Irving Still Matters
ANDREW BURSTEIN
— ix —

Introduction
ANDREW BURSTEIN & NANCY ISENBERG
— 1 —

PART I. ANOTHER TIME

Rites and Times of the Grand Tour
MICHELLE SIZEMORE
— 19 —

Washington Irving Reimagined as Father of His Country
SHIRLEY SAMUELS
— 42 —

Reading the *Sketch Book* from Its Clattering Hooves Up
NANCY ISENBERG
— 62 —

Irving's Relicts
MATTHEW DENNIS
— 82 —

Irving's Investment in Time
ALEXIS McCROSSEN & ANDREW BURSTEIN
— 99 —

PART II. ANOTHER WORLD

Tracing Northern Slavery in the Knickerbocker Stories
ELIZABETH L. BRADLEY
— 123 —

A Toast to, and Distillation of, Rip Van Winkle
TRACY HOFFMAN
— 139 —

The Revolutionary War Lives On
ERIK WEISELBERG
— 154 —

Irving Family Manuscripts
CATALINA HANNAN
— 175 —

An Actor's Reflections on the Theatrical Irving
CURTIS ARMSTRONG
— 190 —

Contributors
— 205 —

Index
— 209 —

PREFACE

WHY WASHINGTON IRVING STILL MATTERS

A pandemic prevented the scholars featured in this volume from assembling in the shadow of the Hudson River to mark the bicentennial of *The Sketch Book of Geoffrey Crayon, Gent.* Our 2020 symposium was canceled, but we have communed on the page as a fruitful alternative, in recalling to mind the prolific author who grabbed the world's attention with that best-selling collection of stories, among which are two unforgettable tales, "Rip Van Winkle" and "The Legend of Sleepy Hollow." Washington Irving (1783–1859) was a Manhattanite who took up his pen in Liverpool, England, as the family trading business he'd come to help his brother manage was collapsing. Writing was the only job he could imagine himself sticking to, and he happened to be adept at what we now style "networking," so when the *Sketch Book* launched him onto the English literary scene, it fed his hopes even as it rescued the reputation of American letters abroad.

Among the rising generation in today's America, Irving has become almost like one of the nearly forgotten authors at whom he marveled in the authorial guise of a wanderer named Geoffrey Crayon. Irving's tale "The Art of Book-Making" is a case in point. It appears in the middle of the *Sketch Book* and captures the storyteller's adoration for (and compulsive pursuit of) preserved texts. Crayon, an American, is on an exploratory mission when he opens a door and enters the hushed silence of a mysterious otherworld. He is surrounded by "great cases of venerable books." Before him sit the devoted members of a scholarly breed, "pale, studious personages" lost in the pages of "mouldy manuscripts," their pens dashing across notebook pages as they seek wisdom and inspiration from withering words to incorporate into their own embryonic writings.

They copy. Most of the tales Irving spins are adaptations in some manner or other; originality does not preclude the act of borrowing. The "manufacturing of books" that Irving addresses in "The Art of Book-Making" is not a study in typography, just as this is not a print shop he has entered. "I was, in fact, in the reading-room of the great British Library, an immense collection of volumes of all ages and languages, many of which are now forgotten, and most of which are seldom read: one of these sequestered pools of obsolete literature to which modern authors repair, and draw buckets full of classic lore, or 'pure English, undefiled,' wherewith to swell their own scanty rills of thought."

From this quasi-confessional essay, we perceive how our author, in his whimsical treatment of language and cheerful interrogations of memory, acknowledges his own shortcomings as a creator. At the same time, he offers a defense of the copyist: "May not this pilfering disposition be implanted in authors for wise purposes? May it not be the way that Providence has taken care that the seeds of knowledge and wisdom shall be preserved from age to age, in spite of the inevitable decay of the works in which they were first produced?" Literature, he tells us, undergoes a "metempsychosis," reemerging in a form more palatable to later times. A "ponderous history" is resurrected as a bright romance; an "old legend" becomes a modern play. "Thus it is in the clearing of our American woodlands," he analogizes. Just as nature acts to restore life, so these book-makers act to refurbish knowledge.

Two hundred years ago, Washington Irving was America's best-known author, the first American fiction writer to become a major sensation abroad. The *Sketch Book,* his breakout work, was published serially in 1819 and 1820, and thereafter bound. "Rip Van Winkle" and "The Legend of Sleepy Hollow" live on. The several Christmas tales, all set in the English countryside, are retained in memory by an interested few. The other pieces are pretty much forgotten.

In the decade of the 1820s, Irving's fan base rivaled Lord Byron's—indeed, the tale teller and the exalted poet shared a powerhouse London publisher in John Murray. The American republic's first professional author came to be treated almost as one who had sprung from the pages of literature. His charming Dutch cottage facing the Hudson River, Sunnyside, became a tourist attraction at midcentury, and the aging icon found his privacy compromised.

One hundred years ago, Irving was still a cherished literary figure, widely read in a host of languages. In addition to the *Sketch Book,* which has never gone out of print, and its similarly framed successor volumes, *Bracebridge Hall* (1822), *Tales of a Traveller* (1824), and the so-called Spanish Sketch Book, *Tales of the Alhambra* (1832), he authored multivolume biographies of Christopher Columbus (1828) and George Washington (1855–1859), which retained their broad appeal for decades. While readers had access to many biographies of the first president by then, Irving's extended treatment of the voyages of Columbus was the first ever in the English language and saw 175 editions published before 1900. Western adventures added to Irving's body of work. At home after seventeen years abroad, the author redirected his story-spinning eye to the frontier in *A Tour on the Prairies* (1835), *Astoria* (1836), and *Captain Bonneville* (1837). The insurgent satirist who first obtained a substantial U.S. readership with his mock epic *A History of New-York,* or "Knickerbocker's History" (1809), had by the 1830s grown into a genteel historian and lover of country, which suited the times.

Over the past half century, however, through no conscious decision in or out of academic circles, Irving's star has gone into apparent decline. His contributions to American culture were never explicitly rejected, yet he has aroused less interest. His image was printed on the one-cent stamp in the 1940 series "Famous Americans"; in the motion picture age, his tales "Rip

Van Winkle" and especially "The Legend of Sleepy Hollow" have been variously adapted. The post–World War II "baby boom" generation grew up on Irving tales, in part through anthologies and in part by way of comic books and television. But in large measure, Sleepy Hollow and Irving's literary-cultural geography have been hijacked to the point where the original author's contribution has become irrelevant. The modern edition of his *Complete Works,* a masterfully annotated series that includes Irving's diaries and correspondence, was published in the late 1970s and the 1980s without jump-starting a commensurate amount of new scholarship—it is a rarity to find these works cited in the present century.

I tried, as the author of *The Original Knickerbocker: The Life of Washington Irving* (2007), to recover the historical Irving as a multidimensional figure, an innovative writer who became a "citizen of the world," a celebrated biographer, and a respected diplomat. The present-day literary canon recollects Irving but no longer treats him as the literary force he was formerly. One reason for the appearance of this volume, then, is to reconnect with a major figure who was immersed in transatlantic culture at the moment when a British-influenced "Americana" took shape. Irving's writing style was molded by English authors such as Oliver Goldsmith and by the literary giant who befriended him, Sir Walter Scott. The *Sketch Book,* in turn, had a profound impact on Charles Dickens. It gave voice to an American as he traveled about and sized up British history, the English countryside, the British class system, Old World folklore, and quaint relics.

Although his writing later took on a nationalist tone, during the *Sketch Book* period, Irving avoided the patriotic gloss that American newspapermen and various other politicos were applying as they proclaimed the uniqueness of their young nation. He displayed a debt to English customs yet preserved his American tone and perspective. Taking note of that fact, our volume reveals more of the cultural environment of the 1820s, a decade in which the romanticized past confronted the emergent industrial age of timekeeping. A rising commercial nouveau riche came to include middle-class Americans who flocked to the former mother country and the European continent beyond, to see, to learn, to compare.

This volume correspondingly acknowledges the importance of literary geography. Whether it is rural England or colonial America (both English- and Dutch-accented), the meaning of place and contested culture necessarily belongs in any conversation that addresses Washington Irving. New Yorkers' dislike of New Englanders is as much a feature in his stories as unresolved tensions in the ongoing displacement of Native Americans and, to a lesser but still significant extent, the practices that shaped racial estrangement and slavery in the North. Nor should we ignore Irving's immediate backyard of Tarrytown. The creation of local legends—before, during, and after Irving's lifetime—demonstrates how Americans continued to invent their history by following Irving's lead. It is not just that he takes readers through castles, roadside inns and taverns, rural ruins, and, notably, Ichabod Crane's breathless race on horseback across one particular bridge; it's that wherever Irving's alter ego rambles, there's a sense of movement and an atmospheric mood. In short, the *Sketch Book* emits a vibrant geo-cultural sensibility.

It would be folly to confine Irving to the narrow contours of one or two of his stories or to attach solely to the Knickerbocker phenomenon that has long since lost its earlier distinctiveness. The essays collected here range widely, but they all recognize Irving as a storyteller who never abandoned the vital spark he brought to his social criticism. As a leading citizen in a contentious republic, he reacted to democratic politics and imperialistic expansion. Make no mistake: what happened in the early American republic impinged upon Rip's fictional republic. That republic may have lacked legislative authority, but it did represent "the people" in its emphasis on engaging characters who exist within the painted scene—the product of a painter's palette. Irving's colorful sketches capture the authentic manners of the places he goes (or imagines).

This book is called *Rip Van Winkle's Republic* because Irving, despite his cosmopolitanism, remained a creature of the momentous decades following the American Revolution. It matters that this namesake of George Washington was born the year the Treaty of Paris secured national independence and the commanding general led his troops down Broadway, just blocks from the Irving family home. Washington Irving breathed the hopes and fears of an expectant generation, prudently skeptical about any democratic future. His writings embody real contradictions: the familiar trio of race, class, and gender encompasses many of the anxieties of his age. Yet his humorous inflections, his pungent prose, capture a real world, an insecure world. As such, the match and mismatch between his lived experience and the stuff of his writing are sought after by the contributors to this volume. The early nineteenth century is never truly hidden, despite Irving's wily purpose: his attempts to defy time.

Irving warrants study by literary scholars for a multitude of reasons, but especially because he thoroughly understood the marketplace of literature, the nuts and bolts of the book publishing trade as it came to life in Philadelphia and New York. Speculative ventures infiltrate plots and frame a good many of his character sketches. One version of Irving was gaily amused, another dredged up dark thoughts. He oscillates between open sky and Gothic shadows, presenting the enterprising spirit of men along with the conflicting notions of their rude democracy. In the opening decade of his career, he launched powerfully subversive satire decrying the treatment of Native Americans; later on, he retrenched, able to rationalize Jacksonian Indian removal. He cannot be categorized easily.

Irving ought to be of interest to historians because he came to his professionalism through an immersion in several professions: participation in the Anglo-American import trade and wholesale merchandising, through his family's ongoing concern, P. & E. Irving; study of the law in turn-of-the-century Manhattan; and close observation of the fur trade on the U.S.–Canadian border—he later helped put together the millionaire fur trader John Jacob Astor's self-centered history-for-hire. Irving knew the wealthy and the titled, and he knew bad investment and bankruptcy firsthand. In politics and the arts, Washington Irving knew most everyone, and everyone knew him.

Accordingly, we ought also to give renewed consideration to the so-called Knickerbocker school of writers that Irving helped spawn. They include Empire State natives such as the prodigious James Fenimore Cooper and Irving's lifelong friend James Kirke Paulding, author of the popular *Westward Ho!* and numerous other novels and poems. Likewise, a good many adoptive New Yorkers profited from Irving's example. Notable among these is the prominent newspaper editor William Cullen Bryant (who was also a prodigy poet and short story writer) and the renowned poet-satirist Fitz-Greene Halleck.

Tireless doers in the decades when New York City became the hub of American publishing and a center for the arts, they were all bent on developing a distinctive "national literature" that would place a young country on more or less equal footing with Europe. *Knickerbocker Magazine,* which began publishing in 1833, kept the sentiment and wit of the original Knickerbocker alive through the Civil War. Yet, with the clear exception of Cooper—a giant of early American literature, who roundly criticized Irving for his middle-class rearing and desire for money—the Knickerbocker crowd has left fainter footprints than Irving in the sands of literary time.

A criticism of Irving has been that he lacks "edge," that his tales are too smoothly crafted, too wondrously drawn. His actual complexity has at times been obscured by a reputation for literary comfort food. True, he gave us an amped-up American Christmas in the form of jolly St. Nicholas (1809), while restoring to memory old English holiday traditions (1820). He also produced an Admiral Columbus (1828) who was uncomfortably close to being a mirror image of that fanciful General Washington who could not tell a lie. The discoverer had a "loftiness of character" that enabled him to alter the "destinies of nations." Like America's "First of Men," the enterprising Genoan was "controlled by a powerful judgement, and directed by an acute sagacity."

But Irving, in his maturity, wasn't just about manly adventurers or dutiful daughters. With his passion for description, whether of individuals or of picturesque landscapes, he did not ignore the crude, the transgressive, or the disorderly. It's just that he gained more traction with his bright-minded characterizations of an imaginary environment where "rambling" folk—willing wanderers like himself—found means to escape the ravages of time.

There is no need to defend Washington Irving against critics, living or dead, who fail to appreciate his penchant for provocation. The author's humorous treatment of outgoing President Jefferson in *A History of New-York*, when he was a daring twenty-six-year-old, is arguably as damning as ex-slave William Wells Brown's *Clotel; or, the President's Daughter* (1853), which purports to tell the story of a victimized biracial woman, Jefferson's unacknowledged offspring. Irving's Jefferson stand-in, colonial New Netherland's William the Testy, was an overeducated bore who "had withered, in fact, not through the process of years, but through the tropical fervor of his soul, which burnt like a vehement rushlight in his bosom, inciting him to incessant broils and bickerings." He was in possession of a "busy, meddling mind." Wielding his pen with a purpose, Irving cut his "Dutch" ruler down to size: "Your passionate little men, like small boats with large sails, are easily upset or blown out of their course; so was it with William the Testy, who was prone to be carried away by the last piece of advice blown into his ear. . . . He gave none a fair trial; and by endeavoring to do everything, he, in sober truth, did nothing." Jefferson's words impressed a whole lot of people, but for the author of this deft caricature, they remained unfulfilled in executive action.

What drew me, as a professional historian, to the historical Irving was his deliberate manipulation of common understandings of time itself. Understanding each generation's treatment of time is the job of historians of every age, whether or not they choose to address the phenomenon directly. Irving wrote to probe the human psyche. He played upon Americans' estrangement from their colonial past, and later captured the modern echoes of Moorish Spain, all the while trapping the ghosts of ages and places past in both the Old and New Worlds. With a combination of adolescent joy and aging suspicion, he remained, throughout his life, committed to recovering a strong, vibrant yesteryear.

Irving resurrected lost cultures by giving them storied histories, but not without serious purpose. In prefatory comments to the 1848 reissue of his parodic "Knickerbocker's History," he said he wished to do more than poke fun at authorial pedantry; behind the burlesque were "the facts and personages of the olden time rescued from the dust of oblivion, and elevated into whatever importance they may actually possess." He hinted at something similar in "The Art of Book-Making."

He read widely with the purpose of engaging the forces of history in imaginative ways. From his opening gambit in "Knickerbocker's History," he wants his readers to understand that chronological time is meant to be attended to reverently before being toyed with unsparingly. "I treat of times long past, over which the twilight of uncertainty had already thrown its shadows," he writes, in the guise of the mock-historian Diedrich Knickerbocker. His way of reclaiming the lost was, he explained, to attach "pleasant associations and quaint characteristics" to it. He tells us precisely what he's bent on doing: creating a timeless setting that only *seems* to fit a particular era.

The mock history continues on the Jersey shore, where the primordial Dutch settlement of Communipaw rose. If not for the eccentric Knickerbocker, "this invaluable history, the great Communipaw, like Babylon, Carthage, Nineveh, and other great cities, might be perfectly extinct—sunk and forgotten in its own mud. . . . Let me, then, piously rescue from oblivion the humble relics of a place which was the egg from whence was hatched the mighty city of New York!"

It should be clear by now that Irving did more than spin yarns, even before he took an active role in national affairs. While never espousing a too-obvious partisan identity, he could not avoid the jumble of politics. Reared on the skirts of New York's financial district, he was introduced into the commercial city's high-toned political circles as the youngest in a patriotic family that included not only merchants like his unsentimental father but also a newspaper editor, a judge, and a congressman.

He came of age in the Manhattan of Aaron Burr and Alexander Hamilton, both of whom he admired (which already suggests his lack of hardened partisanship). Though he lampooned the slippery President Jefferson, he lavished praise on Jefferson's handpicked successor, James Madison, and the naval heroes of the War of 1812. Later on, he familiarly advised President Andrew Jackson, toured the English countryside with Martin Van Buren, and fortuitously bumped into Sam Houston in Oklahoma.

Rejecting a career in law, Irving chose a path that allowed him to express his plain curiosity about the human condition. As the nineteenth century opened, he first found his voice as a theater critic, and then, sequentially, as a social and political satirist, *mock* historian, magazine editor, short story writer, *reputable* historian, and senior U.S. diplomat. He was useful to his country in all of these ways. He was, to put it in broad terms, a passive opinion maker. He was a writer adored by readers for giving more than he asked in return.

Once he put Diedrich Knickerbocker to rest (or at least relegated him to the background), Irving's avatar became Geoffrey Crayon of the *Sketch Book,* a traveler who jotted arresting character portraits. Kings and queens; bankers and squires; anglers, vagabonds, and treasure hunters; townspeople and strangers all found their way into Irving's narratives of the *Sketch Book* period. Most everyone he wrote about was robust and friendly, displaying foibles and managing in one way or another to work through an affair of the heart.

In an Irving piece, the human spirit remains unbroken by forces of malevolence. The author had something better in mind for his readers than mere melodrama. His language exploits sensory deceptions but minimizes suffering; in only one ghost story, "The German Student," is there a gruesome outcome. Irving's legends never escape their storybook character, and his hauntings have reasonable explanations. He muses, he rouses, he dreams, he stirs, he provokes smiles, he celebrates peculiar customs.

And what of his personal legend? Though the affiliated Hudson River School of painting continues to be well regarded, we are at a moment in literary history when there is no obvious center of Irvingiana outside of the Historic Hudson Valley library and archive in Pocantico Hills, New York, a pumpkin's throw from Sleepy Hollow. I began my biography, as yet the only sustained treatment of Irving by a historian, by questioning whether we should regard him as a versatile word artist, adept at multiple genres, or as an uneasy chameleon, shy of commitment to social causes and consequently lost in a tame nostalgia. I'm still not sure that I answered the question to my own satisfaction. This is yet another reason for the present collection of original essays.

I am a historian who has profited from the work of literary scholars. I feel that it's crucially important, whenever possible, to communicate across disciplines. With the present volume, my coeditor and I pick up a conversation that has lapsed, enlisting new scholarship from perceptive students of Irving who are active today.

Before the American Revolution, Washington Irving's iconic character Rip Van Winkle went squirrel hunting in the Catskill Mountains. He encountered a party of quaint Dutchmen from Henry Hudson's era and awoke from an alcohol-infused sleep twenty years later to learn that George Washington was president. Rip could now enjoy a kind of liberation he hadn't known before his time-bending adventure. As Michelle Sizemore writes in her book *American Enchantment* (Oxford, 2018), "The *Sketch Book*'s moments of enchantment advance new ways of thinking about time and historical processes, providing a crucial alternative to familiar and cyclical histories" (108). Rip embodies an American conceit that later became the source of Hollywood magic: as much as we claim to be a country of industrious go-getters and innovators, we love our mischievous vicarious lives no less.

In Rip's fantasy republic, a penchant for storytelling makes inquiries into historical memory almost a civic obligation. It's what a free-spirited citizen does. In Rip's republic, history is a composite of memory and imagination. Here, we see time in terms of generations, allowing for changes of heart but not for withdrawals of affinity. The beauty of Rip's republic (and Irving's sensibility) is that one is at once never and always out of time.

—Andrew Burstein
April 2022

RIP VAN WINKLE'S REPUBLIC

INTRODUCTION

ANDREW BURSTEIN & NANCY ISENBERG

When he left New York for Liverpool in 1815, Washington Irving believed his writing career lay behind him. His breakout collection of stories, *The Sketch Book of Geoffrey Crayon, Gent.*, published in 1819–1820, emerged after a period of financial distress and emotional uncertainty. He tended to write in bursts amid struggles in appraising his self-worth. Never had a writer's world changed more than Irving's did with the praise heaped upon him for the originality of his new work. "The eulogiums," he wrote to his close confidant Henry Brevoort, "completely overwhelmed me. They go far, far beyond my most sanguine expectations." His sudden reputation opened doors, and as he went on to produce new collections modeled on the same format, the *Sketch Book* flew from American presses in reprint editions nine more times before the Author's Revised Edition came out, in 1848.[1]

Our volume was conceived in view of the bicentennial of the *Sketch Book's* publication. Some essays confine themselves to *Sketch Book* essays and tales, while others encompass more of Irving's literary and cultural legacy. The contributors reflect distinctly different backgrounds, roughly divided between the disciplines of history and literary analysis. This is intentional; the blurring of academic boundaries, we feel, makes for a more dynamic conversational structure.

Academics wrote about Washington Irving far more in the first half of the twentieth century than they have since. The two-volume biography by Stanley T. Williams of Yale, published in 1935, while wonderfully rich in detail, was darkened by the author's dismissive attitude toward his subject. Williams saw Irving as a popularity-seeking "dilettante." Damning the *Sketch Book* as "tepid," and driven by its sentimentalism, Williams saw it as pleasing to read but not especially profound, and regarded its successor, *Bracebridge Hall*, as "feeble" and "bloodless." Williams saw Irving as a writer of shifting moods, a "brooding" man with depressive tendencies. Fleeing from everything coarse, Williams's Irving privileged imagination over accuracy.

In time, the strongly biased Yale professor would express his clear preference for Herman Melville's more muscular prose, rescuing that author from obscurity in the 1940s and 1950s through the doctoral students he advised. Yet he did not publish work of significance on Melville or Nathaniel Hawthorne, another of his pet authors. How odd that he should have done so much as a mentor to resuscitate one great writer while more famously seeking to crush the reputation of another.[2]

In contrast to the disdain expressed by Williams, Pete Kyle McCarter drew up a strong assessment of Irving's prowess just as Williams's biography was circulating. His extremely thorough, very readable, unpublished dissertation at the University of Wisconsin (1939) is titled "The Literary, Political, and Social Theories of Washington Irving." As we write, a brand-new entry into the field effectively channels McCarter, this time coming from a professor of religion and philosophy, J. Woodrow McCree. *Washington Irving's Critique of American Culture* (2021) bemoans the diminution of Irving among scholars in the humanities generally and sets out to prove that the author was more than the sum of his parts, that he was supremely well informed in historical subjects and influenced by the intellectual giants of the ancient world. For McCree, Irving was "American Ovid, American Virgil," wise and subtle. He was, no less, a meditative bridge between the conscious skepticism that informed the Enlightenment era and the power of mind that stirred the Romantic spirit.[3]

The slow eclipse of the author in the modern literary imagination cannot be attributed to any lack of source material. From 1976 to 1987, Twayne Publishers released Irving's *Complete Works,* which included the author's personal journals and correspondence along with excellent commentaries from documentary editors. This trove of Irvingiana has scarcely been tapped by the living generation of academic historians and literary scholars.

As cultural historians, we recognize in Irving's well-documented travels, in his ever-expanding political and social networks forged over five decades, material ways to incorporate into modern scholarship the author's conscious interrogation of memory. His words concern the anxious character of transatlantic communications; they uncover nostalgia in the nature of forgetfulness; they touch upon literary life as a reflection of inner life.

Two insightful books published during the second half of the twentieth century analyze Irving's rise to literary fame and have truly stood the test of time: William L. Hedges, *Washington Irving: An American Study, 1802–1832* (1965), and Jeffrey Rubin-Dorsky, *Adrift in the Old World: The Psychological Pilgrimage of Washington Irving* (1988). While offering a Williams-like critique of the *Sketch Book*'s sentimental elements as "wallowing in abstractions and stock metaphors," and taking Irving's alter ego, Geoffrey Crayon, at face value as "a prompter of good feelings," Hedges also captures the volume's value as a restless text: "There is a network of relationships among the various items in the miscellany that . . . lifts up out of the murk of the past, tentative, half-formed, anxious attitudes toward questions of national character, heritage, and culture." The Irving who interests Hedges dwells on pertinent issues: class-inflected manners, competing sympathies, successes and failures, cultural strangeness and alienation, personal inadequacy, historical preservation and waste. To Hedges, then, the *Sketch Book* Irving is not strictly the inauthentic tourist whom Williams deplored.[4]

The implicitly psychological questions Hedges exposes are addressed by Rubin-Dorsky, who found Irving to be emotionally complex. Americanizing the Anglophilic New Yorker, Rubin-Dorsky shows that Irving's writing from abroad spoke to a country that shared much of his own self-doubt. The idea of home as "sanctuary" was key to Irving's proud yet agonizing search for financial and emotional stability, to "own" himself, to find comfort in belonging somewhere. It was as though separation anxiety was central to the personality of the Irving who authored the sketches; he tries too hard to separate himself from his surrogate persona Crayon. The same notion can be gleaned from the tales of "Rip Van Winkle" and "The Legend of Sleepy Hollow." Rubin-Dorsky states that, like Irving himself, "Rip and Ichabod desire nothing more than to live tranquil lives, primarily by inhabiting a safe, ordered, unchanging environment."[5]

One of the strengths of our volume, we feel, is how several contributors reopen an unfinished conversation by "reawakening" an interest in the cultural typology presented by the character of Rip Van Winkle. They tease out new meanings in Rip's lowly identity: Are we to celebrate his democratic character or bemoan his foolish impulses, his general laziness and lack of ambition, as a downside of the republican freedom to just exist, wallow in the banal, and act out fantastic stories? In creating him, was Washington Irving trying to charm or to mock?

We know that Irving himself had elitist tendencies when it came to democratic politics, at least at the time of his Jeffersonian-era writings in *Salmagundi* and *A History of New-York,* but in the *Sketch Book* and in his further publications through the decade of the 1830s, he embraced the frailty of the human condition with outstanding compassion, which is why he tends to be classed as a Romantic. Yet, as McCree's study also suggests, the moony idiom of Romanticism, if it applied to Irving, did not derail him from his larger determination, once again, to enjoy the "safe, ordered, unchanging environment" that he eventually found at Sunnyside.

The author traveled a long and winding road before he obtained that goal of finding his writer's retreat. Beginning in 1819, when the first *Sketch Book* numbers appeared, Richard Henry Dana, writing for the *North American Review,* lamented the loss of "home qualities" in the former satirist's new, mannerly style, wondering why Irving felt the need to go to England for his English to be artificially "improved."[6] As time pressed on and he sank deeper into the Old World, Irving, still struggling to become an independent writer, suffered again when critics at home accused him of having abandoned his people. He proved otherwise in stages: assuming a diplomatic position in London in 1829, then joining US Army Rangers on a rustic "tour" of Indian Territory (Oklahoma) soon after his return home in 1832. After the mid-1830s, when he acquired Sunnyside, along the banks of the Hudson, Irving completed his quest, confining himself thereafter, with few exceptions, to American themes.

In whatever locale he situated his stories, he aimed to recreate moods of quiet mystery or homely endurance. The "when" had something to do with the "where": either he'd recently journeyed to a place or he was fondly remembering home. What most animated his pen was the reconstitution of something precious in a lost past. Conjuring tiny places that lent themselves to quaint vignettes, he revealed character in short strokes. Immersing himself in country villages where kindly, credulous, preoccupied inhabitants indulged mysteries, he toyed with tradition. Or he found a corner of a city where the passing of time proceeded but softly and books came to life. Irving, as Crayon, interposed between the unreal and the possible, injecting mood-changing atmospherics. He always knew what to do with the improbable: grant it enough power to allow for both an intrusion and an escape.

Like Irving/Crayon, who implicitly asks us to explain the world he occupied in terms of the times and places he reinvented, we rescue pieces of the past from the jaws of forgetfulness. In the opening essay of part I, "Another Time," Michelle Sizemore presents Irving as an experienced traveler, fascinated by habits and customs, whose globe-trotting laid the foundation for his tales. She takes on the genre of the travel narrative and the meaning of the Grand Tour, a European ritual that select Americans took to in the wake of Irving's 1815 voyage to England and his subsequent movement about France, Germany, and Spain. As an author aiming for financial security, Irving thought of travel as an opportunity to enhance professional connections and, as Professor Sizemore writes, to "launch his career on a grander stage." The Grand Tour made that possible for the presumptuous middle-class Manhattanite.

In "The Author's Account of Himself," as the *Sketch Book* unfolds, Irving details the purpose of his Grand Tour: it is for a citizen of the United States, a nation "full of youthful promise," to experience "masterpieces of art" and means of refinement that would only be accessible to him in Europe, where "the accumulated treasures of age" reside. Sizemore goes on to expose the discreet meanings and pointed implications of the travel motif throughout the *Sketch Book*. Embedded in this discussion is Irving's Anglo-American pride, seen in the context of the "cyclical timeline of empire."

"England is a place of the past," Sizemore explains. "Americans are primitives bereft of civilization" and Britons are the "remnants of a once-great civilization." Washington Irving's purpose is to find common ground. Yet nothing is so central to the *Sketch Book* as the rituals of literary pilgrimage that seem to mean everything to the undisguised antiquarian Irving. In "A Royal Poet," "Stratford-on-Avon," and several others of the sketches, Geoffrey Crayon finds spiritual communion in books and authors.

In the following essay, Shirley Samuels looks at some of the haunted feelings from which history cannot turn, as they suggest themselves in Irving's imagery. Among the contradictions she identifies in the *Sketch Book* tales is the preservation versus the "pilfering" of the past, and the interplay of disturbance and frolic more generally. The early Dutch haunt "Rip Van Winkle" without posing any real danger, and yet there remains a disquieting element of "misrecognition" in that tale. More menacingly, the very idea of America is challenged by the dispossession of Native Americans, about whom Irving comes up with a multiplicity of narrative strategies, none entirely satisfying.

Perhaps it all began, as Professor Samuels tells us, with the name the youngest Irving carried. Washington was the nation's father, whose legacy haunted as much as it inspired. General Washington/President Washington died in 1799, before Irving came of age, and he left much to be done. If he gave posterity a way forward in defining public service, his sense of white

America's accountability for its treatment of Indigenous peoples was poorly focused. He did little to advance an understanding of the rights of the country's earliest inhabitants, their numbers ever declining.[7]

With respect to Irving's "Philip of Pokanoket," a lament in the *Sketch Book* centered on the defeated Wampanoag chief whose father had welcomed the *Mayflower,* Samuels writes, "The sons of Philip and the son of Rip Van Winkle become oddly juxtaposed here as displaced persons whose fathers have been absent." Thus, not all hauntings are equal. She argues that "the stories we most associate with Washington Irving concern a loss of memory so profound that the rest of his career can be seen as an attempt to reclaim and reassert the power of memory through historical fiction." Ownership of the past is, at best, a mirage of a sort that shadows all historical study.

Moving from issues of national belonging to issues of social identity, Nancy Isenberg engages in a reading of Irving's class politics, which, if obscure in his mature correspondence, is roughly approximated in his stories. With all the attention paid to "The Legend of Sleepy Hollow" over the years, no one has made much of the "broken down plough-horse" that carries Ichabod Crane on his fear-filled adventure. Well, that shameful omission is finally remedied! In several of Irving's tales, Isenberg notes, "horses function as key markers of rural life and class identity." Old Gunpowder, the hapless Ichabod's hapless horse, is a character in the story, not simply a bestial conveyance. Gunpowder's lack of breeding is a revealing social commentary embedded in a tale that is more complex than is generally thought.

Class is an unbanishable feature in Irving's stories. It extends from the country squire to denizens of small villages. It is encompassed in horse pedigree and in the coachmen who manage teams of horses. Most notable among this latter breed is the character of Coachey, who is, as Isenberg writes, the center of attention. "When a stage-coach rolls into a village, any village, something awakens among the lower ranks." Irving's coachmen are news suppliers, raconteurs. The slangwhanging Coachey is a kind of working-class hero.

Class follows Irving west to Indian country in *A Tour on the Prairies*, where a Swiss nobleman mixes it up with a French Creole named Tonish, a pastiche of American ethnic and class confusion, who is as much a braggart as Coachey, "master of the horse" and frontier guide. Chivalry—a nobility drawn from horsemanship—lends distinction to many an Irving narrative. Knights-errant vie for attention, just as Brom Bones, "famed for his horsemanship," fights for Katrina Van Tassel's hand in Sleepy Hollow. Ichabod's Gunpowder gallops into storybook fame as the class-conscious author draws from the past to forge imaginary worlds that toy with time, joining the reader's willing credulity to an inherited taste for magic, mystery, and quixotic characters.

In a fresh take on the nature of historical memory, Matthew Dennis introduces an intriguing premise by way of an etymological variant. The uncommon word *relict* denotes a widowed individual, a survivor. "Relics (or relicts) are objects that exist simultaneously in the present and the past," he writes. "They make the past itself present." Their vitality resides in their power over the mind.

The return of the Marquis de Lafayette to American shores in 1824, after an absence of four decades, is placed beside the return of the fictional Rip Van Winkle after a twenty-year sleep. Lafayette, surrogate son of General Washington and himself the last survivor among the Revolution's generals, excited imaginations as he visited each of the twenty-four states. And of course Rip's reappearance in his quiet village aroused more than a little curiosity. These two venerable "relicts" were alike in stimulating the historical imagination, amplifying the sense of bewilderment over time's mutability while questioning the permanence of historical knowledge. The political implications of Professor Dennis's essay are not to be minimized: "Relics can arouse awe and enthusiasm, foster strong feeling and emotion, promote identification and loyalty, and galvanize people to accept authority as legitimate."

In the final essay of part I of the volume, Alexis McCrossen and Andrew Burstein examine time multidimensionally. Irving lived in major cities, on two continents, where time-measuring devices framed daily life. He was a fastidious record keeper, and yet in scouring his personal journals, one cannot tell whether he made use of a pocket watch, as many gentlemen did. In his literature, time is painted impressionistically, intentionally nonspecific. It supports the author's escapist purpose.

Precision is an encumbrance to Irving's characters. Rip Van Winkle lacks a work regimen, while Ichabod Crane surrenders to superstition. When Irving delineates hours of a day, he does not fix upon a moment; on the contrary, his hours mostly pass unheeded. In "The Spectre Bridegroom," as a bride awaits her betrothed, "hour rolled after hour." In "Westminster Abbey," the numbered hours flow past as "billows" on the sea. In "The Voyage," Irving's narrator, Crayon, is able to "muse for hours." Time-oriented sea metaphors proliferate in the *Sketch Book:* in "Westminster Abbey," once again, as efforts to track the hours go nowhere, one becomes "a wreck on the distant shore of time." Sleep, dreams, and reveries permeate Irving's tales, of course, marking those extended moments when powerful questions form and imagination soars. Timepieces are of greatest use to the author when they serve his real agenda: hypnotizing readers into joining a time-bending journey. Indeed, Irving's appreciation for the present seemed to require that he bring the past to life.

Part II, "Another World," is less about wonderment—that is, less prone to flights of fancy—and more grounded in the physical realm. These essays engage directly with the lived history that exerted its influence on Irving while also shaping cultural identity for a generation that came of age in the post-Revolutionary decades. The American republic that Irving grew up in was combative and contradictory, divided along partisan lines and mired in published invective. As the youngest Irving was initially trying out his critical writing skills, he combined with his older brothers and their prankish friends to belittle grandstanding statesmen and to mock self-importance. His *Sketch Book*–era stories suppressed some of that pique in picturesque description, yet he would have grossly misled himself if he'd pretended that issues of political moment did not exist or that feelings of social alienation were not real.

American history has had to contend with nothing as powerfully felt as race inequality, in both its overt and covert exhibition and expression. Irving grew up in New York City and State when slavery was still practiced. He may have castigated white America for its ignorance and for presumptions made about the Native American peoples who preceded by thousands of years the Europeans' fledgling East Coast settlements, but he did not write a single sentence deploring the cruel imposition of slavery upon the Africans brought involuntarily to American shores.

Addressing these facts head-on, Elizabeth L. Bradley opens part II of the volume with a nimble discussion of the enslaved people who populate Irving's Knickerbocker tales. Across decades, the author's Black characters, though most often cast as objects of condescension, were also endowed with "far-famed powers" and "amazing skill." They were present to mourn the dead and to celebrate when the workday concluded; they retained a sense of community and made distinct contributions to the vibrant culture the author details. "We reject Irving's breezily offensive treatment of slavery and enslaved individuals," Bradley writes, "but as historians, we can read around his prejudices and shortcomings to find evidence of a past—and a community—many chose to ignore or erase."

Tracy Hoffman examines "Rip Van Winkle" in light of the temperance campaigns of the 1820s, mulling the drinking practices of the main character, both in village life and in his mystifying encounter with the seventeenth-century Dutch, whose "wicked flagon" of good cheer sends Rip on his time-bending journey. When Irving writes about drinking customs in his Bracebridge tales, featuring celebratory Christmas activities, he acclaims "the richest and raciest wines, highly spiced and sweetened, with roasted apples bobbing about the surface." Irving was playful in this way, willing to take chances on the page, but in his own life, toast making—a recognized skill in the early republic—created anxiety for him, if not outright embarrassment. Hoffman looks at alcohol consumption from multiple angles, tying moral reform to literary representations of male and female society. In the end, she dismisses any suggestion—and some have indeed made them—

that Washington Irving had a problem with (that is, expressed any moral criticism of) spiritous drink.

Community lies at the heart of Irving's literary universe, which makes it so interesting to consider the real-life impact of the author's geographic embellishments. Erik Weiselberg specializes in long-standing controversies that extend in all directions from the Revolutionary War as it was fought in Westchester County, New York. Here, he takes account of centuries of historical awareness among the residents of Tarrytown, Sleepy Hollow, and environs.

Beginning in 1776, the Hudson River was itself a site for spies, where divided loyalties persisted for several chaotic years. Major John André of the British army was dramatically captured in Tarrytown after meeting with the traitorous Benedict Arnold, and "The Legend of Sleepy Hollow" was written with this famous historical episode in mind. The headless Hessian whom the locals assume is responsible for haunting the area in the ghostly tale directly reflects wartime experiences that Irving's contemporaries recalled in lurid detail.

Taking the Sleepy Hollow story forward to the modern era, Weiselberg chronicles generations of active citizens whose investment in the legend has matched a passion to memorialize the wartime exploits Irving's tale reflected. In consequence of all this concern, and with tourism in mind, North Tarrytown was officially renamed the Village of Sleepy Hollow at the end of the twentieth century.

Catalina Hannan has had unlimited access to many of the original manuscripts of Irving, his family, and their correspondents, owing to her position as research librarian at the stately Historic Hudson Valley library and archive in Pocantico Hills, New York, outside of Tarrytown. Through the active lives and gossipy letters of Irving's nephews and nieces, she takes an intimate look at his return to New York and his reengagement in American life in the 1830s, after seventeen remarkable years on the other side of the Atlantic. Irving spent his later years in the company of a large extended family, whose stories about the storyteller add a fresh layer to our historical understanding. As in the *Sketch Book,* where he snoops about, cataloging his observations of others, in his personal life, Irving occasionally warranted the charge of being a meddling presence in the lives of the younger generation. They, then, deliver a precious portrait of domestic concerns while reflecting their own ambitions, and they do so in refreshingly uncensored language.

The collection closes with the unusual perspective of an accomplished film and television actor, Curtis Armstrong, who has studied the works of Washington Irving for decades. A significant part of Irving's legacy has been the easy conversion of his stories to stage and screen. How visual culture brought Irving tales to popular audiences over generations, at home and overseas (most notably in Spain), is an important element in our appreciation of his universality. His contemporary Jane Austen has attracted a new generation of readers by way of remakes and biopics. The Romantics seem to have a permanent hold on performance, just as Enlightenment philosophes continue to draw in modern interpreters of Western thought.

Armstrong recalls the fame of the great nineteenth-century American actor Joseph Jefferson III (1829–1905), the third of that name in a family of actors, who toured the United States and England as the star of a play based on "Rip Van Winkle." Because the public knew him best for this one persona, Jefferson's delightful autobiography was titled *"Rip Van Winkle."* Here was someone who, as a young man, performed in a comedy Washington Irving saw in Manhattan, and who lived long enough to make a short film that reprised his gloried role as Rip.

Joe Jefferson had no idea that the prodigious writer was in the audience to see one of his comedies, and only discovered it upon reading a paragraph in the fourth volume of the *Life and Letters of Washington Irving,* written by Irving's nephew Pierre Munro Irving. It said that Irving, a lifelong theatergoer, had been a great fan of Joseph Jefferson II, "one of the best actors he had ever seen." The son, he told Pierre, "reminded him, in look, gesture, size, and *make,* of the father." In the autobiography, Jefferson reflects, "To find myself remembered and written of by such a man gave me a thrill of pleasure."[8]

Rereading the *Sketch Book* in rural Pennsylvania on the eve of the Civil

War, Joe Jefferson was moved to create his own "Rip Van Winkle," though several versions had already been tried, one of which killed off the hero at the end of the second act. His rewrite took him far. In fact, Jefferson so embodied Rip in the theatrical imagination that once, when the actor was visiting Catskill, New York, a waiter at his hotel synthesized the tale for a first-time guest at teatime, and when asked if Rip's experience was meant to be believed, excitedly pointed to the actor who sat at a nearby table: "Why, dat's da man." Meanwhile, the president of the Rip Van Winkle Club in the same town accidentally introduced Jefferson at a reception as "Mr. Washington Irving."[9]

Any confusion between Irving's otherworld and the real world is not entirely a matter of chance. From the late nineteenth century forward, his inventions morphed into entities beyond the author's control. In 1809, *A History of New-York* introduced "good St. Nicholas," who "came riding over the tops of the trees, in that self-same wagon wherein he brings his yearly presents to children," "dropping them down the chimney of his favorites." His remarkable "jolliness," courtesy of Washington Irving's original, presented the broad outlines of what became the popular version of American Christmas. "The Legend of Sleepy Hollow" annually feeds pumpkin-related antics at Halloween, though the holiday is never mentioned in the *Sketch Book* story—it did not enter the U.S. calendar while Irving was alive.[10]

In the twentieth century, "Rip Van Winkle" became shorthand in newspaper stories whenever, for instance, a patient miraculously awoke after years in a coma. The headline "A Modern Rip Van Winkle" might describe a prisoner released into society who could not begin to grasp GPS or the use of phone apps. It's anyone who experiences an identity crisis involving the loss of time, or who metaphorically sleeps through historical events or is oblivious to a social idiom. "The Rip Van Winkle Caper," a 1961 episode of *The Twilight Zone,* narrated by Rod Serling, tells of "four Rip Van Winkles," abetted by a scientist, who are deliberately placed in suspended animation; they expect to wake into a world where their bank heist is forgotten and they can melt into future society as fabulously rich men.[11]

Washington Irving was more than a fastidious prose stylist, and certainly more than a sentimentalist. Even in the lofty dreams that crept into many of his tales, he offset expectations, challenged standards. It was a part of his personal psychology to want to confound, to play with ambiguity; his own "thrill of pleasure" derived from the act of invention. But Irving was also expert at the dissection of English and American manners, in the broader sense of customs, norms, and mores. This is what makes him a powerful source of historical knowledge and not merely a figure in the emergence of an American literary tradition. Perhaps his name is no longer on the tips of tongues; even so, his inventions have endured, embedded in language and holiday rituals. Anyone who has ever been lost in a reverie can still retrieve him.

NOTES

1. Washington Irving to Henry Brevoort, September 9, 1819, in *Letters*, vol. 1, *1802–1823*, ed. Ralph M. Aderman, Herbert L. Kleinfield, and Jenifer S. Banks, 559, in *The Complete Works of Washington Irving* (Boston: Twayne, 1978). See also Andrew Burstein, *The Original Knickerbocker: The Life of Washington Irving* (New York: Basic Books, 2007), chaps. 6 and 7; Washington Irving, *The Sketch Book of Geoffrey Crayon, Gent.*, ed. Haskell Springer (Boston: Twayne, 1978), xxv–xxxi.

2. Stanley T. Williams, *The Life of Washington Irving*, 2 vols. (New York: Oxford University Press, 1935), 1:21, 185–87, 207–8, 308–9. Williams advised on a great many Yale dissertations concerning Melville, including that of Nathalia Wright, who went on to author a book about American writers' travels in Italy (including journeys by Irving and Hawthorne) and was an editor of the modern (Twayne) edition of Irving's *Journals and Notebooks*.

3. J. Woodrow McCree, *Washington Irving's Critique of American Culture: Sketching a Vision of World Citizenship* (Lanham, MD: Lexington Books, 2021). As our volume goes to press, yet another new and challenging Irving study has appeared, authored by an American studies scholar in Austria: Heinz Tschachler, *Washington Irving and the Fantasy of Masculinity* (Jefferson, NC: McFarland, 2022).

4. William B. Hedges, *Washington Irving: An American Study, 1802–1832* (Baltimore: Johns Hopkins University Press, 1965), chaps. 5 and 6. Another useful work of this decade that reclaims Irving as a character of historical significance and literary merit is Edward Wagenknecht, *Washington Irving: Moderation Displayed* (New York: Oxford University Press, 1962).

Contextualizing the author with a measure of objectivity, Wagenknecht takes note of the particular difficulty Irving surmounted in appealing to two distinct reading publics: that of the United States and that of England and the European continent.

    5. Jeffrey Rubin-Dorsky, *Adrift in the Old World: The Psychological Pilgrimage of Washington Irving* (Chicago: University of Chicago Press, 1988), introduction and chaps. 1–3; quote at 102.

    6. Rubin-Dorsky, *Adrift,* 41.

    7. See, most recently, Colin G. Calloway, *The Indian World of George Washington: The First President, the First Americans, and the Birth of the Nation* (New York: Oxford University Press, 2018). Calloway writes, "The bulk of the federal budget during his presidency was spent in wars against Indians" (7).

    8. Pierre M. Irving, *The Life and Letters of Washington Irving,* 4 vols. (New York: G. P. Putnam, 1862–1864), 4:253; Joseph Jefferson, *"Rip Van Winkle": The Autobiography of Joseph Jefferson* (New York: Appleton-Century-Crofts, 1949), 172.

    9. Jefferson, *"Rip Van Winkle,"* 173, 351–52.

    10. Washington Irving, *A History of New-York,* ed. Michael L. Black and Nancy B. Black, book 2, chap. 5 and book 3, chap. 3, in *The Complete Works of Washington Irving* (Boston: Twayne, 1984). On Irving's connection to celebrations of Halloween in America, see Erik Weiselberg, "The Revolutionary War Lives On," in this volume.

    11. "The Rip Van Winkle Caper," *Twilight Zone,* season 2, April 21, 1961. In the present century, massive changes in the direction of a national political party caused a Floridian to muse, "Had a modern Rip Van Winkle, who happened to be a Republican, fallen asleep 20 years ago, he might think that he had awakened now in hell." Martin Dyckman, "Is Ted Cruz Eligible to Be President? The Question Needs to Be Resolved," *Florida Politics,* January 25, 2016, https://floridapolitics.com/archives/199595-martin-dyckman-is-ted-cruz-eligible-to-be-president-the-question-needs-to-be-resolved. In another instance, a man spent six weeks in an isolated woodland retreat, meditating, only to return to a country facing a pandemic. Ellen Barry, "'Did I Miss Anything?' A Modern Rip Van Winkle Emerges, Blinking, into Lockdown," *Irish Times,* June 3, 2020.

PART I

ANOTHER TIME

Oh my dear Brevoort how my heart warms towards you all, when I get to talking and thinking of past times and past scenes. What would I not give for a few days among the highlands of the Hudson with the little knot that was once assembled there. But I shall return home and find all changed, and shall be made sensible how much I have changed myself.

—WASHINGTON IRVING (in London) to Henry Brevoort (in New York), August 15, 1820

RITES AND TIMES OF THE GRAND TOUR

MICHELLE SIZEMORE

> To an American visiting Europe, the long voyage he has to make is an excellent preparative. The temporary absence of worldly scenes and employments produces a state of mind peculiarly fitted to receive new and vivid impressions. . . . All is vacancy until you step on the opposite shore, and are launched at once into the bustle and novelties of another world.
>
> —WASHINGTON IRVING, "The Voyage"

Following the War of 1812 and the Napoleonic Wars, Americans began packing for Europe. The end of hostilities in 1815 revitalized travel to England and the Continent, where throngs rushed to see sights unrestricted by the perils of war. The surge continued beyond the postwar years, with thousands setting sail annually in the middle decades and a great deal more in the second half of the century. Developments in transportation also made the voyage easier and more reliable. By the early 1820s, travelers could choose from five transatlantic passenger services with amenities—this compared to previous transportation aboard merchant ships, with crossings much longer, schedules more unpredictable, and hardships more plentiful. But perhaps the most irresistible reason for European travel was the renewed chance to participate in the Grand Tour, a time-honored English tradition increasingly embraced by Americans in the nineteenth century.[1]

For the second time in his young life (the first was 1804 to 1806), Washington Irving joined this Atlantic passage, in May 1815, spending the next seventeen years abroad and penning several works about Europe that would earn him international fame. He had not planned such a long stay. As he subsequently wrote to an Englishwoman he befriended in Dresden, he had expected that travel would ultimately lead him back to a steady life in the United States: "I trusted to return after a short absence, quite another being & then to settle down quietly beside [my mother] for the rest of my life."[2]

The immediate purpose of his excursion was to assist the thirty-two-year-old in finding direction after his literary success with the 1809 *A History of New-York* ("Knickerbocker's History"). Convinced that a career as a writer was out of reach, Irving had since served stints in politics, the military, and magazine editing. That his journey was propelled by a crisis of indecision aligns with the long-standing account of Irving as a man "adrift" at this stage in his life.[3] Securing a livelihood was the defining feature of his European tour, both during the first few years, while he was tending to the Liverpool outpost of the flailing family shipping business, and for the remainder of his stay, as he was advancing his writing career. Thus, he did find his vocation while away. Although it was not his intent, his ability to write for a living became indisputable after the *Sketch Book* caused a transatlantic sensation.

Europe provided not only the subject matter for much of the *Sketch Book* (1819–1820), as well as *Bracebridge Hall* (1822), *Tales of a Traveller* (1824), *A Chronicle of the Conquest of Granada* (1829), and *Tales of the Alhambra* (1832), but also the professional connections to launch his career on a grander stage. Arriving in 1815 with a national reputation as a man of letters, the Manhattanite gradually expanded his influence by winning his way into British literary circles. Among the luminaries whose acquaintance proved most momentous was the London publisher John Murray. In the summer of 1817, Irving devised a brokering business by which he would obtain copyright for a publisher on both sides of the Atlantic, thereby preventing American piracy of British books and vice versa. Irving showed up at 50 Albemarle Street on August 16 to propose his idea to one of the most prominent publishers in Great Britain.

The House of Murray boasted poets Thomas Campbell and Lord Byron, Walter Scott, Jane Austen, and more. If Irving was nervous, he held his own with the men already gathered—Murray's famed drawing room colloquies were daily ceremonies welcoming the notable and elite—and he demonstrated himself to be such a worthy guest that he was promptly invited back to dinner that same evening. Murray expressed interest in Irving's proposal, and though a full partnership never materialized, their initial meeting led to Murray's publication of British editions of the *Sketch Book* two years later, granting prestige and legitimacy to the American writer as well as access to a rarefied circle of literati and other British VIPs.[4]

In this regard, Irving was similar to other American artists, intellectuals, and professionals in seeking European credentials or education that could launch or advance their careers. Regardless of their career ambitions, the new leisured classes of educated professionals and wealthy capitalists often approached the tour as an opportunity to demonstrate the requisite refinement for appreciating European cultural achievements and to earn social and cultural distinction. As we might expect, for former colonists who found North American art, culture, and history to be deficient, Europe was an enticing destination that provided exposure to these desirables. Irving characterizes his own motivations as such in the opening pages of the *Sketch Book:* "There were to be seen the masterpieces of art, the refinements of highly cultivated society, the quaint peculiarities of ancient and local custom. My native country was full of youthful promise; Europe was rich in the accumulated treasures of age." The tour thereby functioned as a civilizing trip of sorts, a medium through which Americans mastered taste and manners or exhibited the cultivation already in their possession.[5]

This essay considers the *Sketch Book* through the lens of travel, specifically in the form of the Grand Tour. While literary critics routinely note the *Sketch Book*'s composition in England and introduction as a voyage, few have explicitly examined it with travel conventions at the fore, which is somewhat surprising, given the attention to travel and tourism in Irving's other writings. Nothing so combined the expectations of male cultural privilege with the rising generation's desire for privileged knowledge. He may be most closely associated with the American provincial and a certain kind of rural fantasy, but Irving's lifelong love of theater and attachment to the arts were improved in this manner. He literally *sketched* his way across Europe.[6]

Approaching the *Sketch Book* as a work of travel writing illuminates a project of American national and imperial definition through the cultivation of "Anglo-Americanness," a term I use to refer to qualities of Englishness attained by Americans on their travels, which in turn served a rising American empire. It has become a standard premise that travel literature "*produced* 'the rest of the world'" for European and American audiences within a culture of imperialism.[7] But because "the rest" generally refers to non-European cultures, American travel writing about Western Europe, and about England in particular, is less recognized as a participant in imperialist discourse. In the *Sketch Book*, Irving creates a model Anglo-American identity via his narrative persona, Geoffrey Crayon, whose encounters with English cultural and literary monuments demonstrate both the American inheritance of Englishness and a special relationship between the two nations.[8]

Such instances take part in the wider production of Anglo-American identity in the sketch collection. This hegemonic ethnic identity had been naturalized simply as "American" identity since the colonial period, but after the Revolution, more than ever, the former colonists sought identification with an English ancestral community.[9] It is important to observe in this early nineteenth-century work the self-conscious construction of an Anglo-American avatar in Crayon, a white *gentleman* (he is, after all, identified as "Gent." on the title page) whose polish and sophistication earn him belonging in a metropolitan elite class within the larger British-speaking world. The civility of Crayon and his transatlantic readership distinguishes them from the provincial non-Anglo and racialized characters featured in the sketches—whether the Dutch in "Rip Van Winkle" and "The Legend of Sleepy Hollow," the Flemish in "The Inn Kitchen," African Americans in

"Sleepy Hollow," or Native Americans in "Traits of Indian Character" and "Philip of Pokanoket." Thus, the identification of civility with Anglicized culture and manners—its association with being civilized—is interwoven with the intersecting identity categories of race, ethnicity, class, nation, and region. By virtue of their Anglo-Americanness, Crayon establishes Americans like himself as custodians of civilization, and by extension, as fit for imperial rule.

RITES, TIMES

If Americans were acquiring artistic tastes and social graces through their travels, they were also, importantly, gaining the historical consciousness of empire. American travelers were participating in a tradition of imperial education they were beginning to adapt for their own purposes. Since the late seventeenth century, the Grand Tour had engaged primarily wealthy male Britons for a one- to five-year period after graduating from the university and before beginning their careers. A leading purpose was to complete the gentleman's education, thus preparing him for the leadership position he would assume upon returning home, a program that has been described as a "mobile finishing school for young men."[10]

Beyond exposing them to the beau monde of the Continent, the tour oriented British travelers to their place within the history of empire. At the heart of the tour was Italy, which Western Europeans considered to be the wellspring of ancient and modern civilization, bearer of classical tradition since the Roman Empire and paragon in fine arts since the Renaissance. In the eighteenth century, as their overseas empire expanded, British travelers came to appreciate the experience of Italy for the parallels they perceived between the ancient empire and their modern counterpart. In the nineteenth century, American travelers saw the United States as imperial successor both to Rome and Great Britain.[11]

In the *Sketch Book,* Irving draws upon this well-known theory of imperial succession as if to reverse the order of national prestige established by progressive histories. Unlike succession on the progressive timeline of stadialism, succession on the cyclical timeline of empire theoretically places the United States at an advantage. In the cycle, coming "after" indicates ascension and coming "before," declension; America mounts upward as Britain slopes downward, like spokes turning on a wheel. And if Americans are primitives bereft of civilization in British travel writing, Britons are, notably, remnants of a once-great civilization in the *Sketch Book*. For Irving's Crayon, England is a place of the past. People are nearly obsolete in the sketches set in Great Britain. The few who appear are survivors of a bygone era, as in the Bracebridge Hall sketches, or ghostly presences, in "Westminster Abbey" and "The Art of Book-Making." In lieu of human occupancy, these sketches abound with crumbling monuments, old books, antiques, and other artifacts of British culture.

Irving's depiction of British archaism is integral to the cyclical history of empire developed in the *Sketch Book*, one that asserts the impending, temporary tenure of American supremacy, not its triumphant and conclusive arrival. Irving hints at the perilous continuities between British and American empire in several sketches—"Rip Van Winkle" most forcefully. Yet, even as Irving gestures to a new hierarchy of nations via the cyclical time of empire, he uncovers in the ritual time of enchantment a means of dismantling social and political hierarchies altogether.

Before discussing the egalitarianism of this ritual time, it is necessary to establish the European tour as a social ritual for upper and aspiring classes of Americans throughout the nineteenth century. The tour was a highly conventionalized activity, with abundant travel guides, travel books, and newspaper and magazine accounts not only supplying set itineraries but also modeling the appropriate thoughts and feelings visitors should experience at these sights. Just as importantly, the tour was a ritual because it was a rule governed and repeated activity that bore special significance in the lives of travelers. William Stowe calls these journeys "sacred" acts because they hold substantially more meaning than mundane affairs, especially in their function as rites of passage or "pilgrimages to sacred [cultural] shrines" in search of the ineffable. For many of these travelers, England in particular held the status of a sacred place, because it was regarded as the homeland. Here, Americans viewed sites and artifacts that put them in contact with a transcendent reality where they were rejoined with Britons through shared historical, cultural, and artistic origins.[12]

The framework of ritual allows us to interpret Crayon's excursions within a pattern of symbolic action. He is performing within a set of expectations shaped by previous travelers about the transcendent power and attendant refinements of aesthetic experience. Crayon and Irving follow in a long line of traveling artists and intellectuals who reflected on the enduring power of art and literature: Joseph Addison, James Boswell, Lord Byron, Andrew Bigelow, and James Renwick, to name but a few. At the same time, Crayon modifies patterns and expectations of the tourist abroad, emphasizing his plan in "The Author's Account of Himself," the opening sketch, to depart from the standard travel itinerary by frequenting "nooks, and corners, and by-places," including those tucked away at popular destinations like Windsor Castle or Westminster Abbey. Characterizing himself as a "pilgrim" throughout the *Sketch Book,* Crayon intimates that a journey to these sites, which host aged literary inheritances like the talking book, present opportunities for spiritual regeneration and enriched perception of the eternal through art.

LITERARY PILGRIMAGE

Appearing throughout the *Sketch Book,* literary pilgrimages were rituals that revolved around a visit to a famous author's home, a renowned setting from literature, or some other landmark related to book preservation or production. In "A Royal Poet," a sketch about the life and writings of King James I, Crayon compares the experience of literary and religious wayfaring: "I have visited Vaucluse with as much enthusiasm as a pilgrim would visit the shrine at Loretto; but I have never felt more poetical devotion than when contemplating the old tower and the little garden at Windsor, and musing over the romantic loves of the Lady Jane, and the Royal Poet of Scotland."

Vaucluse is a natural spring in Provence, France, a setting through the ages for communing with the gods and for inspiring intellectual meditation and artistic creation. Irving therefore suggests that the Fontaine de Vaucluse and the tower where young James composed his poetry are as much sacred places as the Marian shrine in Loreto, Italy. Like the pilgrims of the major historical religions, Crayon believes personal exposure to sites of extraordinary activity—the artistic flourishing at Windsor, Stratford-upon-Avon, Boar's Head tavern, and the like—opens up a deeper level of existence. Such destinations, and England more generally, are axis mundi of literary creativity.

A new development in post-Revolutionary travel, literary pilgrimage placed reading at the center of the experience. Reading was an essential part of the traveler's spiritual passage, facilitating an interior salvific journey that complemented the pilgrimage, itself an exteriorized expression of the interior journey. From early childhood, American grand tourists formed an intimacy with England through books, an experience influencing not only their destinations but also perceptions and sensibilities during their travels. As Crayon tells us in "The Royal Poet," the "storied and poetical associations" he brings to the site contribute to his "mood of ... poetical sensibility." Crayon's prior readings of King James's biography and poetry, James's literary contemporaries, and the history of the British Isles intensify his encounter with the location, shaping his expectations about contact with greatness through knowledge of the writer's distinguished place within British literary and national history. Elsewhere, Irving names this mood of elevated feeling and cognitive insight "enchantment." (A philosopher is "shut up in an enchanted library" in "The Art of Book-Making.")

Reading was also an important formulary of the literary pilgrimage because it allowed large numbers to participate in the quest for spiritual communion that England seemed to offer. The rites were repeatable, the effects re-creatable, even if one could not afford to travel to Europe. A survey of the sketches makes clear that American readers and travelers experience pilgrimage through a set pattern. First, the American's journey to the English literary landmark is conducted either through travel or through reading.

Upon arrival, aesthetic contemplation, meditation, and transport occur. Finally, the traveler is reintegrated into the workaday world with the potential to transform previous modes of thought, behavior, and social relations. Common representations of this pattern include trances or visions followed by sleep and awakening.[13]

This rule applies to sketches as different as "The Royal Poet" and, with some modifications, "Rip Van Winkle." In "The Royal Poet," Irving simulates the reader's participation in literary pilgrimage through Crayon's recitation of "The King's Quair," a poem by James. Generous portions of the poem, interspersed with Crayon's interpretation and response, stretch across multiple pages, drawing attention to Crayon's reading and the text's forceful impressions on him. Just as James is moved by Boethius, so is Crayon by James, and the reader by Crayon.

The *Sketch Book* established the literary pilgrimage as a fixture of U.S. travel writing over the next five decades, making the experience available to tens of thousands of readers. Eventually, guidebooks would incorporate these sites into their recommended itineraries. After the publication of the *Sketch Book*, Stratford-upon-Avon became a popular stop, and by 1874 the *American Traveller's Guide* had integrated the *Sketch Book* itself into the suggested tour, recommending the hotel where Irving stayed during his visit (now known as the Washington Irving Hotel) while attracting guests with objects used by Irving or featured in the sketches. Guidebooks such as George Putnam's *A Tourist in Europe* (1838) helped to codify the appropriate emotional response to the site. In his "rhapsody" on Stratford-upon-Avon, Putnam modeled for readers the enthusiasm and reverence that "pilgrims" should experience during "worship at this intellectual shrine!"[14]

Irving's influence is evident in such works of travel writing as Nathaniel Carter's *Letters from Europe* (1827), Henry Wadsworth Longfellow's *Outre-mer: A Pilgrimage Beyond the Sea* (1835), Calvin Colton's *Four Years in Great Britain* (1835), Bayard Taylor's *Views-a-Foot, By-Ways of Europe* (1846), Henry Tuckerman's *A Month in England* (1853), Harriet Beecher Stowe's *Sunny Memories of Foreign Lands* (1854), and Nathaniel Hawthorne's *Our Old Home* (1863). These volumes all followed basic conventions set forth in the *Sketch Book,* wherein the traveler dedicates portions of the book to aesthetic musings at scenes associated with literary fame.[15]

Longfellow, at twenty-one, visited Irving in Madrid in 1827—"travelling for his improvement," as Irving wrote in the letters of introduction he happily provided his countryman.[16] At the beginning of *Outre-mer,* Longfellow describes the "Old World" he experienced as "a kind of Holy Land"; recounting his first sight of its shores, he declares that his "heart swelled with the deep emotions of the pilgrim, when he sees afar the spire which rises above the shrine of his devotion." Although his "shrine" is the Continent rather than England, Longfellow, like Irving, perceives his engagement with European literary culture as a sacred experience.

Outre-mer thus shares with the *Sketch Book* and other works in the nineteenth-century U.S. travelogue tradition the sense of mystical communion between the Old and New Worlds. Literary pilgrims partake in what the cultural anthropologist Victor Turner called *communitas,* during which individuals merge action and awareness with others and enter an egoless state. In the words of Edith Turner (who continued her late husband's work), participants form an "essential 'We.'" This experience of interrelatedness is signaled via a range of descriptors in the *Sketch Book,* including Crayon's "poetical sensibility," "enchantment," or "charm" upon encountering British cultural monuments and artifacts. Five decades after the *Sketch Book,* Henry James would call this fellow feeling "the rare emotion . . . of feel[ing] England." Though the precise terminology may vary, the emotional intensity of the experience is essential, the basis for something deeply shared and communal. A relationship between individuals undifferentiated by social position—indeed, a "spiritual unity" with "something magical about it"—*communitas* makes possible a relationship of equivalent status, a new common ground, between the two nations.[17]

If *communitas* creates a more inclusive social bond wherein national rank and status disappear, this experience is made possible by an interval of sacred time through which participants enter in the rituals of literary pilgrimage. Notably, then, Irving identifies literary pilgrimage with the suspension of mundane time, while he casts Anglo-American communion in sacred time. In "Stratford-on-Avon," for instance, Crayon makes a "poetical pilgrimage" to the birthplace of Shakespeare, where he immediately observes the sacred journey's leveling effect, noting that "pilgrims of all nations, ranks, and conditions, from the prince to the peasant" join in "universal homage" to the bard. These devotees have covered the house's walls with names and inscriptions written in different languages—the contemplation of which engenders in Crayon a sense of *communitas* that spans the *longue durée* of Shakespearean pilgrimage.

Visitation of these sites serves to dispel Crayon's feeling in "The Voyage," upon arrival in England, that he is "a stranger in the land." For the interval of sacred time is a mythic time of beginnings—the pre-Revolutionary epoch of a now-departed European homeland, a time, as much as a place, of communal belonging and common cultural origins. In these moments of enchantment, mundane time temporarily halts and the traveler feels at one with English history, culture, and identity. In truth, the American pilgrim *becomes* English as he is transported to an age preceding political separation. When, for example, Crayon enters Westminster Abbey in the sketch of the same name, he describes "stepping back into the regions of antiquity and losing myself among the shades of former ages." The sketch is a monument to the great men of the past (including writers) memorialized in the abbey, even as Crayon fears that the ravages of time will turn the mausoleum into ruin. Notwithstanding these concerns, "Westminster Abbey" imparts "reverence" for the hoariness of English history and makes clear that the solidarity of *communitas* derives from a deep conviction about Americans' and Britons' shared history, culture, and lineage. Communion is reunion.

BECOMING ANGLO-AMERICAN

American travelers' sense of English homecoming had been kindled by a belief about common ancestry, a belief largely attributable to myths of ethnogenesis. As the dominant ethnic group in America, the English furnished the mytho-symbolic core for American national identity, absorbing non-Anglo populations unevenly into its myths, symbols, and memories. The *Sketch Book* amplifies the mythology of English origins, naturalizing fictive lines of descent. Fellow feeling—"kindred sympathies," in Crayon's naming—is so potent and absolute that it appears innate to the English "race" and their diasporic descendants. The nativist implications of *communitas* in the *Sketch Book* correspond with an outdated sociological characterization of ethnicity's "primordial quality," its existence "in nature, outside time." Through travel, Americans realize their English birthright, becoming who they were all along.[18]

In Irving's *Sketch Book* essay "English Writers on America," kinship between Americans and Britons precedes an archaic British civilization now showing signs of decay, stretching further back to a "land of... forefathers" where nature, not culture, forms the basis of the "kindred tie." In laying claim to *biological* as well as cultural English heritage, Americans confirmed a coveted Anglo-Saxon genealogy. As Reginald Horsman has argued, the first half of the nineteenth century witnessed the consolidation of a myth about America's superior Anglo-Saxon forebears, the Germanic peoples who ruled England and Wales from the fifth century to the Norman Conquest in 1066. This myth, as propagated by English settlers and then by American Revolutionaries, initially declared the supremacy of Anglo-Saxon religious and political institutions, subsequently embracing democratic government. In the years 1815 to 1850, intellectuals in England and the United States racialized the myth, resolving that "the secret of Saxon success lay not in the institutions but in the blood."[19]

"Anglo-Saxon" as a racialized concept arose from a confluence of developments, including the new science of racial classification and Romanticism's insistence on the singularity of the world's peoples and cultures. The noticeable improvement in Anglo–American relations beginning at the war's end suggests that 1815 is a credible date by which to mark Anglo-Saxon racialization as well as the resumption of transatlantic travel. As Horsman explains, "With the easing of British–American difficulties after 1815, there was a renewed interest in attributes shared by English and American Anglo-Saxons," though the fullest expression of English and American Anglo-Saxons as a separate and superior race is better placed in the 1830s to 1850s.[20]

In keeping with this timeline, as well as Irving's sentimental racialism, the *Sketch Book* does not make overt pronouncements about the superiority of Anglo-Saxons relative to other races. Instead, the author subtly inserts white Americans into this racial myth, not only by asserting blood relation to the English, and thereby to Anglo-Saxons, but also by forming implicit comparisons to other races. References to Saxon structures dot the sketches, reminders of the ancient civilization's mark on the present. In "John Bull," a sketch dedicated to the personification of England, Crayon imagines Bull's "family mansion" as a "vast accumulation of parts erected in various tastes and ages"—an embodiment of different eras in English history. With "Saxon architecture" at its foundation, the national metaphor is straightforward: Saxons are the progenitors of the "old English family" (the English people), occupying the "old English manor house" (the nation). Just as significantly, the durability of the Saxon base connotes the durability of its people, who survive in present-day English and American descendants.

In contrast with this portrait of longevity, the *Sketch Book*'s two Native American sketches underscore the demise of Indigenous peoples. Rendered as a "race" distinct from "white men," Native Americans are casualties of progress, a mournful but inevitable outcome in the march of civilization. In promoting the widespread myth of the vanishing Indian, Irving makes a noteworthy distinction in representing literacy as a key measure of civilization.

"Traits of Indian Character" and "Philip of Pokanoket" presume a hierarchy between the literate culture of the English and Americans and the oral culture of Native Americans. The Indigenous peoples' lack of literacy is the inference drawn from Irving's assessment that they are "ignorant," while "superior knowledge and power" resides in "their enlightened neighbors." While increasingly challenged by scholars, the orality/literacy binary was commonplace thinking for nineteenth-century settler cultures that privileged literacy as a technological advancement. The dominant perception of Indigenous oral and graphic traditions as less evolved has, in Christopher Teuton's words, "contributed to the historical and political subjugation of Native communities by characterizing them as oral, nonliterate peoples."[21]

In both of these Irving sketches, orality is an evanescent marker of a passing culture, a condition captured in stray sentences as fleeting as the dead or dying Native people who speak them. In "Traits of Indian Character," for instance, the author includes brief exclamations from vanishing figures in the introduction and conclusion; the final utterance, "We shall cease to exist!," confirms the lament of the epigraph. The brevity of these statements implies that they require no elaboration—a testament to the authority of the written word. In consequence of its wide circulation in print culture, the trope of Native American obsolescence had, as Brian Dippie confirms, "become a habit of thought."[22]

Irving contributes to this trope even as he condemns damaging portrayals by "bigoted and interested writers" who peg Native Americans as barbaric and treacherous without considering the European and American wrongdoing that resulted in "repining and hopeless poverty," a "canker of the mind" previously unknown to Indigenous peoples in their "savage" condition. Despite the detrimental effects of colonization, there is no other conclusion to draw from "Traits of Indian Character" than that the written word constitutes power. The frontier Native peoples are left to "loiter" and "infest," with no means to improve themselves. Their oral tradition appears in the sketch always in reaction to white violence—as fragmentary expressions of lament and vengeance, but never as a robust historical account from an Indigenous perspective.

The larger implication in the paired Indian sketches is that Native Americans exist—more crucially, *survive*—within the colonizers' frame; hence Irving's emphatic charge that writers must be free "from the coloring of prejudice and bigotry." Writing serves as a "memorial" to a dying race, which is fitting, given the lasting properties of print and ink, as relentlessly documented in Crayon's inveterate exploration of libraries, books, manuscripts, and literary shrines during his English travels.

Undoubtedly, Crayon is a model of civility, as much for his literary graces as for his polite speech and manners. By the early decades of the nineteenth century, reading and writing had become closely associated with social improvement for an American bourgeoisie intent on acquiring the gentility that once belonged exclusively to the upper ranks. Reading widely and writing elegantly were central to the curriculum in popular etiquette books. It is no wonder, then, that Crayon's literary sophistication remains in the foreground of most sketches, whether it is his knowledge of British literary history or his use of literary sources (as in "The Boar's Head Tavern, Eastcheap" and "The Art of Book-Making"); his bent toward antiquarianism and philology (as in "Roscoe" and "The Mutability of Literature"); or his appreciation of British authors on literary pilgrimage. Americans themselves were fighting accusations of being uncivilized, which "attacks" Crayon alludes to in "English Writers on America." The offenders were "English travelers" who "give prejudicial accounts of America"—the exact nature of these accounts is such a "hackneyed topic" that Irving assumes there is no need to fill in the details.[23]

British travelers roundly condemned Americans as "vulgar," "primitive," "barbaric," "uncivilized," and "savage." Travel accounts such as Frances Trollope's devastatingly detailed *Domestic Manners of the Americans* (1832) and Charles Dickens's *American Notes* (1842) are representative of the genre, but they are merely two of the best known. British and other foreign travelers had been regularly publishing volumes of disparaging commentary on America and Americans since the late eighteenth century.[24]

Although they had produced a good many works of drama, poetry, and prose fiction since achieving independence, Americans' literary endeavors were dismissed by critics on both sides of the Atlantic who did not take U.S. writers seriously until Irving demonstrated his mastery of British prose style or, in Irving's parlance, "express[ed] himself in tolerable English." Both

British and American reviewers regarded the *Sketch Book* as the first significant accomplishment of an American writer *precisely because* it measured up to British English. (To the least generous of these critics, however, the book proved only that Americans were adept copyists.)[25]

Far more was at stake with his elegant prose than the establishment of America's literary reputation. The *Sketch Book* was a defense against charges of American savagery, as Irving references in his preface to *Bracebridge Hall*. Writing of the *Sketch Book*'s success, he states, "It has been a matter of marvel, that a man from the wilds of America should express himself in tolerable English. I was looked upon as something new and strange in literature; a kind of demi-savage, with a feather in his hand, instead of on his head; and there was a curiosity to hear what such a being had to say about civilized society."

The "feather" migrating from "head" to "hand" is given as proof of Crayon/Irving's and Americans' capacity for cultural achievement. Here, Irving explicitly links a writing instrument with the civilizing process. The playful denomination of the American as a "demi-savage" implies a more serious assignment to an intermediate position between the two poles of savagery and civilization. According to the influential stadialist model of historical progress, society existed on a continuum from savagery to civilization, each stage following the next in orderly progression, irrespective of factors like race, place, or time. Within this schematic, Americans were envisioned to be at an inferior stage of human development, but as this passage clarifies, Americans would soon "catch up" to European cultures through their possession of "tolerable English."[26]

TRANSTEMPORAL COMMUNION, IMAGINATIVE LONGING

Given Irving's centrality to the genres, it is fitting that his own home since 1835, Sunnyside, should become a standard entry in travel guidebooks and in books on literary pilgrimage. By the turn of the twentieth century, Lippincott had published four works on "literary shrines" by Theodore Wolfe—a series devoted entirely to visits to authors' homes and favorite spots and a topic so in demand that the books went through dozens of editions collectively. Regarding Irving's Tarrytown estate, Wolfe assures the reader that "a more enchanting retreat . . . would scarcely be possible to find." Though Wolfe never made the connection, it would seem that Sunnyside's "enchanting" qualities derived in part from its resemblance to the snug cottages and picturesque countryside Irving romanticizes in his British sketches. The antiquated air of the house appealed to Wolfe, as it did to Irving, who esteemed "the little old-fashioned mansion" as he did the cottages in "Rural Life in England."[27]

As I discuss in greater detail elsewhere,[28] enchantment is a ritual mood that collapses both time and space, as seen in Wolfe's description of proximity to a European past at Sunnyside. More than once while exploring England's literary landmarks, Irving's alter ego experiences a fleeting moment of enchantment that initiates *communitas*. For Crayon, who depicts the American setting without comparable cultural monuments, a feeling of enchantment is evoked both by the singularity of British cultural antiquity and by the powerful historical associations he holds with such sites.

In this interval, the past suddenly meets up with the present. The sketch "Stratford-on-Avon" includes Crayon's meditation on a nearby estate that imaginatively calls forth Elizabethan England: "My mind had become so completely possessed by the imaginary scenes and characters connected with it that I seemed to be actually living among them." He imagines himself for a brief period as a contemporary of the citizens of early modern Europe, someone who "seemed to be actually living among them." His mental powers bridge the long distance of two centuries, making possible transtemporal communion.[29]

Similarly, in *Literary Haunts and Homes*, Wolfe experiences transtemporal communion with Irving's era and literary worlds. Missing, however, is communion between the Old World and the New—the imaginative longing to belong to England. Perhaps this is because the process of becoming

Anglo-American was already complete. After all, Irving, "that great pioneer of New-World literature," by Wolfe's designation, had secured the cultural capital of an Old World literary inheritance as a means of legitimizing "New-World literature."[30]

The publication of *Literary Haunts and Homes* indicates that American literature had arrived at the point of reverence for American authors and worship at their shrines. If the establishment of a great national literature was a requirement of a great nation, as literary nationalists believed, it was further a requirement for a great empire. Published in 1898, Wolfe's book about "prominent figures in [American] literature" came out the same year as the Spanish–American War, whereby the United States acquired the Philippines, Guam, and Puerto Rico, annexed Hawaii, and became the temporary protectorate of Cuba. In the span of eighty-three years from 1815 to 1898, the United States had expanded and settled territory across the continent and overseas at a dramatic pace, poised to become the world's superpower in the coming century.[31]

Significantly, Irving writes the history of Sunnyside as one of territorial conflict in "Wolfert's Roost" (1839), the name given to the residence by its first owner in 1656. Introducing Wolfert's Roost, Crayon deems it "an ancient seat of empire . . . and like all empires, great and small, has had its grand historical epochs." The narrative proceeds through several epochs, the first of which involves land disputes among Indigenous nations prior to European contact, leading to the reign of the "wizard sachem." This is followed by Dutch conquest of the sachem's descendants, the English conquest of the Dutch, and lastly, the American Revolution. The Roost was "debatable ground, lying between British and American lines." In the final epoch, tranquility settles over it.

Given the extended discussion of Irving's favorite mock historian in the ending chronicle at the Roost, Crayon might as well have labeled it the "Diedrich Knickerbocker Era." It is during his sojourn there that Knickerbocker lays the groundwork for his literary career. At the Roost, he discovers his archive of sources for *The History of New-York*, and on his rambles he collects materials for "The Legend of Sleepy Hollow" and "Rip Van Winkle." Thus, Irving imagines a region of unrest transformed into a region of "quiet" through the civilizing influences of literature.[32]

The age of settlement arrives with the man of letters—Knickerbocker, a literary persona who embodies Irving, of course—snug and secure. This culminating moment validates the dwelling's two titles, as "The Roost" (from the Dutch *rust* or *rest*) and "Sunnyside," which Irving referred to as his "dear bright little home." Here, history merges with the occupant's private muse; memory and imagination coexist.[33]

The man of civility as man of letters is an understudied archetype of imperialism and settler colonialism. In American literature of the 1820s, we are apt to turn to James Fenimore Cooper's Leatherstocking Tales or the frontier romances of Lydia Maria Child and Catharine Sedgwick for insight into the genocide and repression of Indigenous peoples and cultures and the appropriation and control of others' lands. As this essay has sought to show, however, the literature of English travel and the literature of literary pilgrimage were vital coordinates in a cultural sphere of domination. Such works effectively promoted an English genealogy and Anglo-American identity that granted civility and fostered attitudes of white supremacy, both of which were preconditions for white Anglicized Americans' notion of rightful rule.[34]

NOTES

1. William Sachse, *The Colonial American in Britain* (Madison: University of Wisconsin Press, 1956); Robert Spiller, *The American in England During the First Half Century of Independence* (New York: Henry Holt, 1926).

2. Washington Irving to Mrs. Amelia Foster [April–May 1823], in *Letters*, vol. 1, *1802–1823*, ed. Ralph M. Aderman, Herbert L. Kleinfield, and Jenifer S. Banks, 742, in *The Complete Works of Washington Irving* (Boston: Twayne, 1978). Irving had initially planned to tour England,

France, Italy, and Greece for a year or two. See Ben Harris McClary, *Washington Irving and the House of Murray: Geoffrey Crayon Charms the British, 1817–1856* (Knoxville: University of Tennessee Press, 1969), xxix.

3. Jeffrey Rubin-Dorsky advanced the image of Irving as a "displaced self adrift in a mutable world." Rubin-Dorsky, *Adrift in the Old World: The Psychological Pilgrimage of Washington Irving* (Chicago: University of Chicago Press, 1988), xv.

4. McClary, *Washington Irving and the House of Murray*, 3–20.

5. Spiller, *American in England;* "The Author's Account of Himself," in Washington Irving, *The Sketch Book of Geoffrey Crayon, Gent.*, ed. Haskell Springer (Boston: Twayne, 1978).

6. For the *Sketch Book* as travel writing, see William Stowe, *Going Abroad: European Travel in Nineteenth-Century American Culture* (Princeton, NJ: Princeton University Press, 1994); David Seed, "The Art of Literary Tourism: An Approach to Washington Irving's *Sketch Book*," *ARIEL: A Review of International English Literature* 14, no. 2 (1983): 67–82; and Matthew Pethers, "Transatlantic Migration and the Politics of the Picturesque in Washington Irving's *Sketch Book*," *Symbiosis: A Journal of Anglo-American Literary Relations* 9, no. 2 (2005): 135–58. As for *Tales of a Traveller*, *Tales of the Alhambra*, and *A Tour on the Prairies*, see Brigitte Bailey, "Irving's Italian Landscapes: Skepticism and the Picturesque Aesthetic," *ESQ: A Journal of the American Renaissance* 32, no. 1 (1986); Judith Haig, "Washington Irving and the Romance of Travel: Is There an Itinerary in *Tales of a Traveller?*" in *The Old and New World Romanticism of Washington Irving*, ed. Stanley Brodwin (New York: Greenwood, 1986); Michael S. Stevens, *Spanish Orientalism: Washington Irving and the Romance of the Moors* (Lanham, MD: Lexington Books, 2018); and John Joseph, "*I*-tinerary: The Romantic Travel Journal After Chateaubriand," *South Central Review* 1, no. 2 (1984): 38–51.

7. Mary Louise Pratt, *Imperial Eyes: Travel Writing and Transculturation* (London: Routledge, 1992), 5.

8. Larzer Ziff, *Return Passages: Great American Travel Writing, 1780–1910* (New Haven, CT: Yale University Press, 2000); Bruce Harvey, *American Geographics: U.S. National Narratives and the Representation of the Non-European World, 1830–1865* (Stanford, CA: Stanford University Press, 2002).

9. For the dominance of Anglo-Protestant identity in America, see Eric P. Kaufmann, *The Rise and Fall of Anglo-America* (Cambridge, MA: Harvard University Press, 2004). For discussions of American settler subjects' attachment to English cultural identity after Independence, see Len Tennenhouse, *The Importance of Feeling English: American Literature and the British Diaspora, 1750–1850* (Princeton, NJ: Princeton University Press, 2007); and Elisa Tamarkin, *Anglophilia: Deference, Devotion, and Antebellum America* (Chicago: University of Chicago Press, 2008).

10. Lynne Withey, *Grand Tours and Cook's Tours: A History of Leisure Travel, 1750 to 1915* (New York: William Morrow, 1997); James Buzard, "The Grand Tour and After (1660–1840)," in *The Cambridge Companion to Travel Writing*, ed. Peter Hulme and Tim Youngs, 37–52 (Cambridge: Cambridge University Press, 2002); Jeremy Black, *The British Abroad: The Grand Tour in the Eighteenth Century* (New York: St. Martin's, 1992).

11. By the second half of the eighteenth century, the tour had acquired a set pattern, featuring longer stays in Paris, Geneva, Rome, Florence, Venice, and Naples, and short stops in smaller Italian cities. See Buzard, "Grand Tour and After"; Stowe, *Going Abroad;* Christopher Mulvey, *Anglo-American Landscapes* (Cambridge: Cambridge University Press, 1983); Allison Lockwood, *Passionate Pilgrims: The American Traveler in Great Britain, 1800–1914* (New York: Cornwall, 1981); and Foster Rhea Dulles, *Americans Abroad: Two Centuries of European Travel* (Ann Arbor: University of Michigan Press, 1964).

12. Stowe, *Going Abroad,* 19.

13. See Victor Turner's discussions of liminality. Turner, "Variations on a Theme of Liminality," in *Secular Ritual,* ed. Sally F. Moore and Barbara G. Myerhoff, 36–52 (Amsterdam: Van Gorcum, Assen, 1977); Victor Turner and Edith Turner, *Image and Pilgrimage in Christian Culture* (New York: Columbia University Press, 1978).

14. W. Pembroke Fetridge, *The American Traveller's Guide: Harper's Hand-Book for Travellers in Europe and the East,* vol. 1 (New York: Harper and Brothers, 1874); George Putnam, *The Tourist in Europe* (New York: Wiley and Putnam, 1838), 86–87.

15. Other notable antebellum travel books that demonstrate reverence for European culture include Nathaniel Parker Willis, *Pencillings by the Way* (1835); Robert Sears, *Scenes and Sketches in Continental Europe* (1850); Joel Tyler Headley, *Sketches and Rambles* (1850); William Cullen Bryant, *Letters of a Traveler* (1850); James Freeman Clarke, *Eleven Weeks in Europe* (1852); and Cyrus Augustus Bartol, *Pictures of Europe* (1856). Periodicals such as *American Review, Rural Magazine, Christian Spectator, Souvenir,* and *Knickerbocker Magazine* included travel essays and letters that also paid homage to Europe. In this tradition of travel writing, American writers were generally open-minded, or at least selectively receptive to the value of European culture, manners, and history. Another more consistently nationalistic tradition of American travel writing was relentlessly critical of European culture. Note, too, that while the Grand Tour was historically reserved for elite young men, as early as the 1820s middle- and upper-class white American women began to travel through Europe in significant numbers for an aesthetic education; among these were Catharine Sedgwick and Caroline Kirkland. See Robert Spiller, *American in England;* Alfred Bendixen, "American Travel Books about Europe before the Civil War," in *The Cambridge Companion to American Travel Writing,* ed. Alfred Bendixen and Judith Hamera, 103–26 (Cambridge: Cambridge University Press, 2009); and Mary Suzanne Schriber, *Writing Home: American Women Abroad, 1830–1920* (Charlottesville: University of Virginia Press, 1997).

16. Andrew Burstein, *The Original Knickerbocker: The Life of Washington Irving* (New York: Basic Books, 2007), 195.

17. Henry James, *A Passionate Pilgrim and Other Stories* (Boston: Houghton Mifflin, 1875), 26; Edith Turner, *Communitas: The Anthropology of Collective Joy* (New York: Palgrave Macmillan, 2012), 3.

18. Kaufmann, *Rise and Fall of Anglo-America,* 11–12; Anthony D. Smith, "The Ethnic Basis of National Identity," in *National Identity* (Reno: University of Nevada Press, 1991), 19–42; Anthony D. Smith, *The Ethnic Origins of Nations* (Oxford: Basil Blackwell, 1986); "English Writers on America," in Irving, *Sketch Book.*

19. Reginald Horsman, *Race and Manifest Destiny: The Origins of American Racial Anglo-Saxonism* (Cambridge, MA: Harvard University Press, 1981), 24.

20. Horsman, *Race and Manifest Destiny*, 95.

21. Christopher Teuton, *Deep Waters: The Textual Continuum in American Indian Literature* (Lincoln: University of Nebraska Press, 2010), xv.

22. The lament in the epigraph is an excerpt from Logan's speech, first made popular in Thomas Jefferson's 1787 *Notes on the State of Virginia*. Gordon Sayre observes, "With Logan's speech, the craze for Indian oratory reached a singular extreme: the oration became the most frequently reprinted, most hackneyed text of the genre." Sayre, *The Indian Chief as Tragic Hero: Native Resistance and the Literatures of America, from Moctezuma to Tecumseh* (Chapel Hill: University of North Carolina Press, 2005), 162. Brian W. Dippie details the propagation of this "rhetoric of doom." Dippie, *The Vanishing American: White Attitudes and U.S. Indian Policy* (Lawrence: University Press of Kansas, 1982).

23. John Kasson, *Rudeness and Civility: Manners in Nineteenth-Century Urban America* (New York: Hill and Wang, 1990), chap. 2.

24. See "American Notes: Travels in America, 1750 to 1920," Library of Congress digital collections, https://www.loc.gov/collections/travels-in-america-1750-to-1920. "America watching," James Chandler states, "became something of a British national hobby." See Chandler, *England in 1819: The Politics of Literary Culture and the Case of Romantic Historicism* (Chicago: University of Chicago Press, 1998), 453.

25. For discussion of the *Sketch Book*'s reception, see Rubin-Dorsky, *Adrift in the Old World*, 32–41; and Stanley T. Williams, *The Life of Washington Irving*, 2 vols. (New York: Oxford University Press, 1935), 1:168–91. Despite resounding praise, Irving drew criticism for imitating British literary models and cultural subjects. Among his most vocal critics, U.S. nationalists condemned what they viewed as Irving's Anglophilia and conformity to English tradition. See, for example, Edward Everett, "Review of Bracebridge Hall," *North American Review* 15 (1822): 209.

26. See George Dekker, *The American Historical Romance* (Cambridge: Cambridge University Press, 1987), 73–98.

27. Theodore Wolfe, *A Literary Pilgrimage among the Haunts of Famous British Authors* (1895); *Literary Shrines; The Haunts of Some Famous American Authors* (1895); *Literary Haunts and Homes: American Authors* (1898); and *Literary Rambles at Home and Abroad* (1900); quote is from *Literary Haunts and Homes*, 175.

28. See Michelle Sizemore, *American Enchantment: Rituals of the People in a Post-Revolutionary World* (New York: Oxford University Press, 2018).

29. Crayon's enchantment closely resembles an affective experience described by the contemporaneous aesthetic theory of "associationism." This theory held that an individual could access history through the imagination, evoking historical associations from present scenes and objects. See Archibald Alison, *Essays on the Natures and Principles of Taste* (Boston: Cummings and Hilliard, 1812).

30. Wolfe, *Literary Haunts*, 176.

31. Robert Hannigan explains that a social evolutionary worldview was foundational to U.S. foreign policy at the turn of the twentieth century. "Old-stock Americans, whose culture, lifestyle, and deportment were taken to define the essence of civilization," considered themselves custodians of new European immigrants (Irish, Italians, and Eastern Europeans), and especially of the "primitive" Filipinos and the Chamorro people of Guam. Hannigan, *The New World Power: American Foreign Policy, 1898–1917* (Philadelphia: University of Pennsylvania Press, 2002), 7. See also Kenneth Hendrickson Jr., *The Spanish–American War* (Westport, CT: Greenwood Press, 2003); Wolfe, *Literary Haunts*, xv; and Ivan Musicant, *Empire by Default: The Spanish–American War and the Dawn of the American Century* (New York: Henry Holt, 1998).

32. Washington Irving, *Wolfert's Roost*, ed. Roberta Rosenberg (Boston: Twayne, 1979). "Wolfert's Roost" was first published as a single story in *Knickerbocker Magazine* in 1839 and subsequently incorporated into a collection of stories with the same title, in 1855. See Burstein, *Original Knickerbocker*, 295, 320.

33. Quoted in William MacDowell Tartt, "Irving at Sunnyside," in *Essays on Some Modern Works, Chiefly Biographical* (London: Tinsley Brothers, 1876), 2:50.

34. Another key contribution to these genres is Ralph Waldo Emerson, *English Traits: A Portrait of Nineteenth-Century England* (1856).

WASHINGTON IRVING REIMAGINED AS FATHER OF HIS COUNTRY

SHIRLEY SAMUELS

> The gloom of religious abstraction, and the wildness of their situation, among trackless forests, and savage tribes, had disposed the colonists to superstitious fancies, and had filled their imaginations with the frightful chimeras of witchcraft and spectrology.
> —Washington Irving, "Philip of Pokanoket"

Haunted by the Revolution, Washington Irving always knew that he had been named after the "father" of the new United States, a country inaugurated the year of Irving's birth, when the Treaty of Paris acknowledged independence. Growing up in the shadow of "founding fathers," fathers whose Revolutionary acts they had just missed witnessing as adults, Irving and his four older brothers found themselves ambivalently managing a legacy: to invent a national tradition.[1]

In this essay I argue not only that such a legacy invokes repeated forms of haunting but also that these hauntings exhibit a fascinating obsession with how the reproduction of identity and the meaning of paternity might operate when a person is cut off from that past—or, literally, cut off from his head. The concept that a head will fall when there's a change in political loyalties haunts Nathaniel Hawthorne's famous preface to a quasi-historical novel about the Puritans, *The Scarlet Letter*. Imagining that his politically sponsored employment will protect him in the customhouse, where his desultory labors enable him to rummage in attics, his narrator professes shock that his "head was the first to fall."[2]

This falling, this symbolic political demise, repeats itself in Irving's writing in ways at first disconcerting and then familiar. As I look through the often disconnected narratives of the *Sketch Book*, I find myself thinking about family legacies and the mythology of the Revolution in my own family history. My maternal grandmother's last name was Winslow before she married a man named Claude Dunbar Briggs. The somewhat better-known Winslow family had already intermarried with the Briggs family since the North American arrivals of both families in the seventeenth century. Both families fought in the Revolution. When my grandmother told me that her father used to joke about trading her to the Indians, I didn't understand that living in Bemidji, Minnesota, in the early twentieth century meant living on the edge of reservations. Because I am immersed in family stories, when I read the *Sketch Book*, I feel haunted by the memories and refusals of memory that Irving repeatedly enacts.

HAUNTED BY THE FATHER

The *Sketch Book* exhibits a compulsion to tell stories about a land marked by recent conflicts as though they were always linked to the Old World—even as Rip Van Winkle famously wakes to wonder why he cannot recognize his own landscape. The young Irving men were always, inescapably, haunted by being born too late for the action, left to ponder the heroes and to travel back to the Old World, either by sea or in the mind. As a lifelong bachelor, Irving tended to make his earliest adventures appear to be those of a flaneur in multiple cultures—initially of New York City and the upstate regions, and then in the cities of Europe.

The bachelor who sits by the fireside and contemplates his marital destiny was a familiar motif later in the nineteenth century, due to works such as Donald Grant Mitchell's *Reveries of a Bachelor*. In this work, the narrator engages the reader in fantasies that resemble dreams while he smokes a cigarette by the fire and wonders if he should marry. His character enacts a peculiarly evasive domesticity that resembles a detached longing as it also promotes the mode of sitting by a fire, like the meditations engaged in by Herman Melville in "I and My Chimney." But the reveries of the bachelor are engaged to avoid marriage, like the escapism of Rip Van Winkle, whose pleasure can only be obtained when Dame Van Winkle is out of the picture. These other sketches might well have been influenced by the evasions and peripatetic wanderings of Irving in the *Sketch Book*.[3]

The ability to transit the ocean on an early version of the Grand Tour forms the backstory of the *Sketch Book:* a narration of money and class privilege crosses with an aspirational longing to find some ability to admire, and yet mock, the libraries and museums that tend to be guarded against just such intrusions. What is the role of the American writer in this view? Irving suggests that it is to stage a "return" to Europe while refusing to feel abashed. Yet he often ventriloquizes forms of haunting that suggest that the books in the libraries and the paintings in the museums have a voice that desires escape. The visits to libraries and museums that suffuse the earliest of the sketches also implicitly frame those stories that purport to be about landscapes or character.

One dominant thread in Andrew Burstein's biography of Irving is an admiration for Irving's capacity for self-invention as well as his insertion of this narrative into the tradition of male writers who are inventing the category of being an American writer. As the youngest in a family of enterprising sons, Irving both engages with and resists being in the family business, which for Burstein means escaping family obligation, as Benjamin Franklin was able to do before refashioning himself as an emblematic American. As a young man, Franklin escapes his apprenticeship to his older brother, the printer James Franklin, only to make printing the metaphor of his autobiography and, to some extent, his incomparable life. As a young man, before mastering the world of print and publication, Irving reluctantly trains in the law, but he is sent off to Europe because of ill health. His health improves, and he learns that his writing can be incorporated into a version of the family business.[4]

The visible and invisible stories of the oral tradition also infuse the inspirations that become the *Sketch Book*. Listening to such stories as he watches the landscape, Irving travels up the Hudson over and over. He has his older brothers to thank for direct exposure to the national politician Aaron Burr and for an awareness of the divided sympathies that existed (even within the Irving clan) in the protracted struggle between Federalists and Republicans in the early republic. What dues must be paid when one dabbles in politics?

As he travels forward and back in the history of his nation, Irving learns that to write is, effectively, to become part of the story. To take his American attitudes to Europe is, for the reader, to watch him watching the cultural landscape. The galleries he visits are in the vein of the Grand Tour, but they also yoke the story of the interloper with the story of the one who rescues the reader from the need to follow the path to Europe.

Irving's sketches increasingly turn to the story of the United States in terms of its ongoing political scuffles around principles. But not just principles. Thanks to Americans' regular recourse to founder-friendly history and literature, lately augmented by the success of the musical *Hamilton*, cultural attention remains focused on the writings of the Revolutionary period as an alive struggle between disparate passionate personalities. The Irving brothers initially aligned with Aaron Burr, who had a captivating presence, and later with President James Madison, who waged a second war with Great Britain (a second revolution, some felt)—activity that made for a keen awareness of the precarious business of political loyalties.[5]

As we read the *Sketch Book* now, we inevitably give renewed attention to the ghost stories. Visual as much as literary memories swirl around the story of the Headless Horseman and the way that Rip Van Winkle looks with some bewilderment at the sign outside the tavern that still says "George" (for King George III) but now refers to the Washington after whom Irving was named. For Irving to travel as a tourist along the Hudson River, to make the journey between Manhattan and Albany into a space for the "Tales of a Traveller," is to find that landscape and history blur.[6]

It has become quite difficult for us to imagine humans jostling shoulders in the small, dirty streets of New York, but it also explains some of the erasure of the historical record. Who belongs in cultural memory? As readers, we still allow for the implied patricide of "Rip Van Winkle" and the brutal courtship of "The Legend of Sleepy Hollow," yet we retain some attraction to violence in our pleasure.[7]

In his biography of Irving, Andrew Burstein begins with a chapter that he calls "New York's Lost Past." Since the book's publication, calls for reimagining that past have reached unimaginable heights, in part because of the success of Lin-Manuel Miranda's *Hamilton*. Given that such a past has reentered the American cultural imaginary, it remains interesting to contemplate the difficulty of inserting other once-notable figures into our historical reframing.[8]

For Irving, the streets of New York became something to escape when he headed to Europe. The British Museum is his restless location in the *Sketch Book,* where he mocks the activity in the rare book room, and those who spend their days summoning books that they pilfer to make other books. A "pilfering disposition" emerges as the way to characterize the researchers who inhabit the reading room. Irving likens the "flights of predatory writers" to carrion crows who distribute seeds. Thus it is in "our American woodlands," he writes, highlighting the organic nature of knowledge that moves in and out of the motifs of farming, as it does for J. Hector St. Jean de Crèvecoeur in *Letters from an American Farmer* (1782). But then, in "The Art of Book-Making," Irving's narrator Geoffrey Crayon falls asleep and dreams that "portraits of ancient authors" have come alive and "seized upon" books that turn into garments. The laughter in his dream wakes him to the disapproval of the reading room and his expulsion from the premises. Might it be that the American is not entirely welcome in England? Or that American and British history are being severed?

Continuing his attention to culture and belonging in "The Mutability of Literature: A Colloquy in Westminster Abbey," Irving returns to meditations on a repository of books. His visit to Westminster Abbey's library invokes tourism and a walk down a long hallway through locked doors that seems vaguely ominous, like the visit described in Edgar Allan Poe's "Cask of Amontillado." What will you find to nurture you down this long hallway? The library makes him muse on the waste of human life that goes into books. The book in his lap becomes alive and talks to him with regret about the difficulty of living in a library: "I was written for all the world, not for the bookworms of an abbey." For an author to present the idea of literature as consumed by worms (or as consumed in order to be regurgitated) suggests a cynicism about the roles of both reader and writer.[9]

When Rip Van Winkle wakes and finds his way back to the village that he thought contained his home, dreading the retributive comments of his wife, he finds his home in ruins and a small, chaotic crowd engaged in frolics and gaming. What turns out to be Election Day frivolity is interrupted by his inappropriately expressed praise for the king. Rebuked, and threatened with the incarceration and dispossession offered to Loyalists, he is further shaken by finding a version of himself, "a precise counterpart of himself as he went up the mountain." Even as the strangeness of the crowd startles him when he returns to his village, it is in looking at the slouching figure of his son that "he doubted his own identity, and whether he was himself or another man." Unable to recognize his son as offspring, Rip shows an odd relationship to the dissimilarity—and possibly the fear of reproduction conjoins with this misrecognition. That is, an incongruity enters the story: a father not understanding that his offspring might bear some resemblance. He is haunted by fatherhood, indeed, this bachelor Irving who will never be a father.

Beneath the haunting possibilities that thread through the story of Rip Van Winkle—most notably, the underlying mystery of what happened to the

Dutch settlers—is the haunting performed by the original inhabitants of the Hudson River Valley. In the second half of the *Sketch Book,* Irving turns to the figure of the Indian. A haunting emerges in "Traits of Indian Character," an essay (more than a tale) that improbably begins with an epigraph taken from Thomas Jefferson's *Notes on the State of Virginia.* Attributed to the onetime Mingo chief with the Anglicized name Logan, the speech that Irving quotes says, "I appeal to any white man to say if ever he entered Logan's cabin hungry, and he gave him not to eat; if ever he came cold and asked, and he clothed him not."[10]

A strange inversion appears here: the epigraph presents the expectation that we are to hear the voice of Logan tracing out what he sees, yet Irving starts the sketch by announcing what the *white man sees* the "savage" seeing. (Of course, Logan defies the very label of savage, since he provides hospitality to strangers, making his cabin a civilized space.) It is rather like what Irving's contemporary James Fenimore Cooper sees after traversing much of the same territory of the Hudson Valley: a man emerging from and then disappearing into a landscape. Writes Irving of the Indian, "He is formed for the wilderness as the Arab is for the desert."

While professing to feel the pain of the Indian, Irving equivocates on the separate qualities of humans who occupy unbounded versus bounded landscapes. He describes the humans of his sketch as though their hearts contained something other than blood, saying of the Indian, "There seems but little soil in his heart for the support of the kindly virtues; and yet, if we would but take the trouble to penetrate through that proud stoicism . . . , we should find him linked to his fellow man of civilized life by more of those sympathies and affections than are usually ascribed to him." The primitive virtue of the land was always a selling point for colonial American settlement, yet the "soil," as the "heart" of the country's virtuous promise, remained unstable for as long as there was no way for it to be shared, for harmonious co-occupancy to occur, among "settled" and "unsettled" peoples.

Irving's message is that "civilized" people, if they could look in a more penetrative way, ought to be able to detect like qualities in those who may have, owing to their greater attachment to the natural environment, less exposure to (superior) settled values. Yet the "civilized" had proven detached and hard-hearted. The Native American was "doubly wronged" by white men, first as a result of land greed, then out of a tragic inability of whites to recognize their common humanity. The colonists "treated them as beasts of the forest," finding, after dispossession, that it was "easier to exterminate than to civilize." Writers went on to "justify" these "outrages." If blame was to be shared, Irving does not apportion it.

By the third paragraph of the sketch, Irving is more direct: "The rights of the savage have seldom been properly appreciated or respected by the white man." He goes on to elaborate. "Certain learned societies have, it is true, with laudable diligence endeavored to investigate and record the real characters and manners of the Indian tribes." But at the same time, he notes, there remains an ambiguous mixed zone, tribespeople who gather at the edges of towns without profiting from the civilized center, whose activities tend to produce the mainstream opinion of Indigenous character. Irving describes these frontier types as the "miserable hordes which infest the frontiers and hang on the skirts of the settlements." His language suggests that they are pests that need to be eradicated from the "skirts"—evoking a form of feminine housekeeping that keeps civilization clean.

By producing his account of the appeal of the "low vices of artificial life" that has "given them a thousand superfluous wants," Irving promotes a classic version of degradation at the edge of civilization: "Thus do we too often find the Indians on our frontiers to be the mere wrecks and remnants of once powerful tribes." Here, they loom as vagrants, "drunken, indolent, feeble, thievish, and pusillanimous." Irving ignores all the white vagabonds who lived on the edge of towns, described by their contemporaries in precisely the same terms. That said, nostalgia for a prelapsarian state emerges when he returns Indigenous people to their traditional habitat, as "undisputed lords of the soil," where they "resembled those wild plants which thrive best in the shades of the forest, but shrink from the hand of cultivation." Again, the soil is "in his heart," the Native American's lifeblood, as it were.[11]

Throughout the *Sketch Book,* as Irving alternates between the archives of London and the uneven, fragmentary dispersals of the frontier, his sketches hint at clarifying the relation between immigrant populations and the *idea* of original inhabitants. While he notes longingly the depredations that have followed on what he calls the "intercourse of the white man with the Indians," he cannot find a place to let his account come to rest. He complains that white people "stigmatize the Indians, also, as cowardly and treacherous." Yet, as Irving also points out, such an accusation of treachery includes resentment of the use of "stratagem in warfare." He reaches back before the time of contact, comparing classic tales of bravery: "No hero of ancient days can surpass the Indian in his lofty contempt of death." In a variety of literary compositions at this time, the poetry of facing danger attached to the idealized Indian.

As he turns to the Pequots in the next section of his account, his manner of expression foreshadows the quality of sympathy expressed by Catharine Sedgwick in *Hope Leslie* for the dismal recorded history of slaughtered Pequot women and children. "Burning with indignation and rendered sullen by despair; with hearts bursting with grief at the destruction of their tribe, and spirits galled and sore at the fancied ignominy of their defeat, they refused to ask their lives at the hands of an insulting foe and preferred death to submission." In the sacrifice was an appeal to posterity.[12]

To haunt is, absent any mystery, simply to frequent a place, to "be about." From its early, nearly unpopulated start, British North America relied upon servants, who were "about," always at hand, and thereby "haunting" places. At the time of the adoption of its federal Constitution and for decades thereafter, the U.S. republic contained voluntary and involuntary immigrants, residents under conditions of servitude. Some were indentured servants whose service had an expiration date, while others were understood simply as bodies for sale whose future held scant prospect of earning citizenship. All can be said to have haunted the landscape.

The first laws restricting immigration in the new nation focused on white people who were refugees from the French Revolution. During Irving's teen years, the Alien Enemies Act (1798) specifically targeted "males of the age of fourteen years and upwards" and directed that they become subject to removal whenever "any invasion or predatory incursion shall be perpetrated, attempted, or threatened against the territory of the United States." The now familiar impulse behind the act was fear of the invasion of aliens, presenting a reality quite opposite the picture Crèvecoeur had earlier painted, when he gloried in the mixture of alien inhabitants in pre-Revolutionary times.

A temporary immigrant in the 1760s, Crèvecoeur returned to Paris to write his fantasy of Americans who had "melted into a new race of man." Jettisoning "all his European prejudices" to become naturalized and truly free, this American went "from the rank of servant to the rank of master." By the end of his letter-driven journey, however, the bright proponent of a liberated people found a dark underbelly in South Carolina, where the agrarian ideal devolves into a horror story and where "no one thinks with compassion of those showers of sweat and of tears which from the bodies of Africans, daily drop, and moisten the ground they till." It is a strange metaphor of melting and moisture, the alchemy of reproduction. Crèvecoeur thought of people as nurtured plants; like the Indians in Irving's story, they had soil in their blood. The Frenchman's narrator bears witness to a Black man in a cage suspended from a tree limb, bloodied and disfigured. "Birds had already picked out his eyes." Caged for resisting the conditions of slavery, the man begged for poison, to bring an end to his suffering. As a witness to horror, the same narrator whose idealism introduced the American pastoral can only retreat in shame.[13]

Read from this perspective, the *Sketch Book* is haunted by the interior landscapes of the Hudson Valley. Traveling north from New York, the reader finds in Irving echoes of concepts present in the earlier work of Crèvecoeur, imagining that it might be possible to cross borders and step onto neutral ground.

Irving's Hudson River Valley is inhabited by the ghosts of the Old World. Even in "Traits of Indian Character," Irving follows his admiration for the stoicism of the Native with an allusion to the Gauls who "laid waste the city of Rome." Irving makes haunting appear a foregone conclusion long before the story concludes. "The eastern tribes have long since disappeared," he writes somberly. "The forests that sheltered them have been laid low, and scarce any traces remains of them in the thickly settled states of New England." With foreboding overshadowed by the odd naturalism of his language, Irving declares that all the Indians shall "vanish like a vapor from the face of the earth."

This entry is followed by an account of the violence of King Philip's War. "Philip of Pokanoket: An Indian Memoir" features a kind of ventriloquist language that raises questions. What does *haunting* mean? What are the ghosts? If the most famous stories are haunted, is the rest of the book haunted? And if you find and name the ghosts, can you find a remedy, or does that act of naming them encourage them to take up residence?

Writing in Ithaca, New York, in late 2020, I have my own questions. What are the appropriate words to use to acknowledge the land grant to which Cornell owes its beginnings, and how should one treat the fact that much of the early wealth of the university depended on trading away lands? These are the traditional homelands of the Gayogo̱hó꞉nǫ' (Cayuga Nation). History and the present collide.

So it is in the pages of the *Sketch Book*. At the outset of "Philip of Pokanoket," Irving is "casually looking through a volume of early colonial history." The scene may be reminiscent of the European libraries he depicted early in his volume, yet here is a history of which he can claim a certain ownership, if somewhat removed. He has traveled through Indian country; he has taken a role in the fur trade of friends and family on the U.S.–Canada border; he senses well "how the footsteps of civilization might be traced in the blood of the aborigines." Irving is able to name the "Pequods, the Narragansetts, the Wampanoags, and other eastern tribes," though they have been removed from his view. The haunting is come home to roost in his revisiting of King Philip's War. And for the modern scholar of early America, it is still possible to say that this war is alive, unresolved. The haunting enacted in the wake of the American Revolution was real to Irving; the violence perpetrated against Indians by General John Sullivan in a series of raids along the shores of Lake Cayuga still haunts the landscape that, "high above Cayuga's waters," my university surveys.

The sons of Philip and the son of Rip Van Winkle become oddly juxtaposed here as displaced persons whose fathers have been absent.[14] The object sustaining participation in the world, for each, is a weapon that cannot fire, a rusted rifle that tells a history and that cannot be carried into the present. And why is the very next piece in the *Sketch Book* "John Bull"? After these forays into ambiguous history, disconnected stories, side by side, we finally reach this other haunted landscape with the immortal "Legend of Sleepy Hollow."

HAUNTED BY A BRIDGE, A STREAM, A TREE, AND HISTORY

"The Legend of Sleepy Hollow" begins with a quatrain from poet James Thompson's "Castle of Indolence" (1748). The first line of the story—"In the bosom of one of those spacious coves which indent the eastern shore of the Hudson"—sets up a welcome to the reader that belies what is to follow. The implied personification of the Hudson River as female runs immediately into the possible dangers of navigating the waters of the Tappan Zee. Set in leisurely sounding "Tarry Town," the story proposes a conflict between harbor and river that has some of the resonance of domestic tension that appears in "Rip Van Winkle"—the name of the town conveys the mild annoyance of "the good housewives" who want their husbands to return from the village tavern more expeditiously on market day.

Gazing up from the town to "a little valley, or rather lap of land, among high hills," the narrator finds "one of the quietest places in the whole world." He had been a "stripling" in this location, although he seems to hold himself apart from the "Sleepy Hollow Boys" who live there. The points that the poignant historical accounts of "Philip of Pokanoket" and "Traits of Indian Character" bring forward seem to belong to a different book. The "drowsy dreamy influence" of the last tale in the *Sketch Book* encourages a somnolent reaction to the preceding stories, even as a somewhat token invocation of the "old Indian chief, the prophet or wizard of his tribe" anchors this story in the historical record.

The haunting in the story is initially traced to the Revolution, to a "remote period of American history, that is to say, some thirty years since," for its staging. Ichabod Crane, who "tarried" in Sleepy Hollow as a teacher, comes from Connecticut with the attributes of the ungainly bird suggested by his name. Other animals enter the description of the unfortunate Crane: "His head was small, and flat at top, with huge ears, large green glassy eyes, and a long snipe nose." Perpetually hungry, with the "dilating powers of an Anaconda," Crane trails from house to house looking to be fed. In nature, cranes stalk, looking for food, which characteristic repeats in Ichabod, a roving, begging vagrant, a strange half-man, half-bird creature.

In his ungainly body, along with a fondness for singing, he also resembles the outlandishly inappropriate singing master David Gaunt of James Fenimore Cooper's slightly later *The Last of the Mohicans*. As a "perfect master of Cotton Mather's History of New England Witchcraft," Ichabod has the legacy of the Salem witchcraft trials trail along with him as well to magnify the story's invocation of inappropriate responses to the accusation of witchcraft.

The appearance of Katrina Van Tassel—at once "plump as a partridge" and ripe "as one of her father's peaches"—causes more disturbing thoughts. Ichabod's fantasy, as Irving presents it, is to cash in on her father's farm and migrate west. His rivalry with the robust Brom Van Brunt, known as "Brom Bones," suggests that his courtship will be limited by his inability to forage food. The surprise—given the general absence of such a figure in the rest of the volume—comes with the appearance of a "Negro, in tow-cloth jacket," who invites Ichabod to a particular kind of party.

The feast appeals in terms of the food that is offered, but more important is how bodies arrive (in the case of Crane, of course, awkwardly) and how they move after they arrive. The emphasis on dancing becomes the location for racialized scenarios: "The musician was an old gray-headed Negro." And as Ichabod, playing the fool, throws his body around, he is the "admiration of all the Negroes . . . forming a pyramid of shining black faces . . . rolling their white eyeballs." The lovelorn Ichabod Crane is again exposed, the outsider desperate to fit in. Against the background of what looks like minstrelsy, his desire to embark on an upward class migration finds its earliest incarnation here.

At the party, stories are told of Major John André, the British gentleman-spy captured near Tarrytown and nostalgically celebrated for his youth and beauty, despite having been executed by the Continental Army because of his involvement with the traitor Benedict Arnold.[15] En route home, in proximity to the tree where André was said to have been hanged, and on the bridge where he was captured, Ichabod revisits stories of the Revolution. He shudders beside that famously "haunted stream," which winds along as a liquid form of the unbanishable memories that adhere to the land. The idea of Tarrytown as a place to tarry is mocked by the inadvertent dawdling of Ichabod Crane, who is rushed out of town by memories that haunt.

Irving's generation, too young to have fought in the Revolution, came of age in a post-Revolutionary society that welcomed its historical satire while still enduring its own destabilizing memories of war and conflict. Though memories recede, generation by generation, I look back casually at the family I can trace to this time. I find among my Maine ancestors the peers of Washington Irving, and I do not have to look far afield to encounter a four- or five-times great-grandfather, Daniel Briggs, who signed up for the Revolution in 1777 in Massachusetts. The handwritten document is almost illegible but the name is clear. An uncle who lived in Turner, a border town once part of British Canada, and who was named Ichabod Bonney enlisted on March 5, 1776. That name—and these other overlaps with Revolutionary histories—make me feel (inappropriately, to be sure) entangled with Irving's Ichabod.[16]

What does *haunting* mean? What are the ghosts? If the most famous of Irving's stories are haunted, does it follow that the rest of the book is haunted? And if you find and name the ghosts, can you find a remedy, or does that act of naming them merely encourage them to take up residence?

Irving gives a partial answer. In *A History of New-York* (1809), which promoted the school of early nineteenth-century writing that satirized the Dutch origins of New York, he used the vehicle of Diedrich Knickerbocker to facilitate a kind of haunting. Ten years later, without entirely disappearing, Knickerbocker gave way to the Anglophilic voice of Geoffrey Crayon in the *Sketch Book*. After one more decade passed, from his new perch in Spain, the author entertained the ghosts of the Moors who, like the headless Hessian in "The Legend of Sleepy Hollow," departed from Spanish history at the time of Columbus. In his various acts of invention, Irving haunted the page while consistently denying that there was anything to fear.

Drawing back two hundred years from the present moment, in visiting a few of the less comfortable stories of the founding era in American history, I want to argue that the stories we most associate with Washington Irving concern a loss of memory so profound that the rest of his career can be seen as an attempt to reclaim and reassert the power of memory through historical fiction.

If we look forward from the awkward reawakening of Rip Van Winkle to the "ruby face of King George" that had "metamorphosed" into "George Washington," we can notice as well how the Dutch-inflected persona of Diedrich Knickerbocker metamorphosed into the multivolume history of George Washington that Irving completed, with his nephew's help, shortly before his death. Throughout his writing career, Irving had an obsession with shifts in patriotic loyalties. Following Irving, the temptation in reviewing the Revolution's grimier stories is to convert these stories into historical fiction, a temptation that Hawthorne clearly gave in to when he wrote "My Kinsman, Major Molineux" (1832), a story that I am about to match, in a Knickerbocker-like manner, with the lamentable tale of Jesse Dunbar.

In a book on Revolution-era Loyalists and their fates, first published in 1847 and revised and expanded in 1864, there is an ambiguous, if violent, story about Jesse Dunbar of Halifax, Massachusetts. Before the outbreak of war, he seems to have purchased cattle from someone aligned with the British. At that time, rebel sentiment decreed that this purchase constituted a disloyal act. Therefore, "after he had slaughtered, skinned, and hung up one of the beasts, [the rebels] commenced punishing him." Putting Dunbar into the belly of the slaughtered cow carcass and throwing him into a cart, they drove him from town to town, charging him a dollar each time he arrived at a new location. After beating him with the entrails of the animal, they threw him into the road. Newspapers asserted that the crowd also stole his horse.[17]

It is entirely possible that this story refers to my four times great-grandfather, also named Jesse Dunbar, also from Halifax, Massachusetts, who was apparently born the same year. The Jesse Dunbar from whom I am descended ended up in Laurens, New York, a town named after John Laurens, a notable figure in the American Revolution and intimate friend of Alexander Hamilton. Jesse Dunbar, his sons, and his grandsons are buried in a cemetery there that I have visited. My grandfather, Claude Dunbar Briggs, carried that Dunbar name with him to South Dakota, where my mother was raised on what is still called the Briggs ranch.

But I am not writing this account in an attempt to prove that they are the same person. Even if they are, the story matters more to me because it resembles Hawthorne's "My Kinsman, Major Molineux," which is an account of humiliation—the humiliation of a man being tarred and feathered. The compiler of the 1847 collection contributed "preliminary remarks," commenting that "the practice of 'tarring and feathering,' however reprehensible, had, perhaps, but little influence." The practice was, he wrote, "confined, principally, to obnoxious custom-house officers, pimps, and informers against smuggled goods."[18] At the time this book was published, Hawthorne was working as a customhouse officer; one wonders if he read these words and winced.

The fear that Ichabod Crane experiences about losing his head—as the story clearly demarcates the haunted horseman as a Hessian soldier—is also the metaphorical fear of losing your head (as absentmindedness) or taking the wrong (losing) side. The Hessian soldier who inspires the story was a mercenary hired by the British. He "lost his head" by losing his way politically, and then he lost his head to a cannonball.[19]

The hauntings in early American history that emerge through Irving's sketches present an alternative understanding of the fathering of the country. If Washington Irving is haunted by the legacy that flows from being named after that father, then he becomes, as the nation's first professional author, a cultural father who leaves a rather uncomfortable legacy himself. Through his stories, readers acquire the sense that democracy's birth occurred in a time of competitive striving between the mocking forgetfulness of Rip Van Winkle and the endangered flight of Ichabod Crane.

Where, between the dangers posed to Loyalists and the crowded anarchy of rebels, does loyalty lie? It's a good question, if you're named after the father of your country and write your most famous tales from the heart of the nation he fought against in earnest. Never knowing whether one should imbibe spirits beneath the swinging tavern sign of King George or George Washington, shrugging off the dangers of useless learning as Ichabod Crane flees Brom Bones, readers of Irving's sketches, like many nineteenth-century readers, can locate themselves on a boat somewhere between the United States and Europe.

Irving's stories of lost memory speak to our national detachment. Whether by forgetting our history or by rewriting it in stories haunted by fragmented memories, Irving reminds us that revolutions turn a new page;

they awaken the dead. Dispossession and disinheritance are as much a facet of America's story as the more heralded demand for liberty.

Washington Irving plainly sought to reconcile his "Washingtonian" with his English paternity. A decade after he reconceived the history of the Dutch settlement of New Netherland (via Diedrich Knickerbocker), and with a glancing eye toward the tragic Indigenous dispossession story, he shook things up in the literary world with his "breakout" work, the *Sketch Book*. As he laid out his deep fascination with the history of print culture, Irving set forth an ambivalent road map for an American escape from English literary imperialism.

NOTES

1. Washington Irving was the youngest of eight. Of his four older brothers, only William (b. 1766), a future member of Congress, was of an age to have understood the stakes while the War for Independence was ongoing.

2. Nathaniel Hawthorne, "The Custom-House," introduction to *The Scarlet Letter* (New York: Library of America, 1983). Historical memory, in this context, calls up Britain's Charles I losing his head, followed by the Cromwell interregnum and the Glorious Revolution—which, in combination, shaped how New Englanders imagined the long prelude to the American Revolution.

3. Donald Grant Mitchell, writing as Ik Marvel, published the first installments of the book that became *Reveries of a Bachelor, or, A Book of the Heart*, in 1849. He was a friend of Washington Irving and dedicated his next book, *Dream Life: A Fable of the Seasons*, to Irving in 1851. Herman Melville, "I and My Chimney" first appeared in *Putnam's Monthly Magazine* in March 1856. On bachelorhood in Irving's world and in his writing, see Andrew Burstein, *The Original Knickerbocker: The Life of Washington Irving* (New York: Basic Books, 2007), 110–12, 118–19, 175–77, 333–35, and elsewhere.

4. Irving's personal story bears a resemblance to that of Benjamin Franklin: both initially profited from their connections to powerful men, and both subsequently displayed an earnest desire to help other young men advance. Irving appealed to Sir Walter Scott to help him get published in London—as he warmly acknowledged in his preface to the *Sketch Book*. Following his own success, Irving helped along numerous American writers, most notably by presenting their work to publishers. Regarding Franklin's experience, see David Waldstreicher, *Runaway America: Benjamin Franklin, Slavery, and the American Revolution* (New York: Hill and Wang, 2004).

5. Of the brothers, Washington Irving was perhaps the most torn politically: he maintained respect for both New Yorkers, Aaron Burr and Alexander Hamilton.

6. To describe Irving as always in motion is at once accurate and misleading. He acquired a home that he loved in Tarrytown, a place, as Burstein points out, where he housed as many as five nieces at a time, in addition to his bachelor brother, Peter.

7. As Burstein notes, there were still hogs rooting through garbage in lower Manhattan. See Burstein, *Original Knickerbocker,* 6, citing Edwin G. Burrows and Mike Wallace, *Gotham: A History of New York to 1898* (New York: Oxford University Press, 1999); also Catherine McNeur, *Taming Manhattan: Environmental Battles in the Antebellum City* (Cambridge, MA: Harvard University Press, 2014). While Irving was still in Europe, Alexis de Tocqueville was charting a path to New York. As he noted the "leveling down" of democracy, Irving went aspirational. The image of the two crossing the Atlantic Ocean in different directions to find cultural knowledge highlights the relation between an investigation of the carceral system in the United States and the different forms of incarceration, notably that of books and paintings, that Irving depicts in the *Sketch Book.*

8. In the twenty-first century, American readers have little memory of the Connecticut Wits, who were followed by the Knickerbocker writers; their humor has become lost, as has the pleasure they took in explaining that there was a "there there" on the barely invaded shores of the American continent. This unofficial congregation included James Kirke Paulding and William Cullen Bryant. To know a person by their friends must also be to notice who it is they don't know—such as, for instance, another writer of sketches, Fanny Fern. She has been paired with Irving by critical commentators. See David Dowling, *Literary Partnerships and the Marketplace* (Baton Rouge: Louisiana State University Press, 2012); Kristie Hamilton, *America's Sketchbook: The Cultural Life of a 19th-Century American Genre* (Athens: Ohio University Press, 1998); Gregg Canfield, *Necessary Madness: The Humor of Domesticity in American Culture* (New York: Oxford University Press, 1997).

9. In its transatlantic crossing and its cynicism about ideas on paper, the story resembles Herman Melville's "The Paradise of Bachelors and the Tartarus of Maids." In that story, the labor of young women in the mills of western Massachusetts makes their skin as white as paper. Meanwhile, the bachelors in London have no concept of the relation of their rags to the production of the paper on which they write. See also the interpretive work on Melville's story in Jonathan Senchyne, *The Intimacy of Paper in Early and Nineteenth-Century American Literature* (Amherst: University of Massachusetts Press, 2019).

10. The first publication of *Notes on the State of Virginia,* in 1785, contained this account by Logan, which Jefferson included along with an indictment of the role of white settlers in the massacre of Logan's family. Challenged about his account, Jefferson published a follow-up account in 1800, but he did not repudiate his original laying of blame. For provenance of "The Speech of Logan" and commentary, see Jefferson, *Notes on the State of Virginia,* ed. William Peden (Chapel Hill: University of North Carolina Press, 1955), appendix 4; Anthony F. C. Wallace, "Introduction: Logan's Mourner," in *Jefferson and the Indians: The*

Tragic Fate of the First Americans (Cambridge, MA: Harvard University Press, 1999); Andrew Burstein, *Sentimental Democracy: The Evolution of America's Romantic Self-Image* (New York: Hill and Wang, 1999), x–xii, 36, 341 note 2; and Bernard W. Sheehan, *Seeds of Extinction: Jeffersonian Philanthropy and the American Indians* (Chapel Hill: University of North Carolina Press, 1973), esp. 109–10.

    11. See Peter Silver, *Our Savage Neighbors: How Indian War Transformed Early America* (New York: Norton, 2008). On white vagrants, see Nancy Isenberg, *White Trash: The 400-Year Untold History of Class in America* (New York: Viking, 2016).

    12. Timeline questions are of interest here. Shortly after the appearance of the *Sketch Book* came related fictional treatments of Native Americans' displacement: Lydia Maria Child, *Hobomok* (1824); James Fenimore Cooper, *The Last of the Mohicans* (1826); and Catharine Sedgwick, *Hope Leslie* (1827). Note, too, that this myth of stoic death supports the vanishing Indian trope—they would rather vanish as proud warriors in historic memory than regress to worthless vagrants without a home or territory to call their own.

    13. Quotes from letters 3 and 9. For an online version, see J. Hector St. John De Crevecoeur, *Letters from an American Farmer,* http://xroads.virginia.edu/~Hyper/CREV/contents.html.

    14. The son of King Philip was sold into slavery, and thus another son was denied his paternity.

    15. The story hit close to home for Irving. One of the "sturdy yeomen" heralded for having captured André was John Paulding, a cousin to the writer James Kirke Paulding, Irving's lifelong friend and literary collaborator. Paulding's sister Julia had married Irving's eldest brother, William, in the early 1790s. For more, see Erik Weiselberg, "The Revolutionary War Lives On," in this volume.

    16. Sylvester, Canada, became a town in a different nation when it was renamed Turner, Maine. Ichabod Bonney set up a meetinghouse in 1782. See William Riley French, *A History of Turner, Maine, from its Settlement to 1886* (Portland, ME: Hoyt, Fogg and Donham, 1887).

    17. Lorenzo Sabine, *Biographical Sketches of Loyalists of the American Revolution* (Little, Brown, 1864), 397.

    18. Sabine, *Biographical Sketches,* 76.

    19. Robert Hughes, "Sleepy Hollow: Fearful Pleasures and the Nightmare of History," *Arizona Quarterly* 61 (Autumn 2005): 1–26.

READING THE *SKETCH BOOK* FROM ITS CLATTERING HOOVES UP

NANCY ISENBERG

Class relations and class issues course through the *Sketch Book*. This should come as no surprise, given Washington Irving's immersion in English life in the years leading up to the serialization of the tales that put the American author on the literary map. Less obvious to most readers, however, is the class dimension of the four-legged characters in Irving's popular stories.

A horse race, a chase scene, and two very different breeds of horses are at the heart of "The Legend of Sleepy Hollow." The humor-laden "horse sense" of old Gunpowder is one of the most memorable aspects of the 1949 Disney version of Washington's Irving's tale. The "broken down plough-horse," as the author styles him, steals the chase scene and becomes the unexpected hero of the cartoon. As in the original tale of 1820, the horse and his "unskilled rider," Ichabod Crane, are a perfect match, in the tangle of coattails and horse tails. In Irving's wry description, the "skirts" of Ichabod's "black coat fluttered out almost to the horse's tail."

Horses are major characters in the *Sketch Book*. They gallop, trot, prance, dash, and clatter their hooves across its pages. Horses of different shapes and sizes make appearances on thirty-eight pages and in thirteen different *Sketch Book* stories. We shouldn't be surprised. In a recent review of horse racing scholarship, "I Got the Horse Right Here," historian (horse-storian?) Katherine Mooney reminds us that "horses were, until very recently in human history, everywhere." They were not just a part of everyday life, Mooney says, but a "vital reality and evocative symbol." To ignore them is to distort the past.[1]

For Irving, horses represent a series of interconnected, recurring themes. In several tales, horses function as key markers of rural life and class identity. They capture the unbridled tension between a natural aristocracy and the crass behavior of the nouveau riche. Horses plod along as they move the plot along; in a strange way, they connect the early nineteenth century to the dreamily misremembered past. Geoffrey Crayon, Irving's alter ego in the *Sketch Book,* observes in "Westminster Abbey" that, as time distorts memory, "history fades into fable . . . the statue falls from the pedestal." The adage neatly encapsulates the fate of Ichabod Crane. At the end of the tale, our poor schoolmaster transforms into yet another of the hazy superstitions that populate Irving's fiction: he falls from his horse and vanishes. The "old country wives" keep his mysterious disappearance alive in their gossip, which contributes to local lore. The very last line in the tale says a lot: as he walks in the vicinity of the haunted schoolhouse, a "plough-boy" is able to hear Ichabod's melancholy psalm tune, whistling in the breeze.

BEATING HOOVES, BEATING HEART

The present is haunted by the past, indeed. But for Irving, that's not all there is to it. He seems to say that the present is haunted by class pretensions. In the stories set in rural England, social hierarchy is reinforced by what he calls "rich morsels of quaint antiquity" that dot the English landscape. One such memorial to the class order is fed to the reader in "The Country Church." Irving describes the elaborate tributes to ancient families inside the building, the elegant workmanship and richly colored marble that adorns the "tombs of knights, and high born dames." His tone as the narrator Crayon is of one who is dazzled yet also somewhat appalled. He remarks, in passive language, that the "eye was struck" with "some haughty memorial" that tried but failed to defy mortality.

The church is a living monument to social rank. The interior is carefully arranged according to class geography: the landed people of rank sit in front in sumptuous pews, with "richly-gilded prayer-books" and family arms on the pew doors. Villagers and peasants fill the back seats; the poor were allotted their lowly perch on benches. Everyone knew his or her place.

Irving seems to admire the unpretentious manners of the titled elites, noting approvingly that they arrive in the "plainest equipage, and often on foot." Their entire demeanor is "easy and natural, with that lofty grace and noble frankness which bespeak free-born souls that have never been checked in their growth by feelings of inferiority." They possess the traits of a natural elite, whose comfort in their own skin commanded respect from those beneath them. Yet Irving points to a problem here: what is "natural" among the old families is that they are untouchable—inured to "feelings of inferiority." Their place is so secure, their privileges so grounded in history and tradition, that they feel no need to flaunt their wealth.

Nothing bespeaks their modest decorum more than walking to church on foot. Horses and carriages, for most of history, had been the mobile symbols of royalty and aristocracy. Private carriages were a luxury, by which the fortunate few avoided the admixture of bodies, the mingling of classes, the dirt and disease uniformly found in city streets and public conveyances. Keeping at a distance and receiving deference from the urban poor—the nameless vagrants and urchins, so unlike Irving's romanticized village neighbors of his country elites—was a privilege of gentility. In London, well into the nineteenth century, carriages unceremoniously ran over poor children in the streets, and gentlemen, from their saddles, whipped rude men without a second thought. In eighteenth-century Philadelphia and New York, only the wealthiest families owned carriages. Irving was not blind to this reality.[2]

Still, he believed, as did many other Anglo-Americans, that genuine aristocrats displayed their power through effortless decorum and disciplined bodies, detaching themselves from mere trappings and things. Horses, however, were more than things. "Horses shared humankind's double allegiance to nature and society," one scholar has observed. Seamless integration into society had made horses appear next in line after humans in the "scale of beings." In a larger sense, the Americans and the English both believed that humans and horses conveyed a *natural register* of station. A well-bred horse was readily identifiable by its coat, gait, mane, pedigree, and pleasing temperament; a well-bred man displayed his tasteful attire, step and deportment, affability, and "healthful hardiness," to use Irving's phrase, along with a proud family lineage.³

Returning to Irving's "The Country Church," the nouveau riche tell a different story. They effectively pantomime their superiors and are capable of little else as social beings. Having purchased a mansion from a ruined nobleman, one family arrives "en prince," decked out in "carriage emblazoned with arms," the crest glittering from every part of the harness. Horses were critical to the new look insofar as they had learned to ape their surroundings. High-stepping steeds projected the arrogance of their owners, arching their necks—they "glanced their eyes more proudly than common horses." As they create a commotion, kicking up dust and stones in a "prancing trot," the villagers are left agape, and in "vacant admiration." Finally, pulled to an immediate stop, the horses rear up on their haunches, setting the scene for a dramatic entrance at the church door.

To Crayon's disappointment, the "august family" in the carriage is anything but venerable. Mere pretenders, they come across as mock aristocrats of the commercial elite. The contrast is stark: pomp and ceremony fail to compensate for the sad human specimens who have stepped out of this carriage. The patriarch is a pompous, red-faced man whose only talent, Crayon surmises, is to "shake the stock market with a nod." His wife is fleshy, vulgar, simple; his daughters supercilious. The sons are dandyish in dress and clumsy in movement, their bodies formed for "common purposes." In short, "Nature had denied them the nameless grace." Plough-horses, all.

A horse was a measure of both man and woman, in addition to serving as a class marker. In an 1826 report on horses by New Hampshire's Merrimack Agricultural Society, published in *The New England Farmer*, the society's chairman echoed the system of classification Irving relied on. He warned against a "dandy's horse" that "partakes of the frivolities and coltish tricks of his rider." They canter at a gentleman's word, "trot, amble and gallop sideways," but, upon closer inspection, their tricks were as superficial as the chain buttons, ruffles, and fancy suspenders of any foppish man about town. According to the same thread of logic, horses trained by ladies were too docile, and warhorses were unsuited to "sensible husbandmen"; horses of "inferior classes," such as the Irish pony or the "clumsy Dutch dray-horse," were no better. Indeed, like young men, horses required a "good education," not in "dead languages" (the chairman joked), but schooled well enough that they were able to follow the commands of a "rational, merciful man." Dandified horses were as artificial and shallow as Irving's nouveau riche of England; dray-horses (or plough-horses) were recognized as the serfs of the horse kingdom. Whether treated as ornaments or companions, horses gave clues to who their owners were. A horse reflected the rider's personality and station.[4]

For Irving, horses symbolized rural life. His arrogant nouveau riche were gate-crashers, despoiling the simple and pure values of the countryside. He drew a line between town and country, urban and rural ways—and the town was always found wanting. In "Rural Funerals," he rebuked showy and gloomy town funeral processions with fancy "mourning horses" as a sham. Manufactured politeness or grief, he felt, destroyed genuine poetic feeling. Once the pompous ceremony ended, and the body was laid in the ground, the deceased was forgotten in the "gay and crowded city." The city was bustling, filled with temptations and constant sensations, "the hurrying succession of new intimates and new pleasures." True feeling, genuine memories, and melancholy persisted in the countryside he favored. There, in tranquil villages, people were less trammeled by the empty conventions of the town. To use an equine analogy, humans were closer to nature, and closer to poetry, when they roamed free, like a spirited horse darting about an open field.

Irving's descriptions of death and melancholy, rustic simplicity and purity of feeling, were well-established British literary conventions by the time of his arrival. More than any other story, "The Pride of the Village" is predictable along such lines. An innocent and beautiful young girl falls in love with a gallant officer, only to be abandoned, left to waste away and die. It is a tale steeped in class politics. The young girl was a child of the "better order of peasantry," who'd learned never to aspire beyond the station into which she was born. Her intrinsic charms nevertheless betrayed a natural superiority; she was "the prettiest low-born lass," "too noble for this place." She's no gold digger or motivated by a secret ambition for the "sordid distinctions of ranks and fortune"; her naiveté is what dooms her. Matrimony is out of the question, because the soldier's father has forbidden a union beneath his titled rank. She knows her "comparative unworthiness." His attempt at seduction (in the aristocratic libertine tradition) fails, and so he abandons her. Class wins out over love.

As Irving retells the story of the girl's demise, "suddenly the clang of hoofs was heard; a horseman galloped to the cottage; . . . it was her repentant lover." Too little, too late, of course. Too weak to speak, she dies as he looks on. This tale is not about redemption, nor does it advocate cross-class marriages. Her death makes the proud soldier a better Man of Feeling, but it does not make him a democrat. It is the horse alone that seems capable of expressing the soldier's natural passions, the beating hooves syncopating with a beating heart. In the end, neither the rider nor his horse can shed their pedigree. The gallant soldier's moment of enchantment, his burst of passion, remains enshrouded in the fading memory of a sequestered village graveyard far from the stately mansion where he will carry on his aristocratic lifestyle.

COACHEY AND CLASS CONSCIOUSNESS

There is little room for social mobility in Irving's tales. If a lovely lass can't marry her Prince Charming, and the nouveau riche are abominations, then what hope is there for the working class? "The Stage-Coach" reinforces the unbridgeable gap between men of taste and laboring men. Down to the last detail, the coachman wears his class identity on his sleeve. To Irving, this "class of functionaries" is easily recognizable by way of "a dress, a manner, a language, an air peculiar to themselves." They could not be mistaken "for one of any other craft or mystery." They were, in short, artisans of the horse trade.

Appearance did not lie, either. His driver has "a commonly broad, full face, curiously mottled with red"; he is fat, filled with "potations of malt liquor"; he wears a strange layering of coats, "like a cauliflower." He has on a brightly colored striped waistcoat and high jockey boots, and while his costume is "maintained with much precision," a strange, awful contrast exists between his neat dress and the "seeming grossness of his appearance."

Curiously to Crayon, and to us, the driver has a following among others of his class. Gathered around him are the village housewives and pretty lasses with whom he gossips along his route, as well as the "stableboys, shoeblacks, and those nameless hangers-on that infest inns and taverns." These sassy boys admire his "cant phrases," his "jockey lore"—they see in him their future. As Irving puts it, "Every ragamuffin that has a coat to his back thrusts his hands in his pockets, rolls in his gait, talks slang, and is an embryo Coachey." The language is rich; Coachey, as a rakish raconteur, is a kind of working-class hero. He is the center of attention wherever he goes, creating a whirl of excitement. When a stagecoach rolls into a village, any village, something awakens among the lower ranks.

His cant, his slippery character, have a near match in the notorious reputation of the horse jockey, whom Irving had earlier disparaged in *A History of New-York*. Horse jockeys were peddlers and hucksters, skilled at selling inferior horses to unsuspecting dupes. They were great storytellers, known braggarts, who hung out at grog shops and taverns. Just like garrulous Coachey, they traded in "jockey lore." An American periodical defined the type, in 1818, as "the despicable character of a horse jockey, who seeks to enrich himself by speculation, lies, and deceit." Yet horse jockeys were comical, and proud of their exploits; they exhibited the same defiant style as the wily coachman who carried himself with an air self-importance.[5]

The coachman had another telling flaw: a complete disregard for his horses, which he saw as simply the tools of his trade. When he arrives at his destination, Irving states, he "throws down his reins with something of an air," for he believes his only duty is "to drive from one stage to another." Irving's obvious disdain for his indifference to the horses reflected another well-established class critique: nobles were known to treat their horses with respect, while the new capitalist commercial economy turned the omnipresent beast into an exploitable resource, left under the command of working-class men. Yet another class-conscious mark against the uncouth Coachey.[6]

Did Irving have a feel (or feelings) for horses? It is not clear from his time in England, though he reveals more of his horse experiences in the following decade, after he sails home and travels west, recording his adventures in *A Tour on the Prairies*. For the demanding trek across Indian country in Missouri, Arkansas Territory, and the future Oklahoma, he had to have a certain degree of skill, balance, and fitness as a horseman. When a working-class character like Coachey joins the team—a French Creole nicknamed Tonish—Irving describes him as "a little, swarthy, meager" man who played the "comic Frenchman." He was someone "without caste, without creed," a "person of inferior rank," and he spoke a "jargon of English, French, and Osage." (The Osage had been a particularly powerful nation of the region, lately having adjusted to the U.S. army presence.) Tonish was made of different parts—peddler, con man, flatterer, liar, and "notorious braggart," much like the horse jockey. He was most pleased when he was given the reins, driving the train of packhorses and becoming "master of the horse."

Irving wryly admitted that Tonish had a "nose for class." He took on the job of guide for the young Count Albert Alexandre de Pourtalès, a Swiss nobleman whose parents were part of Napoleon's court and whom Irving described as a "bold and graceful rider." In Osage territory, Irving described his own mount as a "stout silver gray," "staunch and powerful." For his part, Tonish promised to teach the coltish count how to catch a wild horse. Irving himself participated in the wild horse hunt and came to consider the tricks of that trade to be inhumane—horse hunting wasn't a sport but a ruthless cold cash business. Most appalling was the decision to "crease" the horse's neck with a rifle shot, which stunned the animal. This practice could as easily maim or kill. Irving privately rooted for the horse. Looking upon a captive creature, he deployed class language again, describing its fall from grace: "One day, a prince of the prairies—the next day, a pack horse!"

In the middle of a buffalo hunt, Irving encountered a lone black mare and gave an impassioned description. Startled by his appearance, she "swept up in full speed," ran down the valley and up a hill, so he could see her "flowing mane and tail and action free as air." At this, he cried out that "so glorious an animal might never come under the degrading thralldom of whip and curb."[7]

THE SURROGATE BRIDEGROOM

Horses were supernatural characters in Irving's tales as well. The American author had stepped into a world where true chivalry had recently returned. A fascination with medievalism echoed the Romantic idealism of an emerging naturalism; it conjured a simpler time of heroic codes and a harmonious social character. Updated editions of the fifteenth-century *Le Morte d'Arthur* were giving the British public the imagery of armor-laden knights and brave steeds. Sir Walter Scott, whom Irving admired from afar before a friendship blossomed between them, generated widespread interest with *Ivanhoe: A Romance* (1819). It mattered most, perhaps, that Miguel de Cervantes's immortal *Don Quixote* (1605–1615) continued to wield tremendous influence in the nineteenth century. Ichabod Crane is a quixotic double, described by Irving as a poor imitation of a knight-errant as he trots proudly along on Gunpowder to the grand party at the "castle" of the Van Tassels.[8]

The word *chivalry* goes back to the eleventh-century French *chevalerie*, associating courage with the culture of horsemanship and the horse as a "noble beast." Knighthood was a privileged status. An air of mystery surrounded the elite order in their combat training and in the care they took in selecting superior stallions. In this medieval tradition, the horse symbolically separated kings, lords, and knights from "lesser people"; the lord's elevated station on horseback mimicked his higher rank. The same rules that divided classes and horses developed from the codes of chivalry: the male destrier and courser (or charger) was reserved for knights and aristocrats; the palfrey, a light riding horse, belonged to the untitled classes, pages, and elite women; inferior horses were used for plowing and pulling; the "ambler," or strolling horse, was allotted to women riding sidesaddle. At the top of the horse hierarchy was the destrier, the ungelded male stallion, signifying strength along with the sexual prowess of the male rider.[9]

Irving used this code to define Brom Bones and his horse in every detail. Brom possesses a "rough chivalry in his nature" and prefers to fight Ichabod Crane, his rival for Katrina Van Tassel's hand, like the "knights-errant of yore—by single combat." Brom leads his own "troop," known for dashing through the hollow, and he is "famed for his horsemanship, being as dexterous on his horse as a Tartar." "Daredevil," aptly named, is his favorite, a black steed full of "metal and mischief," difficult to manage, which meant that he was fully endowed as a masculine specimen.

Brom is his horse, and the horse is him. We can appreciate the symmetry. According to the code of chivalry, a knight's stallion was his equal; both had to be of strong build, bold, fearless, and loyal. They formed a "passionate relationship," as Susan Crane has argued in her study of medieval horsemanship. Superior horses were swift, agile, and lively, with a strong, arched neck and a "quick eye." Ichabod's Gunpowder meets none of these standards. The creature is old, gaunt, and thin-necked, with a head "like a hammer"; "one eye had lost its pupil and was glaring and spectral." This is a "broken down plough-horse," Irving announces, the lowest rank of horses.

A lowly horse diminishes the rider. The imagery is pointed and instantly revealing: a noble knight and his noble horse are one, giving them a combined power. A true knight-errant, unlike the pathetically unskilled rider Ichabod, has every reason to glow with pride. As the old English text *Order of Chivalry* went, "He knoweth his horse, and his horse knows him."[10]

Of Irving's *Sketch Book* stories, "The Spectre Bridegroom" is of particular interest, for it indulges all the trappings of knighthood, castles, and the mysterious bond of horse and human. While Brom displays "rough chivalry," the would-be bride and bridegroom in this "wild and romantic tract of Upper Germany" wish to fulfill that fantasy, but fate decrees otherwise. In this rural version of medieval lore, a gallant cavalier, Count Von Alten-

Of the many visual depictions of the famous scene from "The Legend of Sleepy Hollow," this very early action painting captures the drama of the tale particularly well. *Ichabod Crane Flying from the Headless Horseman*, ca. 1828, by John Quidor. Oil on canvas. 22 ⅝ × 30 1/16 in. (57.5 × 76.4 cm). Mabel Brady Garvan Collection. Courtesy Yale University Art Gallery.

burg, and his chivalrous "companion-in-arms," Herman Von Starkenfaust, are waylaid on their trip to the castle of the count's betrothed. Tragically, they are attacked by robbers and the young count receives a mortal wound. He is a man of honor, not an "ardent lover"—the marriage was an arranged one. He begs his friend to finish the journey and convey the news to Baron Von Landshort (a "small man" with a "large soul") and his willing daughter. In his dying moments, the count imagines that he has ordered his horse and is preparing to ride to the castle, only to expire "in the fancied act of vaulting into the saddle." His last act, his last thoughts, are of his horse.

As Starkenfaust arrives at the castle, he is described by Irving as a "tall gallant cavalier mounted on a black steed," bearing "an air of stately melancholy." The pale rider is unable to explain the truth, his voice stilled by the effusions of his host, who has mistaken him for the bridegroom. Starkenfaust falls in love with the baron's daughter at first sight, but he sits gloomily among the revelers at the wedding feast as they retell "wild tales" of supernatural doings. The banquet hall is similar to Irving's country church; it is a museum of the dead. On the walls are hung portraits of the dead "heroes of the house," along with "jousting-spears," "cross-bows and battle-axes," and the grim relics of slain animals—jawbones, antlers, and tusks.

Starkenfaust is devoid of revelrous energy. He makes excuses for needing to bed elsewhere this night, and on parting alone ventriloquizes his friend: "I am a dead man" and the "grave is waiting for me—I must keep my appointment!" He vaults onto his "black charger" and "dashed over the drawbridge, and the clattering of his horse's hoofs was lost in the whistling of the night blast."

The next day, word arrives at the castle that the bridegroom is dead—and had been slain well *before* the wedding banquet. "On the night of the second day," under the moonlight, the bride beheld her "Spectre Bridegroom" from her window. After he wooed and won the young, groomless bride, he whisked her away, they wed, and ultimately they returned to her distraught father's castle. The daughter springs from her horse, accompanied by the cavalier. He stands before the confused baron in his splendid dress, not merely alive but "a noble figure of manly symmetry."

Why the cruel ruse? Starkenfaust feared losing his love because his own family was locked in a "hereditary feud" with the baron. Thankful to have his daughter returned safely, the baron was in a pardoning mood. Irving explains away the stratagems as "excusable in love."

It is an ending that seems strangely forced and unconvincing. Once again, the real moral of the story is that class conquers love. This marriage works because the surrogate bridegroom is "so gallant, so generous—and so rich." The daughter on her "palfrey" and the cavalier on his black steed make a perfectly well-bred couple. Starkenfaust, interchangeable and indistinguishable from the fallen count, is a man of noble birth and a member of the elite brotherhood of knights.

A more humorous tale of a spectral horse comes courtesy of "The Christmas Dinner." At Bracebridge Hall, Crayon meets a modern-day Baron Von Landshort. Scanning the mansion's hall, as the guest of the "squire's son," he finds a replica (or attempted revival) of a medieval castle. The squire, "a country gentleman," lives in a fabled past recreated from "ancient and modern texts," especially writers from two centuries before. He is what we today would call a historical reenactor, or what became known as a Victorian revivalist, who surrounds himself with artifacts, loves old customs, and (to his son) verges on the eccentric. While the servants in their quarters play "hoodman blind, and shoe the wild mare," the children in the main hall play cards or frolic with toy horses. The hall itself is a re-creation of the interior of the castle in "The Spectre Bridegroom." On the wall is a helmet, buckler, and lance, along with an "enormous pair of antlers," whips, and spurs. In this setting, the old squire is seated in his "hereditary elbow chair by the fireside of his ancestors." The squire is a "worthy old cavalier," whose generosity to the poor reflects the "true Christmas spirit of charity."

The centerpiece of the hall's relics is a "great picture" of a "crusader and his white horse." After finding the armor, the squire manufactured his mythic pedigree, convinced that the warrior in the portrait was the family's hero. Crayon hints that he doubts the authenticity of the claim. It is a case of family pride, rooted in a kind of folk genetics, seeing resemblances in the faces of the numerous portraits that cover the walls. The nobler types wore class insignias on their countenances; if the warrior was the sire, then the family portrait gallery was a kind of stud book, a visible record of famed ancestors and a treasured lineage.

The horse at the center of this story is a ghost. The picture of the family hero, a crusader, and his white horse, is thought by the servants to have "something supernatural about it." On Midsummer Eve, a night when ghosts appear, the crusader would mount his horse, "come down from his picture," and visit his tomb. Such superstitions, the squire confesses, are for children, servants, and dairymaids. His education and class background make it impossible for him to believe. Irving suggests otherwise. It is the squire who re-creates the magical chivalric world of ancient lore, games, costumes, dances, and feasts. Poring over ancient texts, he indulges his fancy. The rules of rank are temporarily suspended, much like carnival, for twelve days. The tradition known as Lord of Misrule (or King of Fools) directs the celebration. So class can take a holiday.

Galloping out of the past, out of the portrait, the horse and his rider are the whimsical progenitors of this grand old family. The blood and carnage of the actual medieval crusades had been replaced with the mirth and folly of "Queen Bess" magically coming to life and dancing with glee. This ghostly, nostalgic apparition was a form of misrule, tacit acceptance of the Lord of Misrule, which the "worthy squire" embraces with "childish delight." History blends with superstition; the squire's prized artifacts, like spectral hoof prints, leave misleading traces.

KING FOR A DAY

A horse in a portrait mattered to Washington Irving in yet another way that combined history and myth. Having been named after George Washington, he felt the power of patrimony, and he well knew that the commanding general's national image was deeply bound up in his equestrian ability.

Like the legendary crusader enshrined at Bracebridge Hall, Washington was refashioned as a warrior-king. In numerous paintings, he appears in the saddle or standing next to his mount. The cavalier image was the model for the royal equestrian portrait, and patriot-artist John Trumbull's 1790 *Portrait of George Washington* borrowed from a painting of King Charles I. During his presidency, Philadelphia's famed Ricketts Circus demonstrated equestrian feats and wartime tableaux, or pantomimes, that made Washington the first cavalier of the new nation. John Bill Ricketts, the English-born equestrian turned "American impresario," called himself a "professor of horsemanship." Riding regularly with Washington in the 1790s, he claimed that he had "really" learned to ride under the president's tutelage.

Upon his death in December 1799, Washington received a royal, military-style mock funeral procession in Philadelphia, then the nation's capital. A white horse, festooned with a black and white plume, was marched along, its saddle empty, stirrups turned backwards to symbolize the missing rider. The first president's body was interred at Mount Vernon, but as the nation needed a grand celebration, mock funerals were held. None of this was lost on Irving, then an impressionable sixteen. Virginians saw Washington as a natural aristocrat, a man whose suave manners distinguished him, while his fellow Federalists crafted an image of a republican monarch. The various horse paintings of Washington, as one art historian has remarked, suggested "succession" rather than a rejection of royalism.[11]

In "Rip Van Winkle," Irving pokes fun at grand pronouncements evoking American exceptionalism. After his twenty-year sleep, Rip has missed the entire Revolution, yet he returns to his village to find that few things have actually changed. The image of George III outside the tavern has been easily altered to depict George Washington. The surrogate king, like the surrogate bridegroom, was easily adapted to conform to the seemingly new democratic order.

The need for familiar symbols of class and royal hierarchy persisted. Irving makes only one reference to horse culture in Rip's tale, in identifying the "coltish" ways of Rip's spitting-image of a son. He is idle, unruly, and lacking in ambition. Like the horse that stepped out of the portrait in Bracebridge Hall and came to life, old Rip does a double take when he see his mirror image standing before him, unaware at first that he is seeing his actual son. Pedigree outranks the self-made man in the United States. Democracy does not rule. Horses serve as a reminder of continuity.

Unlike "Rip Van Winkle," "The Legend of Sleepy Hollow" is constantly horsing around. The star of the show is the "Headless Horseman," the "Galloping Hessian," who rides at night searching for his head, races across a haunted bridge, and disappears in a flash of lightning. Brom Bones rides his mischievous Daredevil, and Ichabod Crane lumbers along on Gunpowder. But Gunpowder is, well, explosive in temperament, and certainly more interesting than an old plough-horse. He is nasty, his viciousness imprinted by his "choleric" Dutch owner, that "furious" rider Hans Van Ripper. There is one more horse in the long-lived tale, who makes a brief but meaningful appearance, and that is the "ragged, wild, half-broken colt," mounted by the nameless Black servant (presumably a slave) who delivers the invitation to Ichabod for the Van Tassels' party.

This unnamed horse serves as a prelude to Ichabod's subsequent parade on horseback. Even this lowly slave, Irving tells us, sitting on a ragged colt, is able to imagine himself elevated in station. He "delivered his message with that air of importance and effort at fine language which a negro is apt to display on petty embassies of the kind." His pretensions mimic Ichabod's, as the ungainly pedant heads to the celebration, "gallantly mounted," "issu[ing] forth like a knight-errant in quest of adventures." Ungainly in his riding style, his bent knees up to the pommel of the saddle, with his arms flapping, Ichabod must make quite a sight. Crucially, "he carried his whip perpendicularly in his hand like a sceptre." For that one moment, in his own mind, he is king for a day.

This theme of mock royalty appears in other stories in the *Sketch Book*. We find in "Little Britain" that the lord mayor is looked upon by his townsfolk as "the greatest potentate upon earth" when he rides by in his gilt coach and six horses. In "Stratford-on-Avon," the weary traveler, a "homeless man," finds more than a haven at the Red Horse Inn: he drops himself down before the warm fire, where the "armchair is his throne, the poker his sceptre, and the little parlor, some twelve feet square, his undisputed empire."

Recalling the Lord of Misrule, the dream of every lower-class man is to be a king for a day. It is no different than modern Americans who fantasize about winning the lottery or learning that a long-lost relative has left them a fortune. It is the fantasy of being catapulted to the top of the social hierarchy. Irving's message is doubled-edged: the majority of the population clutches onto an elusive fantasy, yet the lure of this magical mobility is a glue that keeps the class-divided society intact.

In 1790, Vice President John Adams prefigured this phenomenon, so effectively satirized in Irving's tales, when he wrote that fame (along with the fear of obscurity) was the lifeblood that coursed through American veins, as much as it did in any other country. Human psychology attached to every man in every station in society who desired reward, or a sign of respect, so that he could be made to feel positioned above others. Adams trenchantly observed, "What glory is a coach, what shame is a wagon?" If not to be king for a day, what was left for a poor man who possessed nothing? Adams supplied a rather grim answer. "The last and lowest species of humankind," if unable to "attract the notice of a man, woman, or child, . . . must be respectable in the eyes of his dog."[12]

Back to Ichabod. When he arrives in Sleepy Hollow (and later vanishes), he is a poorly paid schoolmaster with few possessions. His schoolhouse is his kingdom, where he "swayed a ferule, that sceptre of despotic power." (A ferule was a stick made of wood, used to punish children.) Ichabod is a man with outstanding appetites, with lip-smacking ambitions. "By hook and by crook," he works his way into the favor of the women of the village and among the Van Tassel circle. He owns but a smattering of learning, which places him one rung below the parson and barely sets him apart from the "country bumpkins." With his quaint tales and his storehouse of gossip, supplemented by an "ingratiating" style, he secures nightly meals from the Dutch matrons. The shrewd Connecticut schoolmaster is a variation on the "Yankee trader," that "beggar on horseback" whom Irving railed against in *History of New-York*. Ichabod isn't selling yards of cloth or broken-down horses—his wares consist of nothing more than dressed-up morsels of arcane knowledge.[13]

His greatest ambition is not simply to win and wed Katrina, to conquer the coquette at her own game, but to inherit the property of her father, Old Baltus. He has no desire to be the next master of the manor. Instead, as he gazes on the rich and fertile meadows that belong to the Van Tassel estate, and he eyes the "plump as a partridge" Katrina, he imagines how the lands might be "turned into cash and the money invested in immense tracts of wild land and shingle palaces in the wilderness." Once a trader, always a trader, Irving reminds his readers. With Katrina, and a whole troop of children, all loaded in a wagon, with Ichabod himself on his mare, he dreams of heading to "Kentucky, Tennessee, or Lord knows where." His wagon is still the peddler's wagon, rattling along with "pots and kettles dangling beneath." The itinerant schoolmaster is forever a carpetbagger, thinking of the money there is to be collected, not the simple contentment of an agrarian existence.

Of course, Ichabod never makes it to Tennessee. Irving leaves his readers guessing about what really happens to his unheroic protagonist. Three separate endings are announced. The most famous is of Ichabod losing the contest for Katrina's hand and vanishing after his race with the "Galloping Hessian." Ending number 2 is an old farmer espying Ichabod in the city, where he has gone from teaching to the study of law, becoming a politician, a journalist, and a "justice of the Ten Pound Court."

Irving's third ending comes in his postscript. Here, a "pleasant, shabby, gentlemanly old fellow," "suspected of being poor," transforms Ichabod into a storybook character. The old chap concludes his entertaining yarn with a syllogism, a conundrum, a joke. Ichabod may have had a spate of "rough riding" with goblins, the old man posits, but "ergo, for a country schoolmaster to be refused the hand of a Dutch heiress is a certain step to high preferment in the state." Despite repeated failures, rumpled honor, and an embarrassing exile from Sleepy Hollow, Ichabod is the perfect quixotic candidate for political success. His "rough riding" prepares him for the topsy-turvy game of democratic politicking to come.

The postscript is Irving's less than subtle way of disparaging American politics, something he has done before in his still-evolving publishing career. He situates Ichabod in a New York the author knows well, where a man—even one lacking in the social graces, even one filled with guile and a pronounced ambition—can reap rewards. Irving's Dutch-American friend, Senator (later Vice President and President) Martin Van Buren, will come to personify that even scrappier New York, where candidates are regularly jockeying for power. Van Buren was a disarming politician, known as the "Magician." Ichabod was not that gifted, though he was endowed with the gift of gab, and as a spinner of tales was well suited for penning outrageous stories, such as those propagated in partisan rags.

The real Ichabod could never ride to power on merit or charisma or a family name. But as that spectral knight-errant, he can write himself into favor among credulous voters. "No tale was too gross or monstrous for his capacious swallow," Irving tells us of Ichabod, and by inference, of his natural constituency. In America, appetites must be fed; preferment will follow. Maybe this last quote is the true takeaway from the twisted tales—and twisted tails—that conjoin the rough-riding Crane and the easily excitable Gunpowder.

NOTES

1. Katherine C. Mooney, "'I Got the Horse Right Here': New Directions in Horseracing Scholarship," *Register of the Kentucky Historical Society* 115, no. 4 (Autumn 2017): 645–66, esp. 653. Mooney's title is a play on the opening number from the 1950 Broadway musical and 1955 film *Guys and Dolls*.

2. On concerns over the mixing of bodies and classes, see Matthew L. Newson Kerr, "'Perambulating Fever Nests of Our London Streets': Cabs, Omnibuses, Ambulances, and Other 'Pest-Vehicles' in the Victorian Metropolis," *Journal of British Studies* 49, no. 2 (April 2010): 283–310, esp. 284–87; on children being run over by coaches, see Clive Emsley, Tim Hitchcock, and Robert Shoemaker, "Transport," *Proceedings of the Old Bailey*, https://www.oldbaileyonline.org/static/Transport.jsp.; on gentlemen whipping rude men from the saddle, see Keith Thomas, *In Pursuit of Civility: Manners and Civilization in Early Modern England* (New Haven, CT: Yale University Press, 2018), 68; on carriages of elites, see Nancy Isenberg, *White Trash: The 400-Year Untold History of Class in America* (New York: Viking, 2016), 72.

3. On decorum, see Thomas, *In Pursuit of Civility*, 65–66, 73, 75; on the "double allegiance" of horses and humans, see Phillip Thurtle, "Harnessing Heredity in Gilded Age America: Middle Class Mores and Industrial Breeding in Cultural Context," *Journal of the History of Biology* 35, no. 1 (Spring 2002): 43–78, esp. 59; also John Borneman, "Race, Ethnicity, Species, and Breed: Totemism and Horse-Breed Classification in America," *Comparative Studies in Society and History* 30, no. 1 (January 1988): 25–51, esp. 26, 28, 47.

4. Thomas H. Pettingell, "Report of Thomas H. Pettingell, of Salisbury, Chairman of the Committee of the Merrimack Agricultural Society, on Horses," *New England Farmer, and Horticultural Register*, November 17, 1826.

5. Washington Irving, *A History of New-York*, ed. Michael L. Black and Nancy B. Black, book 4, chap. 6, in *The Complete Works of Washington Irving* (Boston: Twayne, 1978). On the

braggart horse jockey, see "Stop a Rogue," *Concord* [NH] *Observer,* December 29, 1821; on lying and deceit, see "Extract of a Letter from the Reverend George Newton," *Weekly Recorder,* June 12, 1818; on the horse jockey as a con man, see "Yankee Trick, Latest Edition," *New York Post,* reprinted in the [Keene] *New Hampshire Sentinel,* May 31, 1823. Jeremy Belknap defines horse jockeys as "a set of contemptible wretches" who swap horses. Belknap, *History of New Hampshire,* 3 vols. (Boston, 1792), 3:144.

6. Christophe Traïni, "Noble Gentleness, Vile Cruelty," in *The Animal Rights Struggle: An Essay in Historical Sociology* (Amsterdam: Amsterdam University Press, 2015), chap. 2, esp. 26.

7. Washington Irving, *A Tour on the Prairies,* ed. John Francis McDermott (Norman: University of Oklahoma Press, 1956), 13-15, 19-20, 23, 39, 116-18, 122, 147-49. Also see Andrew Burstein, *Original Knickerbocker: The Life of Washington Irving* (New York: Basic Books, 2007), 263-64, 270; and Peter H. Hassrick, "William Ranney's 'Hunting Wild Horses,'" *Southwestern Historical Quarterly* 110, no. 3 (January 2007): 348-60, esp. 352.

8. Inga Bryden, "All Dressed Up: Revivalism and the Fashion for Arthur in Victorian Culture," *Arthuriana,* 21, no. 2 (Summer 2011): 28-41; Susan Staves, "Don Quixote in Eighteenth-Century England," *Comparative Literature* 24, no. 3 (Summer 1972): 193-215.

9. Cynthia Jeńey, "Politics and Horsemanship in Chrétien de Troes' *Erec et Enide,*" *Arthuriana* 27, no. 3 (Fall 2007): 37-65, esp. 39; Susan Crane, "Knight and Horse," in *Animal Encounters: Contacts and Concepts in Medieval Britain* (Philadelphia: University of Pennsylvania Press, 2012).

10. Crane, *Animal Encounters,* 143, 148, 151, 156-58.

11. John F. Moffitt, "'Le Roi à la classe'? Kings, Christian Knights, and Van Dyck's Singular 'Dismounted Equestrian-Portrait' of Charles I," *Artibus et Historiae* 4, no. 7 (1983): 79-99; Laura Auricchio, "Two Versions of *General Washington's Resignation:* Politics, Commerce, and Visual Culture in 1790s Philadelphia," *Eighteenth-Century Studies* 44, no. 3 (Spring 2001): 383-400; Gerald E. Kahler, *The Long Farewell: Americans Mourn the Death of George Washington* (Charlottesville: University of Virginia Press, 2008), esp. 31-32; Nancy Isenberg and Andrew Burstein, *The Problem of Democracy: The Presidents Adams Confront the Cult of Personality* (New York: Viking, 2019), 131-33.

12. *Discourses on Davila* was introduced to the American public in April 1790 in *The Gazette of the United States.* See John Adams, *Discourses on Davila: A Series of Papers on Political History* (Boston: Russell and Cutler, 1805), 34-35. Also Isenberg and Burstein, *Problem of Democracy,* 137-40; and Isenberg, *White Trash,* 98-99.

13. Irving, *History of New-York,* book 1, chap. 2; book 3, chaps. 3 and 4.

IRVING'S RELICTS

MATTHEW DENNIS

New America emulated Old America, and lavished courtesies, with proofs of congeniality and advancement which the Guest might have doubted as illusions of his fancy and wishes, if they had been less striking and direct.

—*American Quarterly Review* (December 1829),
on *Lafayette en Amérique en 1824 et 1825*

To paraphrase an 1829 review of another literary production, we might say about Washington Irving's *Sketch Book* that *New* America emulated a dreamy *Old* America.[1] For Irving was lavish with literary and historical courtesies that readers might have doubted as illusions of his fancy and wishes, if these had not been so striking, appealing, and useful.

While Irving remained abroad and basked in the success of his *Sketch Book* on two continents, the Marquis de Lafayette sailed into New York Harbor, on August 14, 1824, to the greatest acclaim that America had ever showered on anyone not named George Washington. In an odd way, Irving had anticipated Lafayette. Like Irving's character Rip Van Winkle, the beloved marquis returned after a decades-long hiatus. But unlike Rip, the marquis had hardly been forgotten. The occasion of his reappearance, of course, was the United States' fiftieth anniversary—the Jubilee of Independence.[2]

Americans received the French hero with "a spirit of tender veneration, so active, so inventive, so emulous, so pure," one commenter wrote. Lafayette was venerable to Americans, a blessed living relict of the Revolution, an animate, material vestige and embodiment of their country's mythic founding. Americans showered the Nation's Guest (as Lafayette was now known) with adoration, virtually beatifying him with a "love and reverence" that, as the writer suggested, approached idol worship: "In fact, he was, and is the most wonderful person of the age, considering his original share in our revolution."[3]

Rip Van Winkle was similarly an object of wonder, but in a different sense: his stature and reception were humbler, and his presence represented amnesia about the Revolution. Indeed, in most ways the fictional Rip was the perfect antithesis of the heroic Lafayette, except in one imagination-stirring measure: both were *relicts*.

A LIVING EMBODIMENT OF THE PAST

Relics (or relicts) are objects that exist simultaneously in the present and the past. They make the past itself present. Worked with a certain magic in Irving's hands, as we will see, the relict Rip stretches his current moment languorously, embodying a comforting past, fashioning a happy present, and pushing away an anxious future.

From the fifteenth century, English speakers used the word *relict*—a variation of *relic*—as a synonym for *widow*. By the seventeenth century, the term could apply to both sexes to designate a surviving partner or member of a lineage. No one explicitly called Rip Van Winkle or Lafayette a relict, but each in his own way nonetheless functioned as one—as a revered survivor and symbol of glorious bygone days, as a living embodiment of the past in the present, or as an agent and instructor of American history, American legend (a story with a historical basis), and myth (a story containing a sacred element or sign of destiny).[4]

Lafayette represented the American Revolution through his distinctive service and intimate, nearly scion-like connection to the demigod Washington. The great national patriarch had no children of his own, but he developed a close fatherly relationship with the young marquis that grew throughout the war, culminating in the triumph they shared at Yorktown, which signaled American victory. Washington died in December 1799, and the nation mourned. But to his countrymen he was immortal. He lived on in their hearts—and lived, once removed, in the celebrated Lafayette, who circulated as his venerable relict and avatar in 1824 and 1825.

But this essay is not about the Marquis de Lafayette. It focuses instead on Washington Irving's greatest fictional character, the hapless yet beloved Rip Van Winkle, whose impact on political culture is as an enduring American relict. He slept through the Revolution, offered no military service, displayed no talent or instinct for politics, proved inept at most tasks he undertook, and became beloved only locally, in his humble Hudson Valley village, where he was known for his eccentricity and harmlessness.

Rip had apparently failed to read Benjamin Franklin's *The Way to Wealth*, which became the Bible of nineteenth-century American capitalism. If Franklin's Poor Richard warned, "Be always ashamed to catch thyself idle," Rip felt no shame. If the same Richard Saunders said, "Employ thy time well, if thou meanest to gain Leisure," Rip found ease to be time well spent. If Richard said, "God gives all things to Industry," Rip felt blessed without. If Richard warned, "Trouble springs from Idleness and grievous Toil from needless Ease," Rip transcended such toil and trouble through a practiced indolence. Poor Richard said, "One To-day is worth two To-morrows." Rip was unconvinced by this temporal arithmetic, persuaded perhaps that his languid present was timeless, able to persist despite the passage of time. In his whimsy—in Washington Irving's conjuring—the relict Rip helped Americans construct a useful past and dream themselves into the nineteenth-century future.[5]

Irving loved real heroes, such as Washington and Lafayette, but in the *Sketch Book* he nonetheless tweaks such figures and their chroniclers, picking up where he left off in *A History of New-York*. Via the fictional pen of Diedrich Knickerbocker, he offers a comic, deflating critique of history, written in a solemn, nationalistic mode—great man history as told gravely by great men.[6]

In "Rip Van Winkle" and "The Legend of Sleepy Hollow," Irving suggests an escape not only from conventional history but also from the future. He prescribes the direct opposite of the Archbishop of York's wisdom in Shakespeare's *Henry IV, Part II* (act 1, scene 3): "Past and to come seem best; things present worst." Or perhaps Irving's acceptance of such wisdom led him to transform his present world through storytelling, creating a new fanciful present—an endless, enduring moment to contain things past and to roll ahead through time comfortably, in waves that push away thoughts of unpleasant social, economic, and political transformations.

Even if national development surged on, an endless, dreamy present endured in places like the "sequestered glen" of Sleepy Hollow and Rip's antique village, footing the fairy tale Kaatskills. For example, in Ichabod Crane's environs, the population, manners, and customs "remain fixed," Irving wrote, "while the great torrent of migration and improvement, which is making such incessant changes in other parts of this restless country, sweeps by them unobserved." Rip's and Ichabod's worlds "are like little nooks of still water, which border a rapid stream . . . , undisturbed by the rush of the passing current." For Rip, there was no time like the long present.

The relict Rip is a living embodiment of the past *and* an alternative exemplar of both the present and an indefinitely deferred future. "Rip Van Winkle" blends fact and fancy, allowing each to affect our understanding of the other, highlighting their "truth" as well as the fact of fabrication, whether by storytellers or historians. This marginal "truth" arises from select primary sources: manuscripts, historic sites, objects, and living informants.

Material things—relics and relicts—inhabit Irving's accounts, making them concrete, grounding them, giving them authority, even as we the readers know much of what we read—whether "history" or "stories"—is make-believe.[7] In his storytelling through objects, Irving's relics are both the story *and* its proof.[8]

Irving seeks to conjure—materially, then—a dreamy, mythic tale and to represent it, with a wink, as "history," or at least as an accepted view of the past that needn't be exactly true, or any more true than other chroniclers' nationalistic and hagiographic tales. His reader's awareness of the gambit need not ruin the story or undermine the wistful heritage it has constructed in the place of more troublesome or inconvenient, less usable history. Materiality—even imagined, Knickerbocker-produced materiality—helped consolidate American public memory and identity, giving it delightful form, substance, and an odd authenticity, while offering Americans the opportunity and permission to make themselves up.

> Time is but the stream I go a-fishing in. I drink at it; but while I drink I see the sandy bottom and detect how shallow it is. Its thin current slides away, but eternity remains.
>
> —HENRY DAVID THOREAU, *Walden*

Rip's saga is well known. The beloved, unambitious, henpecked villager escapes his wife's nagging and sets out with his dog, Wolf, to wander and hunt in the charmed Kaatskills. There he encounters a peculiar troupe of antiquated Dutchmen drinking and cavorting, and, after imbibing a few flagons himself, Rip falls into a deep sleep. He awakens the next morning, stiff and disoriented, and ultimately makes his way back to his village, where he experiences even greater bewilderment. The village and its people seem transformed; no one recognizes him. Twenty years have passed, inexplicably. But Rip is quickly embraced by the community, assimilates to his new circumstances, and reassumes his place in the village, "at that happy age when a man can be idle with impunity." The celebrated elder is now a veritable "chronicle of the old times 'before the war.'"[9]

Rip's tale beggars belief. Without narrative pause, he lives through two continuous days, the first culminating in a curious encounter with antiquated Dutch strangers frolicking in the Kaatskills. The second, joined to the first by a night of deep sleep, ends with Rip's confusing return to his village. No interruption, no interlude, occurs between Irving's paragraphs, so Rip's experience—and the reader's experience of these events—at first seems odd but not temporally challenging. Another reality soon clashes with our firsthand understanding of Rip's overnight escapade. His beard grown long, his gun rusted, and his place in the village unrecognized by its inhabitants, we are forced to question our understanding of the passage of time. If stories, and histories in particular, chronicle change over time, what do we make of a world in which time does not pass in a conventional way? "Time waits for no man," except in Washington Irving's magical world.

Irving's credibility—and thus Rip's reliability—is unassailable, because Irving conspicuously trusts the authoritative source of his story. It comes to us, we're told, from one Diedrich Knickerbocker, "an old gentleman of New York, who was very curious in the Dutch history of the province, and the manners of the descendants from its primitive settlers." Knickerbocker's extensive historical researches relied, in turn, on firsthand knowledge, less on books than on the testimony of people, "for the former are lamentably scanty on his favorite topics; whereas he found the old burghers, and still more their wives, rich in that legendary lore, so invaluable to true history."

Where could one find better primary sources, and who could be more reliable about Rip's story than Rip himself, in a story told omnisciently by a trusted narrator and endorsed by an entire community? The "chief merit" of Knickerbocker's earlier work, *A History,* Irving assures us, "is its scrupulous accuracy, which . . . has since been completely established . . . and is now admitted into all historical collections, as a book of unquestionable authority." Irving's prologue and "subjoined note"—not mere appendixes but essential parts of the story—suggest that Rip's saga merits similar credence as "absolute fact, narrated with the greatest fidelity." Knickerbocker writes, "I have heard many stranger stories than this, in the villages along the Hudson; all of which were too well authenticated to admit of a doubt."

Moreover, the opening passages of the story reveal that Knickerbocker himself had been personally acquainted with his subject, as when he writes of Rip, "I have observed that he was a simple good-natured man." Knickerbocker's postscript declares definitively, "I have even talked with Rip Van Winkle myself, who, when I last saw him, was a very venerable old man, and so perfectly rational and consistent on every other point, that I think no conscientious person could refuse to take this into the bargain." Knickerbocker legally authenticates the tale: "Nay, I have seen a certificate on the subject taken before a country justice and signed with cross, in the justice's own handwriting. The story, therefore, is beyond the possibility of doubt." Knickerbocker is not merely a historian, a teller of stories, but also a direct observer, able to offer a true, firsthand account.[10]

What's a reader to do? Some fancy pen work at the end of the tale, where Irving subtly but purposefully shifts the perspective of the narration from Rip to the villagers, helps us to conflate or ignore the irreconcilable time dimensions—the passage of two days versus twenty years. Still, as readers, we are intoxicated by the mutability of time and experience, as if we, like Rip, have drunk the Kaatskill Kool-Aid.[11]

Rip is bewildered by alterations in a most familiar site, where he has routinely lounged and chattered with his friends: "Instead of the great tree that used to shelter the quiet little Dutch inn of yore, there now was reared a tall, naked pole, with something on the top that looked like a red nightcap, and from it was fluttering a flag, on which was a singular assemblage of stars and stripes—all this was strange and incomprehensible." Readers of the post-Revolutionary generation recognize the liberty pole, the Phrygian cap, and the new national flag—products of the American Revolution, about which Rip is oblivious.

Readers are thus obliged to provide the historical context, which merely roils the story's temporal waters. It is Rip who notices something familiar in the tavern sign, "the ruby face of King George, under which he had smoked so many a peaceful pipe," but even that has been "singularly metamorphosed." George's coat was now blue and buff, not red; his scepter had been repainted as a sword, and his head now bore a cocked hat, underneath which it now read, "in large characters, GENERAL WASHINGTON." The transmutation is sensible only to us, as we impose our own (and the villagers') chronology, while Rip remains befuddled.

Many commentators have analyzed the political messages that Irving perhaps sought to deliver to his audience through this temporal trick. One might make the case that Irving means to argue, on the one hand, that the Revolution changed everything, or, on the other hand, that it had changed nothing—just as modern historians have argued about whether the War for Independence did or did not produce a social revolution.

So did Irving mean to suggest that Washington, despite his posture as a republican hero, was in fact a covert monarchist, or was being used posthumously to authorize authoritarian rule, putting the brakes on American democracy? This is not as remote a possibility as it might at first appear. Rip returns to the village during a heated political campaign in an era when electioneering had become increasingly vicious. He is neither Federalist nor Democrat, yet the apparently recrudescent Rip is accused of being a Tory. But politics do not really matter to Rip—and perhaps Irving is implying that they don't matter much to most Americans. As Knickerbocker tells us, "Rip, in fact, was no politician; the changes of states and empires made but little impression on him." Or maybe Irving is suggesting that all politics is local, for Rip focuses on governance at its most local by celebrating the overthrow of the "one species of despotism under which he had long groaned," which is, as Knickerbocker puts it, "petticoat government."[12]

Others have commented on Irving's historiographical purpose: critiquing the first generation of national history writing and hero making, uncritical and hagiographic in its lionizing of Washington and others. The tales that Diedrich Knickerbocker or Geoffrey Crayon tell are no less plausible than those of David Ramsay (the American patriot who wrote the first detailed history of the Revolution) or Mason Locke Weems (who gave the world a certain vignette about a cherry tree–chopping incident in northern Virginia). In the end, the unreliable witness Rip becomes the town "chronicle" or historian.[13]

UNENCUMBERED BY POMPOUS HISTORY

More important for our purposes is a consideration of how Irving performed his social and political magic, using time and objects—most significantly his authorial deployment of the timeless figure, the relict Rip Van Winkle himself.

Through Rip, Irving undermines a conventional understanding of past, present, and future. While in the mountains, Rip lives in and escapes the past: first, the distant era of New Netherland's founding, as embodied in the avatars of Hendrick Hudson's *Halve Maen* [*Half Moon*] crew, with whom he hoisted flagons; and following that, the tumultuous events of the Revolution and early republic. He practically makes evasion of the future a way of life.

To paraphrase the writing of the famously transgressive Henry David Thoreau, Rip went to the woods [mountains] because he wished to live deliberately [blissfully], to front only the essential facts of life, and see if he could not learn what it had to teach, and not, when he came to die, discover that he had not lived. Unlike the mass of men, Rip does *not* live a life of quiet desperation. Anticipating Thoreau in comic fashion—he's a supernaturalist, not a naturalist, after all—Rip lives in the moment. As the bard of Walden Pond would later write, "We should live in all the ages of the world in an hour." Rip, as we know, requires a forty-eight-hour extension.[14]

One literary scholar has termed Rip an "anachronistic vagrant," a wanderer through time with "no place in history," or rather, someone lost *within* history. Rip's disorientation upon his return "occurs because he can find no present which corresponds to his sense of his own," as Jeffrey Insko writes. But he acclimates, and in fact prescribes his new extensive present generally. In Irving's words, "Rip now resumed his old walks and habits; he soon found many of his former cronies, though all rather the worse for the wear and tear of time; and preferred making friends among the rising generation, with whom be soon grew into great favor." Having won over young and old, Rip thus "took his place once more on the bench at the inn door, . . . reverenced as one of the patriarchs of the village." Villagers needn't deny the fact of the War for Independence or the heroic life of a new, improved, republican George, but none of this really matters.[15]

We can comprehend Rip's anachronistic vagrancy by seeing Irving's Rip as a *relict*. Let us, then, reexamine the term. What *are* relics? Broadly speaking, they are ruins, residue, vestiges, souvenirs, mementos, or monuments of the past. Relics or relicts can be objects surviving as remnants of vanishing peoples, types, or species, as traces of otherwise extinct classes or kinds. They have often been distinguished for their durability and resistance to decay. Their ability to transcend time is sometimes matched by their facility in bridging space—they are conventionally transportable, and their mobility enhances their usefulness to their possessors, who are thus able to deploy their power where they might have the greatest effect. Relics can arouse awe and enthusiasm, foster strong feeling and emotion, promote identification and loyalty, and galvanize people to accept authority as legitimate, embrace ideas as self-evident, or understand courses of action as inevitable. *Most importantly,* relics connect the living to the past in a direct, seemingly unmediated way, and this vital link gives relics their unusual power. The alternate spelling, *relict,* as we have seen, once commonly referred to a widow—a woman relicted, or left behind, as the sole living partner in a marriage after the death of her husband. The term fits our comic hero, Rip Van Winkle.[16]

Upon his return, Rip *represents* the past and *is* the past, which he embodies physically in the present. He personifies pastness that persists into the present, like a relic. As the art historian Jules Prown has argued, relics are "objects created in the past [that] are the only historical occurrences that continue to exist in the present. They provide an opportunity by which *we encounter the past at first hand; we have direct sensory experience of surviving historical events.*"[17] Enveloped in narratives and embodying the truth of such narratives by their very existence, revered historic things (such as relics and relicts) occur both as the past and the present. Their timelessness seems well suited to conveying timeless truths, allowing Irving a means here to remake the United States as both new and old. Speaking through Rip (via Knickerbocker and Geoffrey Crayon, delicious layers of faux authority), Irving not only entertains his countrymen but also critiques and enlightens them. With a wink and a nod, he tells us to lighten up, to live in the present, enveloped in a blissful past, unencumbered by pompous history, unconcerned about Americans' overzealous rush into the future.

Irving shows that there is comfort and utility in a romantic past, carefully smuggled into the present by skilled chroniclers. As Andrew Burstein has written, "the past can communicate in such a way that its sentimental truths—our innocence, if we want—can remain with us, being made apparent through supernaturally created new memories. The memorable Rip is part of our consciousness of all that is left behind. *Now we can lose time without losing the past!*"[18] Rip Van Winkle remains with us. Perhaps he is still with us today?

Early in his triumphal return to the United States, the Marquis de Lafayette traveled up the Hudson River toward Albany, leaving Manhattan on September 15, 1824. Lafayette's steamboat, the *James Kent,* soon passed Tarrytown, the haunted terrain of the Headless Horseman who had terrorized Ichabod Crane. At the sight of that "modest village," Lafayette and his companions "pronounced with respect the names of the three militia men, John Paulding, David Williams, and Isaac Van Wart," immortalized by their disinterested service to their country, particularly their arrest of the famous British spy Major John André. They continued toward West Point, where Lafayette was elaborately received, and proceeded upriver with stops at Newburgh, Poughkeepsie, Beacon, Clermont, Catskill, Hudson, and Albany.[19]

At Newburgh, thirty thousand people welcomed the Nation's Guest "with the greatest impatience," reluctant to see him depart. The city's mayor, and then Lafayette himself, addressed the tumultuous crowd from a balcony at the Orange Hotel. Thus satisfied, they released him to his steamboat. Lafayette's party reached Poughkeepsie at dawn the next day and made numerous stops before arriving at Clermont at four o'clock, landing at the elegant residence of Robert Livingston, a signer of the Declaration of Independence and former minister to France. Once again, Lafayette was fêted by the many citizens who assembled from the surrounding towns and by the Livingston family, who detained the marquis until the following morning.

The party boarded the *James Kent* again and headed deeper into the magical world of Rip Van Winkle. As Lafayette's secretary/tour chronicler Auguste Levasseur wrote, "Scarcely had we left Clermont when we came in sight of the beautiful Catskill mountain, which arising at some miles from the river, finely terminates the horizon by its beautiful brown mass which is amphitheatrically developed, in the centre of which shows forth the white house of the pine garden situated 250 feet above the level of the Hudson . . . a place of promenade for the neighbouring inhabitants."[20]

The mountain lodge site offered picturesque views of the Hudson Valley and the Kaatskills, places first made famous by Washington Irving, further delineated by James Fenimore Cooper, and later famously captured by Thomas Cole and the artists of the Hudson River School. As Lafayette continued his tour, Levasseur wrote, "The masses of soldiers and citizens which covered a long pier projecting into the river, by their acclamations informed General Lafayette that the inhabitants of Catskill also expected a visit from the national guest. We remained a few minutes only with this population."[21] And was Rip Van Winkle himself represented in that throng? Why not, if we are willing to embrace Washington Irving's brand of magical realism?

That night, Lafayette triumphantly entered Albany, where new salutations and ceremonies awaited him. He rode up State Street to the capitol and was received in the senate chamber and officially greeted by the mayor. Levasseur wrote:

> In his reply Lafayette could not avoid expressing his astonishment at the numerous changes that had taken place . . . "It is not half a century, since the town, then ancient, it is true, but still very small, served me

for head quarters, upon the frontier of a vast wilderness . . . At present I find Albany a rich and powerful city, the central seat of government of the state of New York, and the surrounding wilds changed into fertile and well cultivated plains."[22]

Yes, Albany and the other upper Hudson villages, towns, and cities were new, transformed and flourishing, but they were also old, legendary, even mythic. In 1824, Lafayette was encountering the landscape and people of these enchanted places not for the first time but as a homecoming of sorts, as his Albany address acknowledged. Reappearing before them after a hiatus of nearly fifty years, Lafayette's moment was, like Rip's, a return after decades.

The Nation's Guest would visit these same environs again in 1825, offering the denizens of hamlets and glens that Rip had trodden one more opportunity to greet him. He was, like Rip, a relic, that man of the hour who made the Revolutionary past present. The return and imprimatur of Lafayette, the selfless hero, and the homecoming of Rip Van Winkle, the lovable antihero, eased anxieties through the wistfulness each conjured for their charmed audiences.

These two relics embodied American *nostalgia*—the word derived from the Greek *nóstos*, "return, homecoming," and the Old English, *nesan*, "to be saved, survive," and *nerian*, "to rescue, redeem, nourish," "to preserve." Each in his own way offered a comfortable, glorious, romantic past to the early republic, a past that affirmed Americans as they were, that relieved their cultural tensions (rather than challenging them to meet impossible historical standards). The heroes' surprising reappearances seemed to grant Americans the liberty to live their lives blissfully in the present and to approach the future in untroubled fashion, bound to each other and their bygone days by mystic chords of fantasy.

NOTES

1. Review of A. Levasseur, *Lafayette en Amérique en 1824 et 1825, American Quarterly Review* (December 1829), 467–93, at 468–69.

2. The Marquis de Lafayette's private secretary, Auguste Levasseur, published a full account of the tour. Levasseur, *Lafayette in America in 1824 and 1825; Or, Journal of a Voyage to the United States*, 2 vols. (Philadelphia: Carey and Lea, 1829). On Lafayette's triumphant return and its historical import, see Andrew Burstein, *America's Jubilee: How in 1826 a Generation Remembered Fifty Years of Independence* (New York: Knopf, 2001), esp. 8–33; Lloyd S. Kramer, *Lafayette in Two Worlds: Public Cultures and Personal Identities in an Age of Revolution* (Chapel Hill: University of North Carolina Press, 1996); Stanley J. Idzerda et al., *Lafayette, Hero of Two Worlds: The Art and Pageantry of His Farewell Tour of America, 1824–1825* (Flushing, NY: Queens Museum, 1989); and Sarah J. Purcell, *Sealed with Blood: War, Sacrifice, and Memory in Revolutionary America* (Philadelphia: University of Pennsylvania Press, 2002), 171–209. Edgar Ewing Brandon has compiled a wealth of local reporting on Lafayette's American tour. Brandon, ed., *Lafayette, Guest of the Nation: A Contemporary Account of the "Triumphal Tour" of General Lafayette . . . as Reported by the Local Newspapers*, 3 vols. (Oxford, OH: Oxford Historical Press, 1957).

3. Review of *Lafayette en Amérique*, 468–69.

4. A special issue of *Past and Present* is devoted to relics and their history. See Alexandra Walsham, "Introduction: Relics and Remains," *Past and Present* 206, supplement 5 (July 17, 2010): 9–36. A signal contribution to the American history of relics is Teresa Barnett, *Sacred Relics: Pieces of the Past in Nineteenth-Century America* (Chicago: University of Chicago Press, 2013).

One might also note, from the same era, another famous and classic example of a relict: the renowned author of *Frankenstein; or, The Modern Prometheus* (1818), Mary Wollstonecraft Shelley. In 1826, at age twenty-nine, Shelley published her second novel, *The Last Man*, a tale of the last survivor of a worldwide plague, set in the early twenty-second century. See F. Clark, ed., *British Future Fiction, 1700–1914*, vol. 8, *The End of the World* (London: Routledge, 2017). A pandemic of cholera, which began in India in 1817, served as the real-life backdrop for Shelley's fiction. After the deaths of her husband, Percy Shelley, their two children, Lord Byron, and nearly everyone else in her family, she wrote in her journal (May 15, 1824), referring to her work in progress: "The *Last Man!* Yes, I may well describe that solitary being's feelings, feeling myself as the last relic of a beloved race, my companions extinct before me." Betty T. Bennett, ed., *Mary Wollstonecraft Shelley: An Introduction* (Baltimore: Johns Hopkins University Press, 1998), 83. Irving was among her visitors when she returned to England in the summer of 1824, as Lafayette was embarking for America.

5. *Poor Richard's Almanack, 1733–1758*, in J. A. Leo Lemay, ed., *Benjamin Franklin: Autobiography, Poor Richard, and Later Writings* (New York: Library of America, 1987, 1997), 441–564, esp. "Poor Richard Improved, 1758," 554–64; quotes at 557.

6. Irving later published biographical works on the heroes Washington and Columbus:

Life of George Washington, 5 vols. (1855–1859); and *A History of the Life and Voyages of Christopher Columbus*, 4 vols. (1828). A chapter included in the *Sketch Book*, "Philip of Pokanoket," represents another biographical work focusing on an admired hero—in this case, the central figure in King Philip's War, whom Irving elevates in his revisionist assessment, transforming him into a hero even while cloaking Philip in the conventions of the Noble Savage. Irving, *The Sketch Book of Geoffrey Crayon, Gent.*, ed. Haskell Springer (Boston: Twayne, 1978).

7. If the noun *make-believe* means "the action of pretending or imagining that things are better than they really are," and if a connotation of *pretend* is, more archaically, "to venture or put in a claim," then many early nationalistic histories might also qualify as "make-believe." Such historians' tales, like Irving's, idealize their narratives, are meant to entertain, function didactically, and make claims on our belief.

8. Though it is beyond the scope of this essay, relics appear in greater number in "The Legend of Sleepy Hollow." In the elusive Diedrich Knickerbocker manuscripts themselves (the supposed source of the tale), we find the supernatural remains of the dead Hessian soldier, especially his missing head, the buried corpse of Major André, and Major André's tree at the site of the British spy's execution. André was of course a real, departed historical figure—*relic* not *relict*. Like Rip, he slept for decades, in a Tappan grave, but his actual resurrection in 1821 was an exhumation, not an awakening to life—the unearthing and transportation of his mortal remains to England for honorific reinterment at Westminster Abbey. On André and his body, see especially Michael Meranze, "Major André's Exhumation," in *Mortal Remains: Death in Early America*, ed. Nancy Isenberg and Andrew Burstein (Philadelphia: University of Pennsylvania Press, 2003), 123–35.

9. Washington Irving, "Rip Van Winkle: A Posthumous Writing of Diedrich Knickerbocker," in *Washington Irving: History, Tales, and Sketches*, ed. James Tuttleton (New York: Library of America, 1983), 783. As Andrew Burstein comments with regard to Rip's tale—"an endearing tale of escapism, alienation, and lost identity"—Rip's misogyny gives us pause, going beyond the merely playful. A gendered reading of the story, however, is beyond the scope of this essay. See Burstein, *The Original Knickerbocker: The Life of Washington Irving* (New York: Basic Books, 2007), 128.

10. The irony (and humor) of Irving's gambit for firsthand authority in his telling of the tale is heightened by the mediation of its telling: Irving, as Geoffrey Crayon, via Diedrich Knickerbocker, plays a veritable game of "telephone" rather than claiming himself an eyewitness. Note, too, that the posthumous attribution to Knickerbocker gives Knickerbocker himself a certain relict status—the manuscript as relic—and its alleged author, able to publish from the grave, similarly seems to live in the present, not merely in the past.

Of course, Irving's mock history of New York also was attributed to Diedrich Knickerbocker, and not everyone embraced it. DeWitt Clinton, for example, wrote of it, "The heterogeneous and unnatural combination of fiction and history is perfectly disgusting to good taste." Burstein, *Original Knickerbocker*, 104.

Though Irving's supposed discovery and publication of Knickerbocker texts was recognized as a delightful gambit, such an event had other proximate, astonishing instances that many deemed credible. A famous example is Joseph Smith's 1823 unearthing of golden plates left near his home in Manchester, New York, by the angel Moroni. Over the next several years, Smith tells us, he transcribed and translated the texts and gave them to the world as the Book of Mormon.

11. Jeffrey Insko perceptively analyzes Irving's "rhetoric of anachronism," his critique of history itself, in the form of historiographical (not merely historical) satire. "Rip Van Winkle," Insko writes, "is at once a parody of the very possibility of absolute historical knowledge and a brilliant confounding of our devotion to chronological, linear time." Insko, "Diedrich Knickerbocker, Regular Bred Historian," *Early American Literature* 43 (2008): 605–41, at 622.

12. Not only does Rip avoid the messiness of the Revolution and subsequent Critical Period, as the 1780s are known, but also his inward, romantic, sequestered focus also avoids—purposefully for Irving?—the turmoil of the economic dislocations resulting from the Panic of 1819.

13. See David Ramsay, *The History of the American Revolution* (1789), or Mason Locke Weems's notorious *Life of Washington* (1800). The next major history of the time, authored by one who lived through it, was Mercy Otis Warren, *History of the Rise, Progress and Termination of the American Revolution* (1805).

14. Henry David Thoreau, *Walden; Or, A Life in the Woods* (1854), excerpts from chapter 2 ("Where I Lived and What I Lived For") and chapter 1 ("Economy"). Burstein, *Original Knickerbocker* comments on Irving's temporal manipulations: "Playing with time, he allows for the imaginative possibility that the death of the past is a delusion. Think of it: the irony of history is that it is so overwhelming that it causes us to simplify and forget" (130).

15. Insko, "Diedrich Knickerbocker," 629, drawing on Robert A. Ferguson, "Rip Van Winkle and the Generational Divide in American Culture," *Early American Literature* 40 (November 2005): 529–44. See also Walter Shear, "Time in 'Rip Van Winkle' and the 'Legend of Sleepy Hollow,'" *Midwest Quarterly* 17 (1976): 158–72. Burstein, *Original Knickerbocker* notes Hart Crane's characterization of Rip as "the muse of memory" and "the guardian angel of the trip to the past" (130). If Rip is, indeed, the muse of memory, his memories are amusing, and his story is meant to *amuse*.

16. See Matthew Dennis, *American Relics and the Politics of Public Memory* (Amherst: University of Massachusetts Press, forthcoming). Note that questions or doubts about the authenticity of relics and relicts do not necessarily destroy their power. Relics remain real enough and potent as long as believers continue to want to believe in them. Knickerbocker, near the end of Rip's tale, writes, "Some always *pretended* to doubt the reality of it, and insisted that Rip had been out of his head, and that this was one point on which he always remained flighty. The old Dutch inhabitants, however, almost universally gave it full credit." Here, doubt, according to the Knickerbocker, is not deep-seated but merely "pretended."

17. Jules Prown, "Mind in Matter: An Introduction to Material Culture Theory and Method," *Winterthur Portfolio* 17 (Spring 1982): 1–19, at 3 (my emphasis).

18. Burstein, *Original Knickerbocker*, 130.

19. The journey is chronicled in Levasseur, *Lafayette in America*, 1:99–111; quote at 100.

20. Levasseur, *Lafayette in America*, 1:110–11.

21. Levasseur, *Lafayette in America*, 1:111.

22. Levasseur, *Lafayette in America*, 1:113–14.

IRVING'S INVESTMENT IN TIME

ALEXIS McCROSSEN & ANDREW BURSTEIN

> The castle clock had just tolled midnight when a soft strain of music stole up from the garden. She rose hastily from her bed and stepped lightly to the window. A tall figure stood among the shadows of the trees. As it raised its head a beam of moonlight fell upon the countenance. Heaven and earth! she beheld the Spectre Bridegroom!
>
> —Washington Irving, "The Spectre Bridegroom"

Most who occupy themselves with the *Sketch Book* tales cannot help but fixate on the tricks that time plays on Washington Irving's characters—most notably Rip Van Winkle. In "The Spectre Bridegroom," the nearest to a Gothic tale in the volume, Irving uses the device of a clock to signal strange doings.

Little thought has been given to *when* the *Sketch Book* was written, that is, to the literal impact of time awareness and time devices in Irving's day-to-day world. These were years when he spent much of his time traveling, when time preparations, dates, and seasonal adjustments had to have mattered to him. Irving incorporated an awareness of measurable time into stories best known for the mystifying possibilities he attached to unreal time. When he treated time elastically, he became the envy of the literary set.

The contrasts are curious, to say the least. America's first professional author came of age as both technological and political revolutions were remaking European and American temporal practices and ideologies. All across the Atlantic Protestant world, the mandates of a reformed calendar coincided with extensive investments in mechanical timekeepers. Most red-letter days (holy days marked in red on church calendars) had been purged from the Anglo-American calendar, and Sunday was now observed as the only holy day. By 1752, when the British adopted the Gregorian calendar with its leap day every four years, established towns had at least one bell, if not clock dials. There was a brisk trade in pocket watches and tall-case clocks.

The first decades of the nineteenth century saw a growing demand for all sorts of timekeepers. Due to innovations in design and production, clocks of all sizes and watches of all makes were plentifully available. Almanacs still stressed the seasons, while other calendars, schedules, and periodical publications together contributed to the development of daily, weekly, and monthly periodicities. The American and French Revolutions and the Napoleonic Wars occurred as "new and old, fresh and corrupt" were expressed in "absolute terms," resulting in what the historian Peter Fritzsche describes as an "explosive sense of time as something sudden, thunderous, and clandestine." Contemporary literary observers like Victor Hugo and Charles Dickens were keen to chart the impact of political revolution and war, along with the tightening grip of clock and calendar, on individuals and society. But not Irving, who dwelled on the power of the past over susceptible minds. In the *Sketch Book,* he decentered calendars and clocks as part of a strategy to furnish time with extraordinary properties.[1]

YES, IRVING KNEW WHAT TIME IT WAS

We begin by exploring evidence related to Irving's time awareness, particularly during his travels prior to writing and publishing the *Sketch Book*. Next, we look at how Irving builds the temporal sensorium in these tales to express a temporality that was by and large against the American grain. Instead of seeing the present as the portal to the future, Irving casts it alluringly as a bridge to the past. His temporality has no use for days and hours but is deeply attuned to the cosmic unfolding of time.

Everywhere Irving went as he gathered observations for the *Sketch Book*, he encountered what two geographers have identified as a "dense infrastructure of public and private clocks."[2] London and environs were home to the Greenwich Observatory, the prime meridian (for all but the French, who kept Paris as theirs), and active workshops of clockmakers and watchmakers catering to the domestic and foreign markets. London boasted many prominent public clocks, including St. Dunstan's clock, the Bank of England's gallery clocks, a large bracket clock at the entrance to London Bridge, and a tower clock installed in 1816 on Horse Guards near Whitehall. At street level, too, clocks could be seen in the shop windows of jewelers

OLD ST. DUNSTAN'S CHURCH, 1814 (*see page* 135).

Washington Irving was not the first to marvel at the unusual St. Dunstan's clock. In the early eighteenth century it was said that, for many, the two giants striking the hours were more admired than the most eloquent preacher in the pulpit on Sundays. Image from Wikimedia Commons.

ST. DUNSTAN'S CLOCK (*see page* 47).

The clock of old St. Dunstan's church in 1814, engraving reprinted in Walter Thornbury, *Old and New London* (London: Cassell, Petter and Galpin, 1872). Image from Wikimedia Commons.

and watchmakers, above markets, inside taverns. Dandies, barristers, businessmen, and others conspicuously carried gold and silver pocket watches.[3]

Leaving the streets, Irving would have seen clocks cased in handsome cabinets or cast in gold and silver in the homes and salons that he frequented. St. Dunstan's clock, which Irving mentions in the sketch "Little Britain," was installed in the late seventeenth century in London's publishing district. The first public clock in London with minute hands, it featured mythical figures drawn from the Old Testament—Gog and Magog—who struck the hours and quarters. Such triumphs of mechanical wizardry and artisan skill sparked the imaginations of the many who encountered them.[4]

In addition to being visible, clocks were audible. Bells rang the hours and tolled calls to evening prayers, funerals, and Sunday services. Visiting Oxford in 1815, Irving twice notes "the sound of bells" in his journal, and he does so again while visiting the English town of Buxton in 1816, and France in 1820.[5] In "Little Britain," he mentions in passing the St. Paul's bell, which "sours all the beer when it tolls." Westminster Abbey's bells, adjuncts to its three clock dials that had only hour hands, toll in the *Sketch Book,* underscoring the passage of day into night. To be sure, Irving had seen clocks and heard bells in parts of the United States, and almost as wide an array of Americans as Britons carried pocket watches and decorated their homes with clocks. In Europe, however, an even denser network of timekeepers surrounded him than in the United States.[6]

Not only were there clocks and watches nearly everywhere Irving went in England, but also community norms produced what scholars have identified as "clock time." In the early eighteenth century, no nation other than England was "so time-bound in its activities and consciousness," according to historian David Landes. National and local legislation had used clock time since the 1700s to set market and banking hours, closing times for alehouses, working hours for some trades, and the duration of breaks for some workers. In Regency-era England, the practices associated with clock time were robust, evidenced by tens of thousands of court depositions between 1700 and 1830, which show that most men and women in rural and urban areas often referred to clock time to indicate when events happened.[7]

Upending E. P. Thompson's earlier assertion that before the factory Britons did not suffer the tyranny of the clock, social historian Mark Hailwood has definitively shown that preindustrial-era city dwellers *and* rural residents "had a relatively high degree of clock-time awareness." Furthermore, he points out, most Britons could "easily tell the time to within an hour," even if they did not have the use of a watch. The literary historian Stuart Sherman explores how clock time and its attendant practices shaped the consciousness and output of diarist Samuel Pepys, novelists Samuel Richardson, Laurence Sterne, and Daniel Defoe, and poets Samuel Coleridge, William Blake, and William Wordsworth. Irving's alter ego Geoffrey Crayon seems for the most part untouched by the diffusion of clocks and watches, indifferent to the habits of mind and routine that accompanied them, and impervious to how English writers were limning clock time.[8]

But this is not entirely the case, as we observe when Irving sets tales in rural England. The popularity of these pieces in the *Sketch Book* led him to elaborate in his next collection of sketches, *Bracebridge Hall* (1822). Here, "the servants of old English families" keep the squire's house in perfect shape, "as if by magic, but it is the magic of system." And what does "system" mean at Bracebridge Hall? "Nothing is done by fits and starts, nor at awkward seasons; the whole goes on like well-oiled clockwork, where there is no noise nor jarring in its operations." Clockwork, as we see here, is already society's familiar metaphor indicating regularity and reliability.

Much of Irving's embrace of time-honored traditions in *Bracebridge Hall* involves the household servants and their close consideration of time. It is the good "old family servant" whose reminiscences are the most sweet and comforting. Before retiring at night, he will "linger about the room to have one more kind look, and one more pleasant word about times that are past—who does not experience towards such a being a feeling of almost filial affection?" The "oddities" of the household flow downward from the old-fashioned squire to the servants' quarters, and because it is Irving's stock-in-trade to manipulate time and consciousness, superstitious traditions are revealed in "mystic ceremonies," and spells are cast. Bringing everyone back to reality, an alarm sounds in the clearest way possible: "On the striking of the great house-clock in the servants' hall, they were seized with a sudden panic."

One other episode proves the point. A threat to domestic peace is occasioned by the appearance of gypsies. To deal with the challenge, the squire sits in a chair ceremoniously placed beneath "an enormous clock," while the possibility looms that the gypsies, who are known thieves, will make off with the "house-clock" itself. The clock is a symbol of stability in the rural England of Irving's reconstructed experience. Without it, the regular flow of events will be compromised. And yet, in the end, none of this matters, because the author's delight is in his description of instability: in spite of its good clocks, confusion prevails at progress-resistant Bracebridge Hall.[9]

If his literature minimized the mechanical, Irving's journals, notes, and letters across the years reveal him to be personally responsive to calendars, clocks, and clock time, whether in New York or in Europe. He headed nearly all of his letters and many of his journal entries with complete dates (though rarely the day of the week). His journals (as well as some letters) give evidence of the time of the day, indicating that he tracked time according to a clock as much as he paid heed to natural events (the light of day) and the temporality of social events. In the summer of 1803, for instance, reporting on a sail up the Hudson, Irving referenced departure and arrival times: "We sat off about 3 Oclock"; light events: "We left Sheldon's at day light," and social events: "an early breakfast." Touring Wales in 1815, he noted departure and arrival times with some precision: "left Birmingham at 10 oclock," "return by 8 oclock," "about 5 oclock arrived at Chester." Also on that tour, he continued to mark time in relation to social events, as in "walk before breakfast," and by light events, such as "arrived before sunset." A pattern of mapping the time of his movements courses through Irving's adult journals.[10]

But how did Irving tell the time? Here, the evidence is marginal. Did he carry a pocket watch? Did he ask a companion for the time? Did he look for visible and reliable clocks? Did he listen for bells ringing the hours and quarters? We have direct evidence only in his commentary on a man's attachment to his pocket watch, when Irving wryly notes that a companion on a journey from Philadelphia to New York "travels with watch in hand" and expressed annoyance in "several minutes' delay." It seems Irving himself did not travel with watch in hand, though when he noted departures and arrivals, he sometimes did so to the quarter hour.[11]

Watches barely figure at all in his private correspondence, journals, or expense accounts. If he did not own one while writing the *Sketch Book,* evidence suggests he eventually came to possess one.[12] That said, Irving was not one of those who craned his neck to make out the time on a clock dial; well attuned to the temporality of social events, phases of the day, sunrise and sunset, and the tolling of bells, he experienced time as a "feeling" more than he tracked it. As a dutiful journal keeper and inventive author who adopted a literary guise in Geoffrey Crayon, Irving attended to an all-embracing sense of time far more so than he fixed upon the days and hours.

GEOFFREY CRAYON, TIME'S FREESTYLE ARCHITECT

Though they are widespread in the places the narrator traverses, forms of temporal reckoning rooted in calendar and clock are significantly underplayed in the *Sketch Book.* Irving-as-Crayon is an impressionist who muses, broods, and thrives on serenity—these are his descriptors in the text. Rather than reach for customary forms of "temporal specificity," which according to modern scholarship enhanced the authority and credibility of courthouses, banks, stock exchanges, histories, and even novels, Irving deploys vague temporal conceits and other seductive uncertainties. We might call what he does a fetish for "temporal unspecificity," at least as it pertains to mundane timekeepers. As a storyteller, Irving thrives on obscuring and prefers a slow unfolding to a neat solution.[13]

Indeed, timelessness pervades Irving's sketches. Readers feel contemporaneous with Crayon, while lacking access to the exact dates of Crayon's visits or knowing when he heard his stories. Only three months are mentioned by name in the *Sketch Book:* March, May, and December ("December snows"). Irving occasionally mentions Sunday, but the other days of the week remain undifferentiated and unnamed. He appreciatively names customary holidays (Guy Fawkes Day, Valentine's Day). Irving casts both Sunday and Christmas as remnants of a wholesome past, despite the fact that the observance of each was being revived in the nineteenth century as regularized breaks (weekly or annually) from a capitalist calendar of intense, regularized work routines, in which there were few spaces of time immune from market pressures.[14]

If clock time is largely buried in the *Sketch Book,* it is entirely by design. Each of the seven clocks in six separate sketches sound the time rather than show it. They either tick, strike, or toll, as do bells in eight tales. The bells that ring do so to call auditors to Sunday, Christmas, funeral, and evening church services, and as such convey the time as occasion rather than as measure. The only bell that really does ring the time is St. Dunstan's clock in "Little Britain," with its "figures that strike the hours." In "Stratford-on-Avon" and "The Spectre Bridegroom," bells strike midnight, a time stamp that serves as an index not of the hour but of an enchanted nighttime moment. The clocks that accent a London Sunday, a country Christmas, and a visit to Stratford-on-Avon convey the existential time of the past, of loss, of death, of immortality. These clocks, which Irving describes as "ancient" or "old-fashioned," tick in the corners of a tavern, the kitchen of an inn, and a sexton's cottage; the time they tell is of an antiquated past, signified by brass candlesticks, pewter mugs, warming pans, and Shakespeare's boyhood. That they are ticking serves to underscore the "presentness" of the moment when Crayon notices them. In ticking, old-fashioned clocks testify to the ongoing life of the past.[15]

Irving activates a temporal sensorium whereby the sound of time is like a clock ticking, a phase of day is like a sunset, a light event is like the extinguishing of candles. A social event may superficially signify a particular time of day, while actually drawing attention to cosmic time. This is literally the case when Ichabod Crane regales the women of Sleepy Hollow "as they sat spinning by the fire" on "long winter evenings" with his "speculations upon comets and shooting stars, and with the alarming fact that the world did absolutely turn round, and that they were half the time topsy-turvy!" Their spinning matches his account of the world's spinning.

The author's temporal tapestry evokes a harmonious attunement between past and present. Consider, for example, Irving's description of how the sound of a distant clock "gave token to the slowly waning day" at Westminster Abbey, just as "the shadows of evening . . . gradually thicken." Here, time cues work together in a sketch meant to emphasize the vast and mysterious past. Once again, Irving deploys clocks and bells to evoke not the measure of time as quotidian hours or minutes, nor really even to draw attention to temporal occasions such as church services, but to underscore modalities of past and present. In depicting a clock, he enfolds it into an expansive historical temporality rather than the narrow temporality of "clock time." Doing so, he denatures the clock, destroying its characteristic properties as a mechanism that tracks seconds, minutes, and hours, and allows it instead to convey the time of a fleeting present and a receding but still living past. The rupture between past and present is one that intuitively haunts Irving's work—with a vengeance, of course, in the time warp of "Rip Van Winkle," where the American Revolution happens during one night's sleep.

As a narrator of human events, Irving manages the rupture in such a way that temporal forces are most often indeterminate, interacting with forces generated from within. Rip Van Winkle's most prominent characteristics are an easygoing temper, a penchant for idle conversation, and an unregulated approach to work. As an escapist, he lacks any interest in measurable time. Ichabod Crane, a scarecrow-like fellow, is too easily arrested by his head, where a frightful past lives because of an apparition that returns at night in search of its own lost head. The schoolmaster's mind is filled with facts, but his temper is constituted by all things *temporary*—dreamy, transient. Perplexity, poor perception, and an inability to seize control of time and circumstance mark both of these iconic Irving characters. We know the amount of time that has passed Rip by, not through his own calculation but by the testament of "old Peter Vanderdonk," a descendant of the village historian, who explains the phenomenon by stating that Hendrick Hudson "kept a kind of vigil" in the mountains "every twenty years."

When Irving invokes hours, they are imprecise, conveying timelessness, endlessness. Perhaps the best example is the fairy tale disguised as a ghost story, "The Spectre Bridegroom," set in a castle in the woods where "hour rolled after hour" as a bride and her family wait for the arrival of the bridegroom. Hours again appear as waves in "Westminster Abbey," where the author casts the hour as a "billow" that "rolled us onward towards the grave," and, quite naturally, while shipboard in "The Voyage," Crayon muses "for hours" on the "tranquil bosom of a summer sea," as "gently undulating billows" keep "rolling their silver volumes" in support of his preoccupation.

The ocean's vastness captured Irving's imagination from early on. He grew up in lower Manhattan and regularly gazed out at multitudes of sailing ships on the near horizon. In "The Voyage," which introduces Crayon as a passenger en route to England, he writes, "At sea all is vacancy," and there for the daydreamer who "delighted to loll," "lost in reverie," content to "muse for hours." Crayon is an idle observer, a speck on the vast ocean, marveling at the sturdy vessel that has "triumphed over wind and wave" and "brought the ends of the world into communion."

The vagueness of measured time returns in "Roscoe," the tale that follows "The Voyage." Crayon announces that "grave-looking personages," studiously absorbed, are constantly visible at the Athenaeum library: "Go there at what hour you may," the scene will be the same. This is where he runs into the eminent Mr. Roscoe, historian and banker, who makes the most of "hours of leisure" and has left his imprint on his native city. "Wherever you go, in Liverpool, you perceive traces of his footsteps in all that is elegant and liberal." Impermanent "traces" are an Irving specialty, in this case the amorphous leavings of a scholar who knows the value of "pure thoughts and innocent hours." For Irving and his wandering alter ego, unclocked hours count. What matters most to him is not what is captured *in* time but what time subtly reveals when—and only when—the imagination is engaged and the senses are activated.

Irving's interest in what might be called the "lived experience of time" is in keeping with his practice in letters and in journals of building a temporal sensorium. "The Legend of Sleepy Hollow" piles detail upon detail drawn from nature and society, which ultimately is meant to situate the reader in the midst of a dark night in late autumn and in a place, Sleepy Hollow, where nothing has changed despite the Enlightenment and the American Revolution.

As we follow "gallant Ichabod" on his hobbled horse headed to the Van Tassels' harvest party, the narrator reminds us that it was "a fine autumnal day." He visualizes this through a clear sky, the browns, oranges, scarlets, and purples of the forest, the wild ducks overhead, flying south. The season is audible in the songs of birds, the small ones chirping as they take "their farewell banquets," the blue jay "screaming and chattering." To underscore the liminality of the moment, as Ichabod passes yards crowded with baskets and barrels of apples, heaps of corn, and ripening pumpkins, he smells "fragrant buckwheat fields."

As his journey continues, the sun begins to set, and Irving describes it as carefully as a member of the Hudson Valley School might have painted the scene. At the Van Tassels' "castle," the mouthwatering treats piled high tell us it is the "sumptuous season of autumn." The eating, the dancing, the singing, the storytelling are all social events that convey the twinned temporalities of evening and leisure. But as moments in time do not last forever, the sun sets, the sky darkens, the party is over.

When the Van Tassel maiden puts an end to Ichabod's courtship, his dream of prosperity and ease dies, and another sort of dream, his long nightmare, begins. In his "credulous" imagination, there are no temporal barriers between past and present, or between reality and fantasy. What was past (the ill-fated British spy, Major André) and what never was (the Headless Horseman) come to life in the deluded pedant's lived experience as he passes through Sleepy Hollow. In Irving's hands, time is elastic, at once dilating and contracting; time is as real as the harvested apples and as unreal as the old Dutch women's stories about ghosts and goblins.

In "Rip Van Winkle," the sense of time as a compliant vessel comes through in the opening paragraph, where Irving describes the wild Catskills: "Every change of season, every change of weather, indeed, every hour of the day produces some change in the magical hues and shapes of these mountains." One does not watch time pass here. The light events of "dusk" and "a bright sunny morning" serve as imagined bookends for two decades, which in Rip's experience was "as one night." We find, in many of Irving's stories, that a fateful fluidity in time's passage is expressed by way of social events: backwoods partying, electioneering, or reuniting with family, to name a few.

As with Ichabod, social events frame Rip's lost years and, in fact, set in motion the simultaneous compression and dilation of time. In the weird, time-altered world Rip confronts, natural time and social time orient and disorient at once. Again and again throughout the *Sketch Book,* the author warns his reader that time may appear to proceed in a regular way, governed by the natural universe or ordinary sociability, but that such appearances are deceiving. As Crayon puts it in "Westminster Abbey," eventually, no matter how carefully you track the hours, you will end up "like a wreck on the distant shore of time." Naturalized time is a contemplative experience, relatable to watching and absorbing the ocean's hypnotic beat. It is a force that overwhelms; humans are too meek to contend with it rationally.

We can see the extent of Irving's naturalism by turning our attention to another set of timekeepers: physical objects, buildings, and customs. Far more numerous in the *Sketch Book* than calendars, clocks, or bells, objects demonstrate the corrosive effects of time's passage. Rip's gun after twenty years' sleep is rusted and worm-eaten. In a quarter of London known as Little Britain, apartments are "time-stained," as is the abandoned Liverpool mansion of the ruined banker Roscoe. Consider, too, Rip's "empty, forlorn and apparently abandoned" house, which had "gone to decay." At Westminster Abbey, "everything bears marks of the gradual dilapidations of time," and the tombs of abbots, knights, and kings are "reliques of times utterly gone by," "mementoes which show the dust and oblivion in which all must sooner or later terminate." Wooden tombstones of ordinary folk rot and disappear; after Rip returns to the village, the innkeeper Nicholas Vedder is "dead and gone," his wooden tombstone "rotted and gone." These are all significant, almost obsessively invoked, features in Irving's literary world.

In terms of practices, Crayon, like the quirky squire of Bracebridge Hall, laments in "Little Britain" the "deplorable decay" of "holyday customs and games of former times." He describes them as "daily growing more faint," as are the three effigies of abbots on Westminster Abbey's floor, which are "being gradually worn away by time, but still more obliterated by modern fashion." In stark contrast, the same sketch smiles upon an "old-fashioned house kept by a jolly publican of the name of Wagstaff," which brings "the sunshine of good-humor over the whole neighborhood."

Irving does not disguise how he feels on the subject of fashion. In "Stratford-on-Avon," which directly follows "Little Britain," the "old-fashioned wood fire, formerly the rallying-place of winter festivity" recovers an imagined community for him. As he rejects all that is flashy and impermanent, he finds his most authoritative timekeepers in "old-fashioned" registers of interior moods. He speaks his mind at the end of "Little Britain," with a pert, "I have determined therefore to beat a retreat in time, and am actually looking out for some other nest in this great city, where old English manners are still kept up."

Many Americans of Irving's generation issued warnings about the ravages the years took on all things, animate and inanimate, typically followed by admonitions to "redeem the time." But not Irving. If he were interested in people who "economize their time," as he puts it in "Rural Life," or in how they did so, then clocks and calendars might have done the work of regularized timekeeping in his sketches. But they do not. He aims to preserve rather than redeem. He wishes to take that which was and make it live again. So we get ghosts, a time travel spectacle, and preservationists like the squire of Bracebridge Hall.

Time, Irving brazenly insists in "The Royal Poet," "delights to obliterate." His remedy is not redeeming or economizing time but slowing the effects of its passage with beauty and poetry. In "The Mutability of Literature," which probes once-heralded literature's loss of its audience over time, Crayon hears schoolboys shouting and a bell tolling as he wanders through a hall filled with books. He observes that the "boasted immortality" that books grant is but a "temporary rumor," akin to "the tone of that bell which has just tolled among these towers, filling the ears for a moment—lingering transiently in echo—and then passing away like a thing that was not!"

In the preceding passage, Irving enlists a powerful metaphor in pursuit of an ontological question: How does the present relate to the past? The present is like the ringing of bells, whose tones fade and at some imperceptible moment disappear. Did that present even exist? Is the past a series of discontinuous present moments, or is it a whole and unified sliver of time?

THE FAR-REACHING PAST

Something interesting occurs as Irving moves from his first two *Sketch Book*–style collections to the third iteration, *Tales of a Traveller* (1824). The Gothic element is repeated often in this volume, in consequence of which the narration attends to measured time more often as a means of timing events that are out of the ordinary. We have "a late hour" repeatedly invoked, "a certain hour of the night," "the hour for retiring," odd doings "past the hour of midnight," "an evil hour," "the fearful hour." Counting the hours suddenly matters more: a servant's daughter is "permitted to enter the house for an hour each day"; the speed of a carriage slows to a precise "seven miles an hour"; a watchman is "relieved every two hours." The narrator bemoans, "For an hour I was kept in this state of peril and anxiety." In "The Adventure of the Mysterious Stranger," a nervous fellow keeps looking around, jerking unsteadily, "as if something painful had met his eye." The same pattern repeats "at intervals of about a minute." There's "the brown hour of twilight, when the owls began to hoot and the bats to flit about," in opposition to "the warm sunny hours of mid-day." As he experiments in *Tales of a Traveller* with a form of storytelling that more directly evokes fear and threatens future tragedy, Irving uses measured time to intensify the emotional experience of his reader.

Thus, in a few short years, having left England and situated himself in France and—most profitably, from a story-collecting perspective—parts of Germany, Irving made a concerted effort to fix his pen on somewhat more realistic characters and unrestrainedly cursed events. But then he unceremoniously put this phase of his career behind him and returned to reimagining the storied past for which he is best known, reaching for Moorish lore in *Tales of the Alhambra* (1832). This is the volume that became known popularly as the "Spanish Sketch Book," imbuing a new series of folk tales with more fantastic imagery of a magical, not-quite-datable past.[16]

Returning to the original *Sketch Book,* from which we mark the most enduring traits of this author, one cannot help but marvel at the temporal spaces he produces. Although the present is not yet the past, the two commune on a regular basis. To make the present manifest, Irving's narrator takes a confiding step, or what we might call a "walk by my side in real time" tone, where he uses the present verb tense to introduce historic sites and ancient customs. Crayon escorts readers around both rural and urban England, entering cemeteries, taverns, athenaeums, manors, the streets of London, its medieval churches—anywhere he finds it possible to dissolve into the past. Irving's temporal mind-set is that of a particular kind of historian, not one who narrates events that progressively build upon each other, leading to either triumph or disaster, but one who never quite leaves behind the picturesque that describes nature's enduring power over the mind.

We tend to call historians such as Irving "antiquarians," collectors of remnants and vestiges, fascinated by the sheer pastness of their quarry. Near the end of his life, in a letter to a namesake, the son of a cherished Sunnyside neighbor who had married into the family, Irving identified himself as a "hunter of the picturesque and historical."[17] This characterization is more than a throwaway line, and it is readily apparent throughout the *Sketch Book*. In resurrecting old English Christmas in the eponymously named tale "Christmas," for instance, Irving revives holiday games that "flourished in times full of spirit . . . , times wild and picturesque, which have furnished poetry with its richest materials." And what else does he find "picturesque"? Each "remnant of old times," "morsels of Gothic architecture," and "romantic solitudes" worthy of an artist's sketch book.

"Romantic solitudes" is yet another key to this author's sentimental search for historical permanence. In the melancholy sketch "Rural Funerals," we have a perfect reminder of the marriage of picturesque nature and fond remembrance. Here, "the stroke of death" upsets the "tranquil uniformity" of a rural village, and "the passing bell tolls its knell in every ear," yet "the fixed and unchanging features of the country" succeed in keeping alive a deceased friend's memory. The picturesque in nature speaks to the revival of feeling; it stimulates recollection of companionate strolls amid sweet sensations of the rising and setting sun in familiar haunts. The natural cycles of time, as captured in familiar seasonal scenes, pacify the otherwise unnerved survivor. From recollection comes recognition, acceptance, and a kind of gratitude.

Throughout his writings, Irving liked to dwell on the form of a landscape, the interior of an old but durable structure, or the call of a homely habitation—scenes that served him as frames for time-related adventures designed to combat decline and resist physical decay that was inevitable. The battles Irving entered most determinedly were ones that pitted memory against forgetfulness. He needed to "breathe" the past in order to preserve all that is good in the human spirit.

As Peter Fritzsche reminds us, "disconnection from the past was a source of melancholy" in this era. Yet Irving did not find melancholy depressive, or even disconnecting. He did not count the numbers who fell in war or see ruins as "the debris of quite specific historical disasters" made by men.[18] He saw differently: death renewed the commitment to memory; physical ruins were the result of a natural wearing out wrought by time. Abstractedly, he begged for a better lesson from history than degeneracy or accumulated misery. Born into a world that had endured calamitous wars caused by royal willfulness and territorial greed that severed the present from the past, Irving, in his prose, offered a way to reexperience sensations of coherence in eras of imagined continuity. Whether standing inside Westminster Abbey or at Shakespeare's graveside, or, later in his career, giving new life to the bold aesthetic of Moorish Spain, he treated the present as a portal to the past, available through the senses.

He was more than a dreamer with a pen, though. We are learning from neuroscience research in our own century how the mind constructs and visualizes time, and it is not entirely divorced from Irving's methodology. The perceptual world we know is a collection of information from outside ourselves that skips over visual input the brain does not need; we in fact perceive beyond what we see with our eyes alone. Illusions readily occur to us, because the brain is constantly making assumptions. According to David Eagleman, whose specialty includes time perception and involuntary sensations, "There is a looming chasm between what your brain knows and what your mind is capable of accessing." Not all of memory is accessible, and our sense of time is purely a construction. He seems to have Rip Van Winkle all figured out.[19]

In contrast to Irving, who saw the present as a portal to the past, some of his American contemporaries who toured Britain around the same time were decidedly future-oriented. They commented on sites associated with the industrial, capitalist, and imperial power of England, seeing them as portents of the future, some more bleak than others. The merchant Francis Cabot Lowell toured British textile mills shortly before the War of 1812, absorbing technological and organizational details that he and his successors would use to industrialize New England. Lowell was less interested in how yarn was *once* spun, or how textiles were *once* woven, or how capital was *once* amassed than he was in how Britain's great mills were *presently* spinning yarn, weaving fabric, and deploying capital. His interest was in building a future out of the present. When, in 1823, the six buildings of the Lowell Mills opened along the banks of the Merrimack River, their centerpiece was a clock tower. When its bell rang, it called mill workers to the factory gates. There was no time for communion with the past.

What more obvious contrast to Lowell's plan could there be than Irving's imagining of a future anterior? There is no future in Irving's world, except when he imagines how the future will appear once it is past. He gives us the bride as widow in "The Spectre Bridegroom," the youngish man as an old man in "Rip Van Winkle," and the memorial as ruin in "Westminster Abbey." In temporal zones such as these, calendars are incidental, clocks convey the feel of the past rather than the hour of the day, and nothing is of greater consequence than what once was.[20]

NOTES

Alexis McCrossen would like to thank Tom Allen, Annie Rose, and Nick Yablon for their help with this essay.

1. Peter Fritzsche, *Stranded in the Present: Modern Time and the Melancholy of History* (Cambridge, MA: Harvard University Press, 2004), 31.

2. Paul Glennie and Nigel Thrift, *Shaping the Day: A History of Timekeeping in England and Wales, 1300–1800* (New York: Oxford University Press, 2000), 17. Timekeeping was vital to the economy of Liverpool, where Irving lived while writing the *Sketch Book*, dependent as it was on shipping and commerce. The city was home to one of England's most accomplished makers of chronometers and watches, Robert Roskell.

3. John Styles, "Time Pieces: Working Men and Watches," *History Today* 43 (January 2008): 44–50.

4. On the ubiquity of clocks in eighteenth-century urban England, see Hans-Joachim Voth, *Time and Work in England, 1750–1830* (New York: Oxford University Press, 2000), 53; and Glennie and Thrift, *Shaping the Day*. On Bank of England clocks, see Anne Murphy, "Clock-Watching: Work and Working Time at the Late Eighteenth-Century Bank of England," *Past and Present* 236 (August 2017): 100–132; and Christina Juliet Faraday, "Tudor Time Machines: Clocks and Watches in English Portraits, c.1530–c.1630," *Renaissance Studies* 33 (2018): 239–66.

5. Irving, "Notes, 1815–1821," in *Journals and Notebooks*, vol. 1, *1803–1806*, ed. Nathalia Wright (Madison: University of Wisconsin Press, 1969), 55, 73; Irving, "Journal, 1820," in *Journals and Notebooks*, vol. 2, *1807–1822*, ed. Walter A. Reichart and Lillian Schlissel (Boston: Twayne, 1981), 321–22.

6. St. Paul's enormous bell had been hanging from the south tower of London's tallest building for more than a century when Irving encountered it; it only rings for the deaths and funerals of the royal family and other important personages. King George III died on January 29, 1820, while Irving was living at 21 Edward Street, Portland Place, some twenty miles from St. Paul's. See Irving to John Howard Payne, January 28, 1820, in *Letters*, vol. 1, *1802–1823*, ed. Ralph M. Aderman, Herbert L. Kleinfield, and Jenifer S. Banks, 574–75, in *The Complete Works of Washington Irving* (Boston: Twayne, 1978); and Alexis McCrossen, *Marking Modern Times: Clocks, Watches and Other Timekeepers in American Life* (Chicago: University of Chicago Press, 2013), chaps. 1 and 2.

7. David Landes, *Revolution in Time: Clocks and the Making of the Modern World* (Cambridge, MA: Harvard University Press, 1983), 227. On banking hours, see Murphy, "Clock-Watching," 101, 108–12. Regarding the concept of "clock time," see Glennie and Thrift, *Shaping the Day*. Hans-Joachim Voth, who studied the period 1750 to 1830, found that "basic patterns of daily life" in rural and urban England were quite similar, with a workday of about twelve hours, regardless of the season. Voth, *Time and Work in England*, esp. 67, 76, 94. See also Mark Hailwood, "Time and Work in Rural England, 1500–1700," *Past and Present* 248 (August 2020): 87–121; and Keith Wrightson, "Popular Senses of Past Time: Dating Events in the North Country, 1615–1631," in *Popular Culture and Political Agency in Early Modern England*

and Ireland: Essays in Honor of John Walter, ed. Michael Braddick and Phil Withington (Boydell Press, 2017), 91–107.

8. Hailwood, "Time and Work"; E. P. Thompson, "Time, Work-Discipline, and Industrial Capitalism," *Past and Present* 38 (December 1967): 56–97; Stuart Sherman, *Telling Time: Clocks, Diaries and the English Diurnal Form, 1660–1785* (Chicago: University of Chicago Press, 1996).

9. Drawn from the sections "Family Servants," "Love Charms," and "The Culprit," in Washington Irving, *Bracebridge Hall,* ed. Herbert F. Smith (Boston: Twayne, 1977). For full contextualization of the effects in *Bracebridge Hall,* see Jeffrey Rubin-Dorsky, *Adrift in the Old World: The Psychological Pilgrimage of Washington Irving* (Chicago: University of Chicago Press, 1988), chap. 4.

10. Irving, "New York Journal, 1803," in *Journals and Notebooks,* vol. 1, entries of July 30, August 8–9, 1803; "Tour in Wales, 1815," in *Journals and Notebooks,* vol. 2, entries for July 31, August 10, and August 14, 1815. During his first year back in the United States after seventeen years in Europe, Irving's travel journals continue to mix clock time, social events, and light events. In 1832, he "left Cincinnati at 5 oclock," on another evening "after dinner drove out," and again noted "sunset" when a "party breaks up." Irving, *Journals and Notebooks,* vol. 5, *1832–1859,* ed. Sue Fields Ross (Boston: Twayne, 1986), 42–93; see esp. entries of September 3–8, 1832. Irving's last extant travel journal, from a trip made in 1842 to England and France, notes arrival and departure times and the duration of travel, but otherwise marks the time only with notations referencing phases of day, and mostly "evening."

11. "We arrived here Sunday between four and five, having experienced several minutes' delay on the road, to the great annoyance of Cooper, who travels watch in hand." Irving to Joseph Gratz, New York, March 30, 1808, in *Letters,* 1:254. As early as the mid-seventeenth century, "clock-watchers" sprang up in cities, comparing their chronometers with public clocks and noting deviance. See Michael J. Sauter, "Clockwatchers and Stargazers: Time Discipline in Early Modern Berlin," *American Historical Review* 112 (June 2007): 685–709.

12. In the miscellaneous entries of a notebook Irving kept in 1818, he included a watch on a short list of items he either purchased or intended to purchase. Irving, "Notebook 1818, Number 2," *Journals and Notebooks,* 2:284. After nephew Edgar Irving visited him in Spain in 1829, Irving wrote, "When you were here you mentioned something about your having no watch; and that you liked the French watches of a flat construction. I shall write to your Uncle Peter to procure one and send it out to New York for you & you must wear it for my sake." Irving to Edgar Irving, Alhambra, May 26, 1829, in *Letters,* 1:431.

In the 1840s, Irving's personal expenses show that he owned and cared for at least one if not more pocket watches; in February, April, and August of 1840, he either bought watch parts or had a watch repaired. As one notation specifies "silver watch," he may have owned another watch, likely of gold, which would have been fitting for a man of his position. In 1841, he paid to have a watch repaired four separate times. Irving, "Account Book, 1840–1841," in *Journals and Notebooks,* 5:449–50, 469, 471. For men and women who carried their watches, repair work was a typical and not infrequent expense. See Alexis McCrossen, "The

'Very Delicate Construction' of Pocket Watches and Time Consciousness in the Nineteenth-Century United States," *Winterthur Portfolio* 44 (Spring 2010): 1–30; and McCrossen, *Marking Modern Times*, chap. 4.

13. Murphy, "Clock-Watching," 108. Murphy draws on Glennie and Thrift, in assigning to public clocks and related objects the power to enhance the "value and credibility of evidence." On the temporality of novels, see especially Sherman, *Telling Time*.

14. "December snows" are mentioned in "Philip of Pokanoket." December: "The Stage Coach" and "Christmas." May: "A Royal Poet" and "Pride of the Village." March: "Stratford-on-Avon." Sunday: "Rural Funerals," "Rural Life," "The Widow and Her Son," "Christmas," "The Pride of the Village," "The Spectre Bridegroom," and "The Legend of Sleepy Hollow." Valentine's Day and Guy Fawkes's Day: "Little Britain." May Day: "The Pride of the Village." Christmas: "The Stage Coach," "Christmas Eve," "Christmas," and "Christmas Dinner." On these developments, see Alexis McCrossen, *Holy Day, Holiday: The American Sunday* (Ithaca, NY: Cornell University Press, 2000); Stephen Nissenbaum, *The Battle for Christmas: A Social and Cultural History of Our Most Cherished Holiday* (New York: Knopf, 1997); and Leigh Eric Schmidt, *Consumer Rites: The Buying and Selling of American Holidays* (Princeton, NJ: Princeton University Press, 1995).

15. Clocks: "The Boar's Head Tavern, Eastcheap," "The Stage Coach," "Stratford-on-Avon," "Westminster Abbey," "Little Britain," and "The Spectre Bridegroom." Bells: "Rural Life in England," "Christmas Day," "The Pride of the Village," "A Sunday in London," "Westminster Abbey," "Little Britain," "The Widow and Her Son," and "The Mutability of Literature." In "Rip Van Winkle," Irving compares the innkeeper Nicholas Vedder to a sundial, his movements regularly tracking those of the sun. "An old-fashioned clock ticked in one corner" of the Mason's Arms in "The Boar's Head Tavern, Eastcheap." "A clock ticked in one corner" of an inn's kitchen on Christmas Eve in "The Stage Coach." "An ancient clock, that important article of cottage furniture, ticked on the opposite side of the room" in "Stratford-on-Avon."

For Irving's focus on historical time and the experience of time, and his fascination with the past more broadly, see Michael Warner, "Irving's Posterity," *ELH* 67 (Fall 2000): 773–99; Jeffrey Insko, *History, Abolition, and the Ever-Present Now in Antebellum American Writing* (New York: Oxford University Press, 2018), 29–55; and Insko, "Historicism," in Thomas Allen, ed., *Time and Literature* (New York: Cambridge University Press, 2018), 180–92.

16. Andrew Burstein, *The Original Knickerbocker: The Life of Washington Irving* (New York: Basic Books, 2007), chaps. 8 and 10.

17. Irving to Irving Grinnell, October 28, 1858, in *Letters*, vol. 4, *1846–1859*, ed. Ralph M. Aderman, Herbert L. Kleinfield, and Jenifer S. Banks, 666–68, in *The Complete Works of Washington Irving* (Boston: Twayne, 1982). Irving writes in response to Grinnell's lament that while on a tour of England, Scotland, and Ireland, he, a young Columbia College graduate, did not seem to take in the full import of what he was seeing. "I stand looking with all my eyes and senses open, and feel as though I were deficient in some faculty which prevented me from really appreciating and enjoying all that I see." Irving responded that most travelers, after

the fact, "invent what they think they ought to have felt." To Grinnell's sister Julia, Irving had written a short time earlier, "Sightseeing is at times rather fatiguing and exhausting; but the fatigue is amply repaid by the stock of recollections hung up in one's mental picture gallery." Irving to Julia Grinnell, September 2, 1858, in *Letters*, 4:665. Moses Hicks Grinnell (1803-1877), the father of this brother and sister and briefly a member of Congress, is buried alongside his wife, Irving's niece Julia Irving Grinnell (1803-1872), at Sleepy Hollow Cemetery.

18. Fritzsche, *Stranded in the Present*, 56-57, 97-101.

19. David Eagleman, *Incognito: The Secret Lives of the Brain* (New York: Pantheon, 2011), 51-57.

20. On the future anterior as an archetypal mode of American thought, see Nick Yablon, *Untimely Ruins: An Archaeology of American Urban Modernity, 1819-1919* (Chicago: University of Chicago Press, 2009), 246-85.

PART II

ANOTHER WORLD

> Writers, like bees, toll their sweets in the wide world; they incorporate with their own conceptions, the anecdotes and thoughts current in society; and thus each generation has some features in common, characteristic of the age in which it lives.
> —WASHINGTON IRVING, "A Royal Poet"

TRACING NORTHERN SLAVERY IN THE KNICKERBOCKER STORIES

ELIZABETH L. BRADLEY

It has been more than a century since Edwin W. Bowen first described Washington Irving as the "father of the American Republic of Letters," in a 1906 panegyric for the *Sewanee Review*. He emphasized both the "firstness" of Irving's achievement and his "sunny disposition" as it was transferred onto the page. The paternal epithet, however well-intentioned, has dogged the author's literary reputation ever since and has led some critics to deride his best-known works as nursery classics, suitable for classroom anthologies and pop culture adaptations, but little else.[1]

It is true that Irving's most popular Knickerbocker tales have engendered a litany of interpretations and homage over the past two hundred years, for audiences of every age and interest. On the strength of this claim, we must agree with Bowen's literary paternity suit. Yet readers who seize on Irving's deeply satisfying and seemingly familiar tropes of forests primeval, Dutch damsels, and scouring ghosts neglect a very different kind of imagery that is also vividly present in his stories of old New York: the unapologetic depiction of American slavery, and of the experiences of enslaved people in and around the Hudson Valley.

Born in New York City in 1783, a few months before the end of the Revolutionary War, Irving was sixteen when New York State passed a gradual emancipation act, and thus he lived in the midst of slavery. The transatlantic slave trade and widespread use of unfree labor had been the engine that powered colonial New York when the port city was second only to Charleston in the sheer number of households with enslaved residents, and it remained a major component of New York's economy after independence. The emancipation act was, in fact, designed to protect the interests of enslavers, not the rights of those held in bondage, and included provisos that allowed slave owners to claim as property future children born to enslaved mothers, among other cruel exemptions. This inhumane compromise ensured that the landscape of Irving's New York childhood and early literary career included enslaved Africans in every context.[2]

As a young man, Irving would have encountered enslaved individuals in businesses and in private homes, often working in highly skilled professional capacities, and almost always without compensation or hope of gaining legal selfhood. The Irving family would have taken the presence of slaves throughout the city as a given, for even if the family were not enslavers themselves, their neighbors certainly were. An advertisement placed in *Rivington's New-York Gazette, and Universal Advertiser* on December 2, 1783, testifies to this fact: "ONE GUINEA RUN-AWAY from the Subscriber this morning, about nine o'clock, Two Negro Lads, called STEPNEY and PRINCE," the notice begins, before enumerating the features that distinguish twenty-year-old Stepney and seventeen-year-old Prince in the eyes of the person who considers them as property. The advertisement concludes: "It is supposed they have gone on board some vessel immediately bound to sea. All Masters of vessels are requested not to harbour or take them off. Any person delivering them to Capt. Nicholson, No. 92, William street [sic], shall have Five Guineas Reward for each."[3]

The large Irving family lived at 75 William Street.

Slavery was also a significant feature of the largely agrarian Hudson River Valley, where many of Irving's most famous tales are set. Slave labor was used by white plantation owners, as well as by tenant farmers, rural business owners, and households looking for domestic staff—all of whom could legally buy, sell, rent, and inherit enslaved men, women, and children. The Van Cortlandts, who are generally thought to be a model for the Van Tassel family of "The Legend of Sleepy Hollow," had a retinue of enslaved domestic servants, including at least one enslaved family.

By the time Irving purchased Sunnyside in 1835, slavery had been legally abolished in New York, but little had changed in practice: enslaved New Yorkers appeared on the state census rolls into the 1840s, and in family documents even later. Furthermore, the Fugitive Slave Act of 1850 not only rendered the North dangerous for any enslaved person who had self-liberated from a slave state but also made it risky for free Black New Yorkers, who were vulnerable to kidnappers looking to make a profit in the South. While Irving himself may not have been an enslaver, the business and practice of slavery was taking place around him, all the time. Why, then, have so many readers ignored the slavery in his writings?

The simple answer to this question is that Irving was no more enlightened than the average American pundit in the post-Revolutionary period. His accounts of slavery are not stirring abolitionist jeremiads or empathetic calls to action. In fact, there is not much at all that seems prescient or broad-minded about Irving's depictions of slavery or his characterizations of enslaved and formerly enslaved Black people. While the author never mounted a full-throated defense of slavery (as his older writer friend James Kirke Paulding did), the scenes of enslavement sprinkled throughout his Knickerbocker stories are steeped in a paternalistic racism that has little to recommend it to the contemporary reader. It seems easier to extract the Headless Horseman from his historical landscape, as so many adaptations have done, than to hold one's nose and grapple with Irving's own erroneous perspective. However, this distasteful assignment matters greatly. Sifting through the author's descriptions of life in Dutch New York, one can find pieces of a very different Knickerbocker narrative: that of an enslaved community hiding in plain sight.

The everyday experience of slavery hovers over Irving's Hudson Valley writings. Enslavement is an unexpected through line connecting one book to the next, as the author returns time and again with increasing intensity to a subject that was quickly falling out of fashion in the northern states, as well as in England, where he wrote many of his most famous tales. In so doing, he creates some of the first Black characters in American literature and illustrates, most likely inadvertently, the distinctive contributions that unfree New Yorkers made to the development of the city and the colony.

DIEDRICH KNICKERBOCKER AND THE ENSLAVED RESIDENTS OF COMMUNIPAW

Irving's initial engagement with northern slavery occurs in his first book, *A History of New-York from the Beginning of the World to the End of the Dutch Dynasty*, which was published in 1809. True to form, this satirical history begins facetiously, with a list of reasons why the European colonization of North America is legitimate. These include the "right by discovery," and the "right by extermination, or, in other words, the right by gunpowder," by which the author means the persecution and murder of the Indigenous populations. It is here that Irving's narrator, Diedrich Knickerbocker, first engages with the concept of race-based enslavement. He describes the logic by which the "righteous followers of Cortes and Pizarro" determined that the American Indians were too dark-skinned to deserve the land they inhabited: "Being of a copper complexion, it was all the same as if they were negroes . . . Therefore, so far from being able to own property, they had no right even to personal freedom—for liberty is too radiant a deity to inhabit such gloomy temples."[4]

While the narrator continues on in an ironic vein about how the European settlers handily discounted the traditions, beliefs, and accomplishments of Indigenous peoples, he does not return to the subject of the "personal freedom" of African captives until book 2, when the reader is introduced to the Dutch settlers of Communipaw, and the "Dutch Negroes" who were enslaved there. The appearance of enslaved individuals is registered without apology or preamble: wherever Dutch settlers are, there are enslaved laborers, as far as Knickerbocker is concerned.

The reality in New Amsterdam was not quite as matter-of-fact as Knickerbocker makes it in the pages of Irving's *History*. In 1626, eleven African captives were delivered to New Amsterdam on a Dutch West India Company ship, the first instance of enslavement in the Dutch colony, although by no means the first in North America. These captives, who were initially considered permanent indentures, sued and were ultimately granted freedom for themselves and their wives. However, the company ruled that their children, including those yet to be born, would remain enslaved, a decree that led to the development of the first "half-free" settlement in the colony, which was developed north of New Amsterdam in what would become Washington Square Park and lasted into the eighteenth century.

The meaningful legal and social complexity of a "half-free" condition is nowhere in Irving's account of the Dutch founding, but his narrator's description of life among the enslaved residents of Communipaw, and later "Manna-hatta," bears a strong resemblance to the actual mechanics of urban slavery:

> These negroes, in fact, like the monks in the dark ages, engross all the knowledge of the place, and, being infinitely more adventurous, and more knowing than their masters, carry on all the foreign trade, making frequent voyages to town in canoes loaded with oysters, buttermilk and cabbages. They are great astrologers, predicting the different changes of weather almost as accurately as an almanac; they are, moreover, exquisite performers on three-stringed fiddles; in whistling they almost boast the far-famed powers of Orpheus' lyre, for not a horse nor an ox in the place, when at the plough or before the wagon, will budge a foot until he hears the well known whistle of his black driver and companion. And from their amazing skill at casting up accounts upon their fingers they are regarded with as much veneration as were the disciples of Pythagoras of yore when initiated into the sacred quaternary of numbers.[5]

Knickerbocker's enumeration of the skills and acumen possessed by the enslaved community in Communipaw may be delivered with the narrator's signature condescension, but it still manages to reveal Irving's fluency with the practice of slavery in his own time. From the time of Dutch colonial rule through the mid-nineteenth century, enslaved individuals in urban centers like New York were given considerably more freedom of movement than their rural counterparts. They often served as representatives for their masters, conducting business on their behalf or managing farms and plantations in their enslaver's absence. In a cosmopolitan port such as New Amsterdam, unfree laborers would, in fact, be likely to "carry on all the foreign trade," as Knickerbocker suggests, and to be able strike deals in several languages. Irving, raised at the foot of Manhattan Island, would have witnessed very similar interactions.

The measures of autonomy that slaves were granted in New York should not be confused with freedom. To be a slave was to be considered property under law; as such, the lives of New York's enslaved families were not theirs to control. Knickerbocker gestures at this fact in the *History*, too, in his recounting of Peter Stuyvesant's funeral procession:

> His funeral obsequies were celebrated with the utmost grandeur and solemnity. The town was perfectly emptied of its inhabitants, who crowded in throngs to pay the last sad honors to their good old governor. All his sterling qualities rushed in full tide upon their recollection, while the memory of his foibles and his faults had expired with him. The ancient burghers contended who should have the privilege of bearing the pall; the populace strove who should walk nearest to the bier, and the melancholy procession was closed by a number of gray-bearded negroes, who had wintered and summered in the household of their departed master for the greater part of a century.[6]

Absent the "departed master," the enslaved members of Stuyvesant's household would absolutely have been adrift. The "gray-bearded" elders may have been bequeathed, or sold, and in either case are likely to have been separated from family and community. The breakup of enslaved families on the Stuyvesant compound had already happened during the governor's lifetime, as Joyce Goodfriend has shown. It is unlikely that Irving is gesturing toward this terrible history in his image of Stuyvesant's funeral cortege. But he does give the slave community the final word, and not for the last time.[7]

"PET NEGRO CHILDREN," "MUD SAM," AND "PLUTO"

The success of the *History* and the instant celebrity conferred upon the fictional historian Diedrich Knickerbocker made that narrator's triumphant return all but inevitable. With more tales of Dutch New York come still more detailed depictions of bondage in the Hudson Valley, which is, of course, the setting for Irving's most famous tale, "The Legend of Sleepy Hollow." As in *A History of New-York,* the enslaved Black characters featured in "The Legend" are nameless and grossly caricatured. At the same time, they have a significant narrative function: to hold a mirror up to the interloping Ichabod Crane and bear witness to the schoolmaster's most bald-faced efforts to ingratiate himself in the Dutch community. This is most evident in the description of Ichabod's vigorous dance at the Van Tassel frolic:

> Ichabod prided himself upon his dancing as much as upon his vocal powers. Not a limb, not a fibre about him was idle; and to have seen his loosely hung frame in full motion, and clattering about the room, you would have thought St. Vitus himself, that blessed patron of the dance, was figuring before you in person. He was the admiration of all the negroes; who, having gathered, of all ages and sizes, from the farm and the neighborhood, stood forming a pyramid of shining black faces at every door and window.

The schoolmaster's audience not only throws his antics into vivid relief but also reveals the visibility and open curiosity expressed by the Black residents, and the extent of Van Tassel's slaveholdings. From the "pyramid" of

"He came clattering up to the school door with an invitation to Ichabod to attend a merry meeting." Representation of a Black character from "The Legend of Sleepy Hollow," in *The Beauties of Washington Irving* (1835).

onlookers, the reader can begin to speculate about the multigenerational enslaved community on the Dutch planter's farm.

Historians study inventories, wills, and other legal records to uncover the existence of enslaved families on plantations and in urban centers, even when their enslavers refused to acknowledge these relationships in any formal manner. A pattern of similar names on a census document can reveal an enslaved father and son, just as Knickerbocker's casual reference to "all ages and sizes" of Black onlookers suggests children, parents, and elders. What is intended as light comedy thus becomes, through a different lens, an intriguing record of kinship and enduring family bonds.

While the enslaved community at Baltus Van Tassel's home has been relegated to "every door and window" of the ballroom, they are not, in fact, the outsiders in the frolic scene. Ichabod, fated to be frightened out of Sleepy Hollow that very night, is the foreigner. Unlike the enslaved described above, he has no meaningful connection to Sleepy Hollow. Indeed, unlike the preferred musician at the Van Tassel party, an "old gray-headed negro, who had been the itinerant orchestra of the neighborhood for more than half a century," the tuneless Yankee Ichabod has no history in the village—and no engagement with history to speak of, aside from his beloved *History of New England Witchcraft* by Cotton Mather. The professional violinist, on the other hand, has more than fifty years' forcible experience parsing and navigating the tribal rites that mark this insular, "vegetating" Dutch settlement; his ancestors may have centuries' more.[8]

It is fascinating to note that the Van Tassel musician had a real-life counterpart on the Van Cortlandt homestead in Croton-on-Hudson, where an enslaved man named Ishmael lived and worked as a coachman at the turn of the nineteenth century. Van Cortlandt family correspondence indicates that Ishmael also served as an "itinerant orchestra" in the region—in this case, without the sanction of his owner. A 1799 letter from Pierre Van Cortlandt to his neighbor James Mandiville makes this prohibition clear: "I have understood that my Negro man Ishamael [sic] is one of the Fiddlers that frequents you[r] house at frolicking Times. I shall take it Kind if for time to Come you will not Countenance his being there at any Rate as I do Intend here after to prosicute [sic] any person that Encourages, or suffers him to play the fiddle at Night for their houses."[9]

Whether or not Ishmael is the model for the violinist in "The Legend of Sleepy Hollow," the real and fictional musicians have something else in common. They exist in the historical and literary record only at the points where their stories intersect with those of their masters. As legal chattel, they may truthfully be said to "belong" to their communities, but the kind of belonging that Ichabod seeks can never be within their reach. At the end of "The Legend," the interloper Ichabod is cast out, to find "preferment," as Knickerbocker's postscript hints, in other places. The enslaved person, so often erased from the frame of Irving's most famous story, is in fact the one character who cannot leave it.[10]

Irving's subsequent collections, *Bracebridge Hall, or The Humorists* (1822) and *Tales of a Traveller* (1824), both include Knickerbocker narrations that interpret New York slavery through a similar lens. "Dolph Heyliger," a winding tale of haunted houses and buried treasures, makes a point to establish the picaresque Heer Antony Vander Heyden as a liberal paterfamilias devoted to his wife and daughter, in a scene that includes the Black community on his Albany estate: "There was a great degree of patriarchal simplicity, and good-humored indulgence. The negroes came into the room without being called, merely to look at their master, and hear of his adventures; they would stand listening at the door until he had finished a story, and then go off on a broad grin, to repeat it in the kitchen. A couple of pet negro children were playing about the floor with the dogs, and sharing with them their bread and butter. All the domestics looked hearty and happy."

This story, set during English colonial rule, depicts slavery as a matter of course, replete with "pet" Black children. Albany, the future state capital, had one of the largest enslaved populations in the colony. One possible historical model for the Vander Heydens is the prominent, land-rich Schuyler family, into which Alexander Hamilton married. The Schuylers (and Hamilton, as recent research has shown) were enslavers, like Irving's fictional Heer Antony. Among the individuals held in bondage by the Schuylers was a man named Will, whose wife, Brit, was owned by Schuyler relatives, the Ten Broeck family, on a neighboring estate. Their daughter, Susannah, was considered the property of the Ten Broeck family by law, as were Susannah's children after her own marriage.[11]

The Vander Heydens' "pet negro children" (referred to this way twice in "Dolph Heyliger") are property, like the children of Will and Brit, and the narrator's euphemism does not obscure the fact that the law has effectively orphaned them. Parentless and disenfranchised, the "pets" in Irving's tale have no more rights than the animals with whom they share their repast.

"Dolph Heyliger" offers the first glimpse of a personal relationship between free and enslaved characters in a Knickerbocker story. The narrator reports that "the old black cook" was Dolph's only friend in the household of Dr. Knipperhausen, where he has been taken on as an apprentice. And when Dolph volunteers to exorcise the ghosts in Dr. Knipperhausen's country estate, it is the unnamed cook who provides an "amulet, given her by an African conjurer, as a charm against evil spirits."

This is the last the reader hears of the cook, as she does not feature in his treasure-laden return to Manhattan, and it might be easy to dismiss the episode as trivial. But the detail of her amulet is significant: it invokes the many ways enslaved New Yorkers sought to protect and nurture the cultures from which they had been forcibly separated. A similar use of ceremonial and sacred jewelry can be discovered at the African Burial Ground in lower Manhattan, where archaeologists have unearthed waist beads, necklaces, and rings that speak to the mortuary rituals of the more than fifteen thousand free and enslaved Africans who were interred there. Many of these items carry deep spiritual meaning in traditional African societies, and in some cases may have been carried to New York via the Middle Passage.[12] The cook's amulet is a rare expression of African heritage in a Knickerbocker story, reminding readers that the enslaved characters they meet in Irving's works are dispossessed people rather than possessions.

Another dispossessed person inhabits "The Money-Diggers," the Knickerbocker-narrated final section of *Tales of a Traveller*. This is Sam the fisherman, from "The Adventure of Sam, the Black Fisherman, Commonly Denominated Mud Sam." Despite the eponymous honor done to him, Sam is not the hero of this story—Knickerbocker accords that distinction to the Dutch cabbage farmer, Wolfert Webber—but he is arguably the most intriguing of all the characters, not least because his legal status is never addressed. "Sam was easily found," Irving writes, "for he was one of those old habitual beings that live about a neighborhood until they wear themselves a place in the public mind, and become, in a manner, public characters."

What does it mean to for a Black man to have a "place in the public mind" of colonial New York? Was Sam freed by an enslaver, or did he liberate himself from slavery? Some enslaved men and women were able to purchase their freedom by a combination of negotiation and unstinting work.

Sam's uncanny skills "about the shores of the bay and the fishing grounds of the Sound" may have paid for his autonomy, though the reader never knows for certain. By some means, he is at liberty to be hired by Wolfert Webber in the pursuit of buried treasure, an activity that throws the two men into a surprising intimacy.

When the treasure is found, however, it is not in one of Captain Kidd's fabled hiding places, but in Webber's actual backyard—his "hereditary acres," when developed into Manhattan streets, transform the impoverished farmer into a wealthy landlord. For Sam, on the other hand, there is no reward. If he is enslaved, he cannot own property; if he is free, the opportunities to accumulate wealth are beyond his reach. As far as the reader can discern, Sam returns to his cabin, which Knickerbocker describes as "not much larger than a tolerable dog-house . . . rudely constructed of fragments of wrecks and drift-wood, and built on the rocky shore," there to remain as one of the most poignant mysteries among the Knickerbocker tales.

A variation on the character of Sam returns to puzzle the reader in a story Irving wrote for *Knickerbocker Magazine* years later, in 1839. "Guests from Gibbet-Island" was inspired by the Brothers Grimm, and while not explicitly a Diedrich Knickerbocker story, it picks up the themes of Hudson River piracy where "The Money-Diggers" left off—it is narrated in the Knickerbocker vernacular.[13]

Among the characters in "Guests from Gibbet-Island" is a Black man named Pluto, a "curmudgeon" and "enigma" of unknown origin and legal status in colonial Communipaw, who is taken in by the Dutch proprietor of the Wild Goose Tavern: "Some thought him a negro just from Guinea, who had either fallen overboard, or escaped from a slave-ship. Nothing, however, could ever draw from him any account of his origin. When questioned on the subject, he merely pointed to Gibbet-Island, a small rocky islet, which lies in the open bay, just opposite to Communipaw, as if that were his native place, though everybody knew it had never been inhabited."[14]

Like Sam, who is described as "something more of a fish than a man," it is initially uncertain whether Pluto is "fish or flesh, or a compound of both, commonly yclept a merman." Here, Irving's imagery owes a greater debt to Shakespeare than to Grimm, for Pluto is very much like Caliban, the bewitched half-human figure in *The Tempest,* who is here cast as profane and fearfully magical:

> Lay any command on him, and the stubborn sea-urchin was sure to rebel. He was never so much at home, however, as when on the water, plying about in skiff or canoe, entirely alone, fishing, crabbing, or grabbing for oysters, and would bring home quantities for the larder of the Wild Goose, which he would throw down at the kitchen door, with a growl. No wind nor weather deterred him from launching forth on his favorite element: indeed, the wilder the weather, the more he seemed to enjoy it . . . How he weathered the tempest, and how and where he subsisted, no one could divine, nor did any one venture to ask, for all had an almost superstitious awe of him.

While the residents of Communipaw may be in awe of Pluto, the author is not. It soon becomes apparent that Pluto's function, like Sam's, is to lead the protagonist of the story, a Dutch boy named Yan Yost Vanderscamp, to his destiny—in this case, a fatal rendezvous with vengeful ghosts. It is Pluto who raises the boy up to be a pirate, "[prompting] him to all kinds of mischief . . . until the lad became the complete scapegrace of the village." But it is also Pluto who teaches Vanderscamp to navigate "all the bays, rivers, creeks, and inlets of the watery world around him." No thanks are given for this buccaneering education; instead, murder follows murder, and Pluto is only absolved from possible guilt when he, too, is discovered dead on Gibbet-Island.

How are readers to make sense of the stateless, haunted Pluto? He appears in Irving's canon more than a decade after New York finally declared a legal end to slavery—but several decades before New Jersey (where Communipaw, now Jersey City, is located) did the same. Gibbet-Island, which sits between New York and New Jersey in upper New York Bay, is known today as Ellis Island, the most famous gateway to America. Pluto may be free, or he may be a fugitive. The story doesn't turn on his status, nor does Irving care to settle the matter for the readership of the *Knickerbocker Magazine* (or in *Wolfert's Roost and Miscellanies,* in which the story was republished in 1855).

Whatever else it may be, "Guests from Gibbet-Island" is not intended as a political commentary on slavery. Nonetheless, the reader must be aware that Pluto's liminal identity is not of his own making but has been cruelly manufactured for him by the slaveholding society where he washes ashore. Like the other enslaved characters found at the edges of Irving's Knickerbocker stories, Pluto represents an untenable, inhumane existence. "This thing of darkness / I acknowledge mine," Shakespeare's Prospero says of Caliban. The American "thing of darkness" is the horror of slavery, whether Irving acknowledges it or not.

Among the "firsts" that are generally granted to Washington Irving are the creation of several cherished American myths (including Santa Claus and the quasi-deification of George Washington), along with the coining of a number of well-worn terms and phrases (the Almighty Dollar, Gotham). These contributions are all of a piece with what Michael Warner has described as Irving's "self-conscious production of quaintness." While Warner calls this a "trait" of Irving's style, I would suggest instead that it has, in fact, become a powerful, even dangerous industry, of a piece with Irving's reputation as a literary paterfamilias.[15]

This Knickerbocker industry, which has continued to function for two hundred years, has done an excellent job of obscuring a very different "first" from Irving's repertoire: the first short story writer to engage the subject of American slavery. We don't have to discard the author's stories in order to understand the common assumptions of his historical moment. As readers, we reject Irving's breezily offensive treatment of slavery and enslaved individuals, but as historians, we can read around his prejudices and shortcomings to find evidence of a past—and a community—many chose to ignore or erase.

As a storyteller, Washington Irving adopted a series of strategies and employed multiple personas and voices, some more reliable and original than others. It is notable that the first time Knickerbocker mentions "a string of incredible stories about New England witches—grisly ghosts—horses without heads—and hairbreadth scapes and bloody encounters among the Indians," it isn't he who is spinning the tale, or even Ichabod Crane. It's an elderly enslaved woman, sitting by a hearth, in the founding days of Dutch New Amsterdam. Now, there's an adaptation that deserves to be made.

NOTES

1. Edwin W. Bowen, "Washington Irving's Place in American Literature," *Sewanee Review* 14 (April 1906): 171–83.

2. See David N. Gellman, *Emancipating New York: The Politics of Slavery and Freedom, 1777–1827* (Baton Rouge: Louisiana State University Press, 2006); Shane White, *Somewhat More Independent: The End of Slavery in New York City, 1770–1810* (Athens: University of Georgia Press, 2004).

3. *Rivington's New-York Gazetteer and Universal Advertiser*, December 2, 1783. Digitized by the Freedom on the Move project, Cornell University.

4. Washington Irving, *A History of New York*, ed. Elizabeth L. Bradley (New York: Penguin, 2008), 42.

5. Irving, *History of New York*, 65–66.

6. Irving, *History of New York*, 346.

7. Joyce Goodfriend notes that the enslaved community in the "protective, family-oriented environment of Stuyvesant's *Bouwery* were not immune to the pressures of the marketplace." She goes on to quote a letter sent from Curaçao, apologizing to Governor Stuyvesant for the accidental purchase of "little children" who had been baptized by Judith Stuyvesant in New York. Goodfriend, "Black Families in New Netherland," in *A Beautiful and Fruitful Place*, ed. Nancy McClure Zeller, 147–56 (Albany, NY: The New Netherland Project, 1991), 149.

8. Irving's Knickerbocker does not say whether Ichabod was at all acquainted with another of Cotton Mather's productions, *The Negro Christianized*. In that pamphlet, Mather advances spiritual and economic arguments for the humane treatment of enslaved people, and

for their conversion to Christianity, exhorting, "Man, Thy Negro is thy Neighbour. T'were an Ignorance, unworthy of a Man, to imagine otherwise. Yea, if thou dost grant, That God hath made of one Blood, all Nations of men, he is thy Brother." Mather, *The Negro Christianized* (Boston: B. Green, 1706), 4. Mather does not advocate for emancipation.

9. Letter in Van Cortlandt Family Collection at Historic Hudson Valley library and archive, Pocantico Hills, New York, V. 1708.

10. The last adaptations of "The Legend of Sleepy Hollow" to depict the enslaved community were a 1922 silent film featuring Will Rogers and a 1934 Ubu Iwerks animated short. Neither film improves on the offensive stereotypes of Irving's original. By the time Disney produced *The Adventures of Ichabod and Mr. Toad*, in 1949, Black characters had been excised from the narrative completely.

11. For more on Brit, Will, and Susannah, see Jessie Serfilippi and Ian Mumpton, "Not Two Miles Apart: Brit, Will, and Love in the Face of Slavery," Schuyler Mansion State Historic Site, February 15, 2019, http://schuylermansion.blogspot.com/2019/02/not-two-miles-apart-brit-will-and-love.html.

12. Howard University's New York African Burial Ground Project has produced a fascinating and comprehensive multivolume report on the archeological findings at the African Burial Ground: *The New York African Burial Ground: Unearthing the African Presence in Colonial New York* (Washington, DC: Howard University Press in association with the General Services Administration, 2009). https://www.gsa.gov/about-us/regions/welcome-to-the-northeast-caribbean-region-2/about-region-2/african-burial-ground/introduction-to-african-burial-ground-final-reports.

13. Irving's source was "Gäste vom Galgen" [Guest from the Gallows], a tale in the Brothers Grimm, *Deutsche Sagen* (1816–1818).

14. "Guests from Gibbet-Island," *Knickerbocker* 14 (October 1839).

15. Michael Warner, "Irving's Posterity," *ELH* 67 (2000): 773–99.

A TOAST TO, AND DISTILLATION OF, RIP VAN WINKLE

TRACY HOFFMAN

> I should as soon expect to hear of Cinderella striking for higher wages, or of a speech on Women's Rights from Old Mother Hubbard, as to listen to a temperance lecture from Rip Van Winkle.
>
> —JOSEPH JEFFERSON III, *"Rip Van Winkle": The Autobiography of Joseph Jefferson*

In celebrating the two hundredth anniversary of the *Sketch Book* and its author's legacy, I present an esoteric argument: that Rip Van Winkle's lost twenty years, a consequence of a drinking session during a forest rendezvous, far from being a veiled critique of alcohol consumption, in fact holds overwhelmingly positive connotations. Pull up a bar stool, if you will, and hear me out.

Allow me first a small detour into personal memoir, long enough to set forth one of my favorite stories about Washington Irving. When I get nervous before giving a talk that is beyond the capacity of the small, cozy lecture hall where I typically teach, and as the current president of the Washington Irving Society,[1] I am often reminded of the famous occasion when Irving, celebrated though he was, faced a challenge in introducing Charles Dickens to a large New York crowd.

What does this have to do with the temperance movement that flourished during the heyday of the *Sketch Book?* If you'll just bear with me, I'll make it entirely germane.

In December 2017, after having read the Christmas stories from the *Sketch Book* in my Early American Literature class, student leaders of Sigma Tau Delta, our English honorary society at Baylor University, decided to throw a Washington Irving Christmas party. The Christmas sketches were read aloud throughout the day, and apple cider was served with other treats. The president of Sigma Tau Delta and I traveled to Yosemite National Park over the holiday break to attend the Bracebridge Dinner,[2] where we enjoyed an elegant, madrigal meal complete with the pageantry of the wassail bowl, along with peacock pie. The next year, the Washington Irving Society hosted a related panel, "Washington Irving and Christmas," at the American Literature Association conference in San Francisco. And for a lecture I prepared, the poster announcing the event included the following teaser:

- Why did Mary Shelley, the creator of *Frankenstein*, invite Irving to her tea party?
- Why would Sam Houston meet Irving for a drink?
- Was Rip Van Winkle an alcoholic?[3]

Teaching "Rip Van Winkle," as I do every semester, I like to pose that question "Is 'Rip Van Winkle' a story of temperance?" Students usually look at me sideways—abstinence from alcohol no longer takes that name—so I reword it: "Is 'Rip Van Winkle' an anti-drinking story?" At this point, they laugh. My rationale for asking the question has to do with assessing the story for any moral lesson that might be contained in it. In all the years of posing this question, never once have students, on first reading, thought Rip to be a drunk. Nonetheless, my consideration of temperance in "Rip Van Winkle" has been brewing, if you will, for more than a decade, particularly as I am routinely asked to toast Irving on his birthday each April 3.

"THAT DICKENS DINNER"

The speech Irving rued for longer than seems healthy took place in 1842, more than two decades after initial publication of the *Sketch Book*. He had settled into New York life after being abroad for seventeen years. At fifty-eight, probably bearing the restrained look captured in Mathew Brady's daguerreotype, Irving received papers naming him ambassador to Spain, a position he would hold from 1842 to 1846.[4] According to nephew Pierre M. Irving, his uncle knew about the appointment in advance. However, waiting on documents did not cause the inner turmoil Irving experienced on Friday, February 18, 1842. Instead, he was stressed about a speech he was scheduled to give that evening. By 7:00 p.m., hundreds of guests had gathered at the Carlton House for a dinner honoring Charles Dickens, who had recently arrived in America for the first time, and Irving was slated to introduce him. He bore some responsibility for all this, having corresponded with Dickens, encouraging him to visit the United States. Irving was the obvious choice to make the formal introduction to New York's literary crowd and beau monde.

Despite the hospitable sentiments exchanged with Dickens and the warm audience that greeted them both, Irving dreaded the moment. He was nervous. He felt shy and overanxious. He repeatedly told people beforehand, "I shall certainly break down." But he was prepared. Some sources suggest he had a lengthy script on hand. But break down he did. Receiving tremendous applause as he rose to speak, Irving lost his composure and forgot about his prepared speech. He blurted out a few sentences, skipped the speech, raised his glass, and finally managed a toast: "Charles Dickens, the guest of the nation." The audience drank to Dickens. As Irving returned to his chair, those within range could hear him say, "There! I told you I should break down, and I've done it."[5]

Apparently, the audience did not mind Irving's meltdown. Cheers greeted Dickens as he took center stage. Fortunately, the Englishman was eloquent and made up for Irving's lack. He had extremely kind words for Irving:

> There is in this city a gentleman who, at the reception of one of my books—I well remember it was *The Old Curiosity Shop* [1841]—wrote to me in England a letter so generous, so affectionate, and so manly, that

if I had written the book under every circumstance of disappointment, of discouragement, and difficulty, instead of the reverse, I should have found in the receipt of that letter my best and most happy reward. I answered him, and he answered me, and so we kept shaking hands autographically, as if no ocean rolled between us. I came here to this city eager to see him, and [laying his hand upon Irving's shoulder] here he sits! I need not tell you how happy and delighted I am to see him here to-night in this capacity.

Dickens continues with a quip, often repeated: "Washington Irving! Why, gentlemen, I don't go upstairs to bed two nights out of the seven . . . without taking Washington Irving under my arm; and when I don't take him, I take his own brother, Oliver Goldsmith."[6]

Oliver Goldsmith (1728–1774) embodied wit and waggishness for this generation, and it should not be lost on any lover of "Rip Van Winkle" that Goldsmith's origins, like Irving's, like Dickens's, were modest. A few years after the Dickens banquet, Irving would go on to write a Goldsmith biography that can only be called hagiographic.

As Dickens lavished praise on his tongue-tied host, he fell into a cadence:

Washington Irving—Diedrich Knickerbocker—Geoffrey Crayon—why, where can you go that they have not been there before? Is there an English farm—is there an English stream, an English city, or an English country-seat, where they have not been? . . . Go farther still: go to the Moorish Mountains, sparkling full in the moonlight . . . who has travelled among them before you . . . ? Who embarked with Columbus . . . traversed with him the dark and mighty ocean, leaped upon the land and planted there the flag of Spain, but this same man now sitting by my side?

Before he congratulates Irving for being selected as America's "representative in the country of Cervantes," Dickens brings the audience to the character of Rip: "And what pen but his has made Rip Van Winkle, playing nine-pins on that thundering afternoon, as much part and parcel of the Catskill Mountains as any tree or crag that they can boast?"[7]

The exchange between Dickens and Irving on this February night would later be referred to by Irving as "that Dickens dinner," an event he would rather forget but could not shake. The Irish poet Thomas Moore, who was, incidentally, responsible for bringing Irving and Mary Shelley together, wrote in his diary of the difficulty presented whenever Irving was scheduled to appear at a dinner where a toast might be expected of him: "He told me his mind was made up on the point; that the drinking his health, and the speech he would have to make in return, were more than he durst encounter; that he had broken down at the Dickens Dinner (of which he was chairman) in America, and obliged to stop short in the middle of his oration, which made him resolve not to encounter another such accident." As Moore pestered him to commit to a few—just a few—words, Irving demurred: "'That Dickens dinner,' which he always pronounced with strong emphasis, hammering all the time with his right arm, more suo [in his own manner],—'that Dickens dinner' still haunted his imagination."[8]

His failed attempt at a toast ended up being one of the most embarrassing moments of Washington Irving's life. Literary critic Nina Baym has called him "gregarious,"[9] and it would appear otherwise proper to assume that his social skills and movement in high-society circles—indeed, he was a seasoned diplomat—qualified him for eloquence. But such performances did not suit Irving's personality or come easily for him. This vulnerable, exposed moment, which so affected him, allows for deeper insight into his biography and texts.

BREAKING DOWN THE TEMPERANCE DEBATE

Irving's failed attempt at a toast, and Dickens's bright remarks in its wake, allow for a slight maneuver into the temperance debate to be extracted from "Rip Van Winkle." Revisiting the reception history of the tale, and other specifics of Irvingiana, spotlights the negative and positive consequences of alcohol in the celebrated story.

First, Rip labels the Dutch beverage container "a wicked flagon." But how much should we make of this? In fact, elsewhere in the *Sketch Book* Irving uses liquor not only optimistically but also symbolically, as a gesture toward peace. The wassail punch described in the Christmas stories sets forth strong textual evidence for alcohol having a positive purpose. The Christmas stories were so popular that they were repackaged in Christmas collections, inspiring a sequel to the *Sketch Book,* the composite known as *Bracebridge Hall,* that features the setting of the earlier Christmas stories.

Irving outlines Squire Bracebridge's prescription for the holiday mixture: "The butler brought in a huge silver vessel of rare and curious workmanship, which he placed before the squire. Its appearance was hailed with acclamation, being the Wassail Bowl, so renowned in Christmas festivity." It was the squire himself who prepared "the skilful mixture of which he particularly prided himself . . . , being composed of the richest and raciest wines, highly spiced and sweetened, with roasted apples bobbing about the surface."[10]

Irving's alter ego, Geoffrey Crayon, footnotes all kinds of helpful information about the wassail bowl and the squire's pride: "The old gentleman's whole countenance beamed with a serene look of indwelling delight, as he stirred this mighty bowl. Having raised it to his lips, with a hearty wish of merry Christmas to all present, he sent it brimming round the board, for every one to follow his example, according to the primitive style; pronouncing it, 'the ancient fountain of good feeling, where all hearts met together.'"

Of course, Washington Irving had as much to do with reviving Christmas traditions as Charles Dickens did. In the context Irving presents, the connection between Christmas and social drinking flows naturally. Intentionally or not, Irving's writing encouraged drinking rather than discouraged it.

The *New-York Evening Post* ran a glowing literary notice when the first installment of the *Sketch Book of Geoffrey Crayon* was published in June 1819: "This is a new production said to be from the elegant and racy pen of Washington Irving, Esq." In listing the five initial sketches, the reviewer summed up the last as "a sketch of low life in an inland Low-Dutch village, as it appeared some sixty or eighty years ago, and which is thrown into the form of a story, entitled 'Rip Van Winkle.'"[11] It is worth remarking on a word choice: *racy*, as an adjective, referred to "piquant, pungent, or flavourful" drink (generally of wine), as in the squire's "richest and raciest" concoction, the wassail bowl described above. The *Oxford English Dictionary* cites as one example of *racy* its use in a poem by Irving's friend Thomas Moore.

Amid typesetting issues—slurred speech?—that look like the work of one who has had too much to drink, the reviewer lavishes consistent praise on the collection: "The graces of style; the rich, warm tone of benevolent feeeling [sic]; the freely-flowing vein of hearty and happy humour, and the fine-eyed spirit of observation, sustained by an enlightened understanding, and regulated by a perception of fitness—a tact—wonderfully quick and sure, for wlnch [sic] Mr. Irving has been heretofore so much distinguisded [sic], are all exhibited anew in the *Sketch Book,* with freshened beauty and added charms."

The greatest praise is reserved for "Rip Van Winkle," which the writer calls "the master-piece," relishing its "comic spirit" and playful character. The tale, he says,

> seeks its gratification in the eccentricities of a simple, unrefined state of society, rather than in the vicious follies of artificial life; for the vividness and truth, with which Rip's character is drawn, and the state of society in the village where he lived, is depicted; and for the graceful ease with which it is told, the story of Rip Van Winkle has few competitors. There appears, also, to be a design to exhibit the contrast between the proverbial times, and the state of things subsequent to the American revolution.

Nothing here suggests behavioral problems emanating from tavern culture or Rip's notable lack of drive, which drink might otherwise occasion.

Initial reviews, like Dickens's assessment of "Rip Van Winkle" decades later, applaud the story's merits without reference to drink. Yet no early nineteenth-century reader would have failed to notice the effects of alcohol as a main ingredient in the plot. The scene is memorable, as Rip awakens from his twenty-year slumber. He feels "stiff in the joints," bemoaning his predicament by blaming the Dutch flagon that instigated his drowsy journey. "Oh! That flagon! That wicked flagon!" he laments. Rip's easygoing attitude is early established, for he's a fellow who prefers neither "white bread or brown."

As critical as he is toward his wife, Dame Van Winkle, whom he considers the source of his problems, in her absence he must point the finger at someone or some*thing* else. It isn't the Dutch bowlers who made the beverage available to him, either; he curses the drink. Moments later, he decides to redirect his verbal assaults toward his ghostly Dutch companions. By story's end, Rip's mind has shifted from blaming the liquor to being grateful for the life changes drink has provided him.

So, if Rip initially incriminates the alcohol for his troubles, there is no further temperance message to be had. Rip does not get "ripped," to summon forth the modern colloquialism; nor is he a "rip-roaring drunk." R.I.P. should remind the reader of the calming phrase "Rest in peace." For his tale ends with good spirits and no further tension. Another possible interpretation is that Rip has died and is born again—which makes the tale a conversion narrative, coinciding with the temperance movement's reform agenda.

Cushioning himself behind multiple narrators (Geoffrey Crayon, his traveling American narrator, and Diedrich Knickerbocker, the somewhat grumpy Dutch-American interloper in some of the stories), Washington Irving neither warns readers of the dangers of drinking nor promotes the temperance movement. Rip's creator, like his title character, had a "well-oiled disposition," carefully avoiding any political stance that could be considered staunch. He often satirized politics, but he avoided clear-cut positions on divisive matters. Negating any suggestion of a temperance position in "Rip Van Winkle," his "wicked flagon" is a sign of mixed blessings, an elixir for peace-seeking New Yorkers who drink in, and drink to, their Dutch roots. They indulge in the choice "Hollands" (how the brew is designated in Irving's tale), recognizing as well the unpleasant dregs of the past. America is meant to release its tumultuous past and to rest in peace for the sake of the Union.

The concoction Rip consumes contains a magical element. He overindulges, of course, and he resents his wife, but nothing supports the premise that one of Rip's constitution could become an alcoholic wife beater. So, is Rip Van Winkle a drunk? Hang on; we'll get there.

Irving wrote to entertain, and yes, to make money; he never wrote to press a moral agenda or put forward strong political statements. This was especially true in the *Sketch Book,* most of which he wrote while living in England, with the side aim of mending fences between England and its former colonies (relations were still rather strained at this time).

Only in recalling a "strange man with a keg of liquor," and believing he had been "dosed . . . with liquor," does Rip pronounce an opinion about drink—about the flagon in question, anyway. Away from prying eyes, he finds the brew tempting: "By degrees Rip's awe and apprehension subsided. He even ventured, when no eye was fixed upon him, to taste the beverage, which he found had much of the flavor of excellent Hollands." Rip knows his Hollands, which speaks to his predilection for drinking.

It's hard to ignore. Irving doubles down on Rip's inclination to drink: "He was naturally a thirsty soul and was soon tempted to repeat the draft. One taste provoked another; and he reiterated his visits to the flagon so often that at length his senses were overpowered, his eyes swam in his head, his head gradually declined, and he fell into a deep sleep." Once he awakens, and conveniently blames the alcohol, we glean that this is nothing new for Rip: "What excuse shall I make to Dame Van Winkle?" Amid confusion, "he now suspected that the grave roysters of the mountain had put a trick upon him, and having dosed him with liquor, had robbed him of his gun." Yet Irving would not have his reader believe that nothing would have befallen Rip if he had not imbibed. Irving is not arguing for teetotalism.

Joseph Jefferson III (1829–1905), the actor who toured the country and became famous for playing Rip Van Winkle on stage, thoroughly studied Rip's character. "Rip's sympathy with nature is always very keen, and he talks to the trees and his dog as if they were human," Jefferson writes in his memoir. "The fairy element in the play seems to be attached to it as the fairy element in *A Midsummer Night's Dream*. And because Rip is a fairy, he neither laughs nor eats in the fourth act." Critically, here is what the actor/playwright had to say about temperance in the play: "When they wanted me to reform at the end of the play, I said, 'No. Should Rip refuse the cup, the drama would become a temperance play; and I should as soon expect to hear of Cinderella striking for higher wages, or of a speech on Woman's Rights from Old Mother Hubbard, as to listen to a temperance lecture from Rip Van Winkle. It would take all the poetry completely out of it.'"[12] Joe Jefferson is forceful in his denial: any temperance message in the story would, in fact, "take the poetry out of it." One as temperate in his emotions as our simple, neighborly Rip (who already had been, in Irving's equally decisive words, "rendered pliant and malleable in the fiery furnace of domestic tribulation") required no further reduction in vigor.

Modern Irving scholars and biographers do not index alcohol use or the contemporaneous temperance issue in their books. Other issues arising from "Rip Van Winkle" have been given greater attention, particularly those that concern the main character's escapist persona. In his groundbreaking *Adrift in the Old World: The Psychological Pilgrimage of Washington Irving*, Jeffrey Rubin-Dorsky says that "the need for appropriate, contributory labor and, in opposition, the fantasy of escape from this burden were issues of uppermost importance to Irving's American audience" at this time. Rubin-Dorsky closely examines Irving's fears during his seventeen years in Europe, but alcohol does not enter the picture. Instead of following the drinking cycle, this critic concentrates on Rip's estrangement, which leads him to assume the role of village storyteller, much as Irving hopes his disappearance from New York will afford him the opportunity to return home with literary accolades where it mattered most—Great Britain and the Continent. In Rubin-Dorsky's analysis, "Rip Van Winkle weaves Irving's desire for a settled life (as chronicler) into the fabric of the story.... The *Sketch Book* demonstrates that, for Irving, authorship offers a possible compensation for the experience and alienation and loss."[13]

Other reasons exist that solidify the argument against temperance. First, Dame Van Winkle has a tongue that grows sharper with constant use, but she never mentions Rip's drinking. Second, as Irving introduces him, Rip "was a great favorite among all the good wives of the village, who, as usual with the amiable sex, took his part in all family squabbles and never failed whenever they talked those matters over in their evening gossipings, to lay all the blame on Dame Van Winkle." If Rip Van Winkle had been a drunk who mistreated his wife and children, then the encircling gossip would have alerted the "good wives" to his escapades and they would not have taken his side. Irving's is not an anti-drinking story, because Rip is better off in the end, without any need to change who he is or to adjust his behavior.

FEMINIST APPROACHES

Feminist approaches to temperance terminology in "Rip Van Winkle" provide reasons to question a stance against alcohol on Irving's part. In *The Feminization of American Culture,* Ann Douglas provides helpful biographical details, seeing Irving as a travel writer, nonchalantly touching on various subjects without much energy or gravity. She writes, "They [travel writers] made of apparently aimless wandering a vocation, a vocation which perforce always retained amateur rank. They emphasized the casualness of their journeys, the haphazardness of their impressions, the uncollated quality of their notes. They escaped censure because they did not take themselves seriously." What is more, the type Douglas describes "confessed to indolence," and certainly Crayon's observer status removes him from a too obvious judgmentalism.

To her unambiguous characterization of authorial nonchalance, Douglas notably adds, "They wished to be considered amateurs, even idlers, not men working hard to achieve their literary goals."[14]

We can prove her point by counting the number of times Irving invokes the word *idle* or *idleness* in the *Sketch Book*—twenty times. In "The Author's Account of Himself," on the very first pages of the volume, Irving/Crayon couples his "rambling propensity" with an admission to an "idle humor" that has led him from any more committed depiction of all that the world has placed before him. In "The Voyage" (from America to England), he quietly ponders "a distant sail," which then redirects his imagination to "another theme of idle speculation." At the end of the journey, while Crayon's busy shipmates are eagerly seeking out the faces they recognize on shore, "I alone was solitary and idle."

The idleness grows. In "Rip Van Winkle," Dame Van Winkle charges into an all-male "assemblage" and calls out even the indomitable Nicholas Vedder for "encouraging her husband in habits of idleness." As the story winds down, with his wife deceased, Rip is allowed to find peace as "one of the patriarchs of the village," "being arrived at that happy age when a man can be idle with impunity."

Carol Mattingly's *Well-Tempered Women* establishes possibilities for Dame Van Winkle's character. "Evidence of women's difficulty in coming to public voice after centuries of silence surfaces over and over in temperance women's rhetoric," Mattingly writes. "The difficulty for many women in uttering even one syllable in public presents a painful image of female voicelessness." It is in this context, she clarifies, that "the tremendous coming to voice" among temperance women in public meetings held real significance.[15]

Mattingly's concern for women who would speak up suits a feminist reading of Irving's Dame Van Winkle. She notes that modern scholars undervalue temperance women out of a politicized belief that the pursuit of gender coequality in the nineteenth century should be focused mainly on those "taking a more direct, aggressive approach."[16] Temperance was, in fact, a major thread alongside the dynamic efforts of Lucretia Mott, Elizabeth Cady Stanton, Paulina Kellogg Wright Davis, Amelia Bloomer, and their colleagues to critique gender inequities in society's most prominent institutions: state, church, and family. Mattingly's insight into the voiceless resonates through many episodes in Irving tales. His female characters are almost axiomatically comforting, accommodating figures, neither robust nor eager for notice.

In several of his writings, the late Robert A. Ferguson left scholars much to consider about the archetypal American tale. "Rip Van Winkle and the Generational Divide in American Culture" sets forth the argument that the anti-drinking theme is unavoidable. "The truth of the matter is that Rip has been an alcoholic on a 20-year binge, and many aspects of the story lend themselves to that explanation."[17] To underscore the point, Ferguson says that "the code words of drink and its consequences are everywhere," and gives as a rationale for the claim, "Studies of the use of alcohol in the United States calculate that consumption per capita reaches its highest point during the first third of the nineteenth century, the same years in which Irving wrote his important fiction, including 'Rip Van Winkle.'"[18]

Compelling as the statistic is, just because alcohol consumption was high at the time does not in any way prove that it was exclusively thought of in negative terms, or that Irving would have been concerned enough to cast drinking in that way. In fact, if people loved their liquor so much that tavern culture suffused U.S. cities and towns, it could as easily be argued that a decent percentage of early Americans thought of their beverages as restorative.

The 1810s and 1820s saw the dissemination of medical thinking on the correlation between alcohol abuse and economic instability. Intemperance and depravity were growing concerns, as Matthew Warner Osborn's scholarship reveals. The symptoms of alcohol-induced insanity were by then well known, and this only worsened as a result of the widespread Panic of 1819. But none of this was Irving's concern. Rip served as comic relief; he was not created to mount a temperance platform.[19]

NOTES

1. The Washington Irving Society falls under the umbrella of the American Literature Association. See www.washingtonirvingsociety.org.

2. See www.bracebridgedinners.com for more information on the Bracebridge Dinner, inspired by Washington Irving's Christmas stories. The madrigal dinner and pageant is held annually at Yosemite National Park, though it was canceled in 2020 and 2021, due to the COVID-19 pandemic. See also Curtis Armstrong, "An Actor's Reflections on the Theatrical Irving," in this volume.

3. My answers to the teaser questions are as follows: 1. Because she liked him. 2. They were relaxing together at Fort Gibson, in Oklahoma Territory. 3. No, based on textual evidence outlined below, Rip is not an alcoholic.

4. According to his private journals, Irving "had been commissioned on February 10, 1842, as envoy extraordinary and minister plenipotentiary to Spain; he accepted by letter on February 18, and Secretary of State Daniel Webster's initial full letter of instructions was sent to him on March 19." See Washington Irving, *Journals and Notebooks*, vol. 5, *1832–1859*, ed. Sue Fields Ross (Boston: Twayne, 1986), 269.

5. Andrew Burstein, *The Original Knickerbocker: The Life of Washington Irving* (New York: Basic Books, 2007), 297; Pierre M. Irving, *The Life and Letters of Washington Irving*, 4 vols. (New York: G. P. Putnam, 1862–1864), 3:164–66, 173, 182–85. Pierre M. Irving reprints statements made by President Felton of Harvard University upon the death of Washington Irving. Felton was an eyewitness to the speech.

6. "New York, February 18, 1842," in *The Speeches of Charles Dickens: 1841–1870*, ed. Richard Herne Shepherd (London: Chatto and Windus, 1906), 70–71.

7. "New York, February 18, 1842," 72–73.

8. P. M. Irving, *Life and Letters*, 3:198–201.

9. Nina Baym, *Feminism and American Literary History: Essays* (New Brunswick, NJ: Rutgers University Press, 1992), 89.

10. From "The Christmas Dinner," in Washington Irving, *The Sketch Book of Geoffrey Crayon, Gent.*, ed. Haskell Springer (Boston: Twayne, 1978).

11. "Literary Notice," *New-York Evening Post*, June 26, 1819. Note, too, that "sixty or eighty years ago" would have been 1739 to 1759, and as Rip wakes to find his village tavern named after "General Washington," the reviewer's math is suspect—twenty years after 1739 would have been sixteen years before Washington was even named a general. Rip could not have fallen asleep in the mountains before 1755.

12. Joseph Jefferson, *Rip Van Winkle as Played by Joseph Jefferson* (New York: Dodd, Mead and Company, 1893), 17.

13. Jeffrey Rubin-Dorsky, *Adrift in the Old World: The Psychological Pilgrimage of Washington Irving* (Chicago: University of Chicago Press, 1988), 104–11.

14. Ann Douglas, *The Feminization of American Culture* (New York: Knopf, 1977), 236–38. In assessing the sketch as a literary form, Douglas defines the type of writer Irving and his fellow traveling writers must have been. "The sketch is by definition short; part of the convention behind it is the assumption that it was produced at a sitting, even carelessly" (238). Irving's sketchy approach to these early stories suggests that they were meant to be lighthearted, not morally heavy-handed, on an issue such as temperance.

15. Carol Mattingly, *Well-Tempered Women: Nineteenth-Century Temperance Rhetoric* (Carbondale: Southern Illinois University Press, 1998), 5–6.

16. Mattingly, *Well-Tempered Women*, 21–22.

17. Robert A. Ferguson, "Rip Van Winkle and the Generational Divide in American Culture," *Early American Literature* 40 (2005): 529–44, at 531. See also Ferguson, "Does Nobody Here Know Rip Van Winkle?," in *Alone in America* (Cambridge, MA: Harvard University Press, 2013), 17–34.

18. Ferguson, "Rip Van Winkle and the Generational Divide," 532. Ferguson's assertion is backed up by the scholarship of W. J. Rohrbach, *The Alcoholic Republic: An American Tradition* (New York: Oxford University Press, 1979).

19. Matthew Warner Osborn, "A Detestable Shrine: Alcohol Abuse in Antebellum Philadelphia," *Journal of the Early Republic* 29 (Spring 2009): 101–32; Osborn, *Rum Maniacs: Alcoholic Insanity in the Early American Republic* (Chicago: University of Chicago Press, 2014). See also Michael P. Branch, "Rip Van Winkle's Wicked Flagon," *Nineteenth-Century Prose* 42 (2015): 31–39; and Ian R. Tyrrell, *Sobering Up: From Temperance to Prohibition in Antebellum America, 1800–1840* (Westport, CT: Greenwood, 1979).

THE REVOLUTIONARY WAR LIVES ON

ERIK WEISELBERG

Everyone knows that the Headless Horseman haunts Sleepy Hollow. But not everyone knows that a real-life event provided the historical horizon for Irving's fiction in his story "The Legend of Sleepy Hollow" (1820). Forty years earlier, at Tarrytown, the British spy Major John André was captured by John Paulding, Isaac Van Wart, and David Williams. From 1820 forward, the physical presence of material culture and historic sites maintained the association of Irving's frightful tale with the Revolutionary War episode that inspired it.

By the close of the twentieth century, however, Irving's richly historical text acquired a very different kind of cultural authority, having been supplanted by illustrated books, children's literature, feature films, and other commercialized adaptations. The original tale took on new life as a stripped-down, generic ghost story masquerading as Indigenous, premodern folklore. In short, the "Spirit of '76" that animated Irving's original tale was dispossessed by a pumpkin-wielding Headless Horseman at a Halloween party. We are left to ponder how it was that the region around Tarrytown became associated in the American calendar with Halloween rather than with Independence Day. What is lost and what is gained in the process of appropriation? And can competing testaments to a malleable historic memory be reconciled?

We are concerned here with a pair of factors: first, the nineteenth century's fascination with the ill-fated Major André and the legacy of the Revolutionary War; and second, the twentieth century's twin obsessions with entertainment and consumerism. The rise of Halloween in the late nineteenth century as an amalgamation of Indigenous and imported folk traditions, stripped of its parochial and rowdy elements, produced a children-centered holiday consistent with Victorian-era morality. Halloween's repurposing allowed a somewhat more innocuous Headless Horseman to ride freely through the popular imagination, no longer bound to the time and place that constrained it in Irving's text. Yet even with its loss of any association with the Revolutionary War, the story retained its layers of meaning. That is, it implicitly calls up history's ongoing concern with time-centered memory and historical change. By examining the tale's different receptions by residents of the Tarrytown region from 1820 to 2020, we are able to appreciate the different ways that texts get mapped onto the cultural landscape.

THE MEMORABLE MAJOR ANDRÉ

"The Legend of Sleepy Hollow" is revealing on a number of levels. It recalls actual terror in the War for Independence and themes of self-determination and independence that speak to Irving's personal life at the time he was fashioning the *Sketch Book*. While the story is familiar, it is important to note that its author was living abroad when he set the tale in a part of New York he knew from his younger years, where his friendship with fellow writer James Kirke Paulding (whose first cousin John is integral to the story) developed along with his own interest in writing.

"The Legend" unfolds, then, outside the village of Tarrytown, along the Hudson River in Westchester County. Brom Bones, a rustic lad of Dutch extraction in the village of Sleepy Hollow, aims to keep the interloper, Connecticut Yankee Ichabod Crane, from despoiling the village's quiet isolation and stealing its material prosperity, as symbolized by Katrina Van Tassel, daughter of the bountiful farmer Baltus Van Tassel. To energize this literary battle over Katrina and her attendant bounty, Irving evokes multiple time constructs from the history of the region, and in particular the several English invasions into the Dutch Hudson Valley. He sets the story around the year 1790, at the beginning of what was then called a "Yankee invasion"—indeed, the influx of New Englanders lasted from the end of the Revolutionary War, in 1783, to 1850, as a host of Anglo-Americans migrated west, intermarried, and settled among the primarily Dutch-descended inhabitants of the Hudson Valley region.[1]

In 1790, memories of the Revolutionary War were fresh in the minds of the inhabitants, some of whom (in Irving's tale) give exaggerated accounts of their wartime experiences. As the "neutral ground" or no-man's-land between British forces headquartered in New York City and the Continental Army positions in the Hudson Highlands, Westchester County became a deadly cauldron of civil war and irregular warfare from 1776 to 1783. Military patrols and roving bands of marauders conducted foraging expeditions, took part in vicious skirmishes, and carried out cold-blooded raids.

Irving explicitly identifies Ichabod Crane's plight with that of Major John André, the British spy caught carrying plans of the American fortress at West Point, which were given to him by the traitor Benedict Arnold. André was captured by the three American militiamen on September 23, 1780.[2] Ichabod and André are both educated Englishmen traveling alone in the Dutch Hudson Valley, as interlopers in an alien and hostile climate, scheming to take territory and resources from an Indigenous population that wishes to remain undisturbed in its enjoyment of the natural bounty. Ichabod's mock tragedy mirrors that of André, step for step, including his capture near the giant whitewood, or tulip tree, which is "universally known," Irving tells readers, "by the name of Major André's tree." Here, as well, we reencounter the swamp and brook where at the outbreak of hostilities patriotic men mustered for the local militia.[3]

Traveling alone on horseback near the same giant tree, both interlopers—André and Ichabod—encountered country lads of Dutch descent who were dressed as Hessians and who proved their undoing. André was captured by John Paulding, a militiaman whose Hessian jacket had been acquired in an escape from a British prison a few days prior; Paulding thus deceived André into letting down his guard. Similarly, Ichabod is unnerved and undone by

Brom Bones, who has taken on the appearance of a Hessian horseman, said to be "the ghost of a Hessian trooper, whose head had been carried away by a cannon-ball, in some nameless battle during the Revolutionary War."

In this moment of decision amid fright, Irving evokes the terror in the American psyche about Hessian troops, who were depicted in American propaganda as savages bent on enslaving Americans. The Declaration of Independence characterizes their goal as one of spreading "death, desolation and tyranny." For a large part of the war, Hessian forces under the command of General Wilhelm von Knyphausen protected British-held New York City and played an outsize role in Westchester County to the north. Whether this is true or not, the Hessians had a reputation among American rebels for their bloodthirsty ways. Irving used this perception to advantage in adding intensity to his historically informed story.[4]

The *Sketch Book of Geoffrey Crayon* constituted Washington Irving's personal declaration of independence, his attempt to break out of his financial and social dependence on his family and to pursue his own path to material and psychological happiness as a professional writer. In October 1818, after having just completed "Rip Van Winkle," he rejected an offer arranged by his brothers to take up a position, with a comfortable salary, as a clerk in the Navy Department. He'd been in England since 1815 and would not return to New York until 1832.[5]

Staying with his sister Sarah and her husband, Henry Van Wart, in Birmingham, in 1818, Irving and his host, close in age, sat recalling memories of their earlier years at Tarrytown. This was when Irving began to outline "The Legend of Sleepy Hollow." He borrowed elements from European folk tales, which included headless horsemen and midnight rides, but returned in his mind to places he had been introduced to in his midteens, in 1798, when his parents sent him off to the healthful spot of Tarrytown to escape a yellow fever epidemic that was ravaging their neighborhood in lower Manhattan.[6]

In Tarrytown, Irving stayed with James Kirke Paulding, five years his elder, whose sister Julia had married Irving's eldest brother, William, in 1793. Together, the future authors ranged about the nearby woods. In Birmingham, Irving lodged with Henry Van Wart, whose uncle was Isaac Van Wart. As John Paulding was James's first cousin, through his personal relationships with separate genealogical lines, Washington Irving had direct knowledge about the wartime experiences of two of the three captors of André.[7]

We have, in this way, a pretty good idea of the real world that Washington Irving drew upon in his adaptation. During the nineteenth century, residents of Tarrytown, and Americans more broadly, maintained the association he constructed between the Revolutionary War and "The Legend of Sleepy Hollow." Across the nation, memories of the war were kept alive by such closely followed events as the Marquis de Lafayette's visit to the United States in 1824 and 1825, fiftieth anniversary commemorations of independence in 1826, and fifty years later, the 1876 centennial. In the Hudson Valley, as was true across the country in the 1820s, veterans maintained a living link with the Revolution, telling war stories on back porches, delivering Fourth of July orations, and petitioning the government for well-deserved pensions. Their visibility, as David Schuyler writes, "provided physical and psychological continuity with the past."[8]

In the immediate post-Revolutionary years, natural features served as monuments, including the giant tulip tree that Tarrytown residents called André's Tree, near which the spy was captured. On July 31, 1801, when news of the death of Benedict Arnold arrived in Tarrytown, old veterans sitting on a stoop became animated in recalling wartime exploits. All of a sudden, a storm broke and lightning struck the celebrated tree, causing a raging fire that blazed some twelve or fifteen feet up from the roots. The *American Citizen* reported, "Its destruction has occasioned general regret throughout the surrounding country, and its fragments have been carefully collected and preserved by the inhabitants."[9]

Attempts in the 1820s and 1830s to erect a more permanent monument to the captors failed repeatedly. This was due in part to growing public sentiment against the three men after their failed bid in 1816 to have their individual pensions raised. The petition was orchestrated by captor John Paulding and drew public attention to both the Revolutionary War and questions of patriotism. Benjamin Tallmadge, an intelligence officer assigned to guard André, who went on to serve as a congressman from 1800 to 1816, led the fight against the petition. He denounced John Paulding in Congress as a self-serving fraud, and the others as highway robbers. Tallmadge's objections carried the day, as Congress voted 80 to 53 against an increase in the pensions, reasoning that Paulding's service had been routine and not exemplary.[10]

In subsequent years, Paulding's family came to his defense. In 1818, James Kirke Paulding wrote a poem called "The Backwoodsman," in which he praised his cousin and criticized André. Memorials were later erected at the captors' grave sites in Westchester County, one in 1827 by citizens of New York City to honor John Paulding, and another in 1829 by citizens of Westchester to honor Isaac Van Wart.[11] As veterans disappeared and physical relics of the Revolutionary War era were displaced during the era of industrialization and urbanization, Hudson Valley residents began to encourage the creation of more permanent monuments to honor their region's history.[12]

The dedication of a monument to the captors at Tarrytown in 1853 offered a more permanent symbol to keep alive the memories, emotions, and physical locations of the Revolutionary War that Irving had mobilized to such great effect in "The Legend of Sleepy Hollow." The Monument Association to the Captors of Major André included descendants of John Paulding and other Dutch patriot veterans. They were assisted in locating the site of the capture by Captain John Romer, the last Westchester County survivor of the Revolution and the only person then living to have seen André in person. The 1853 monument, from stone quarried and dressed at nearby Sing Sing prison, still stands.[13]

In the final decade of his life, James Kirke Paulding wrote the monument's inscription, which seemed addressed to the remaining skeptics: "The people of Westchester County have erected this Monument, as well to commemorate a great Event, as to testify their high estimation of that Integrity and Patriotism which, rejecting every temptation, rescued the United States from most imminent peril by baffling the arts of a Spy and the plots of a Traitor." On July 4, 1853, local resident James Alexander Hamilton, a son of Alexander Hamilton, laid the cornerstone. And on October 7 of that year, Governor Horatio Seymour dedicated the monument before a crowd of fifty thousand spectators.[14]

The dedication of the Captors' Monument presented Tarrytown residents with an opportunity to renegotiate the boundaries of patriotism, which had been besmirched by those who, like Congressman Tallmadge, had belittled the militiamen's contributions. Notably, too, with the placement of the cornerstone on July 4 and the ceremony on October 7, Captors' Monument celebrations deliberately linked the Revolutionary War with autumn, simultaneously celebrating Independence Day and André's capture. And they did so in the presence of Washington Irving, whose residency at nearby Sunnyside from 1835 until his death in 1859 further solidified the association of the history of the region with his literary fictions.[15]

In 1876, a nation seeking common ground after the Civil War was eager to make alliances with the English-speaking world. Enough Americans embraced the Revolutionary War as a common, unifying event that John André became an increasingly sympathetic figure. Cyrus W. Field, a resident of the Ardsley neighborhood in Irvington, New York, and a noted Anglophile who had financed the transatlantic cable, sponsored the construction of a monument to André at the site of his execution, across the Hudson River in Tappan, New York. On October 2, 1879, the anniversary of André's execution, the seven-and-a-half-foot granite block was unveiled. While some Tappan residents felt the monument would help advertise the place and bring benefits to their village, only three or four residents attended the ceremony, and many villagers closed their doors and shutters in protest.[16]

Partly in response to Field, and partly due to plans already under way for the centennial of the capture, in 1880 the Monument Association of Tarrytown updated the Captors' Monument, receiving $9,000 in donations from 270 citizens. A series of alterations were designed to make the monument less of a funerary memorial and more of an interpretive installation, including most noticeably the replacement of the gravestone-like obelisk shaft with a bronze statue of John Paulding, clad in accurate dress and with a face modeled from an original portrait. The residents of Tarrytown made their point emphatically: theirs was not a memorial to André but a monument to his captors.[17]

At the celebration dedicating the expanded monument on September 23, 1880, a crowd of seventy thousand gathered to hear addresses by former New York governor Samuel J. Tilden and others. Representatives of neighboring communities were invited, including even Cyrus W. Field. Neighborhood houses were decorated with bunting, and church bells rang continually. At 10:00 a.m., the hour of André's capture, an artillery salute was responded to by warships on the nearby Hudson River. Reverend Alexander Van Wart, son of André captor Isaac Van Wart, spoke a prayer, followed by military processions and a chorus of five hundred. At sunset, artillery salutes reverberated once again, capped off by fireworks.[18]

As part of the centennial celebrations, a twenty-four-page souvenir booklet was issued, with a hand-colored folding map of Tarrytown as it appeared "one hundred years ago." It showed sites visited by both the real Major André and the fictional Ichabod Crane, merging history and fantasy, just as Irving had done in "The Legend of Sleepy Hollow." A fixation with all things André continued through the end of the century.[19]

In the next decade, the Revolutionary Soldiers' Monument was dedicated at the Sleepy Hollow Cemetery—a landscape inviting visitors and that Irving himself had helped to establish. As early as 1838, he had conceived the spot where he wished to rebury his parents and deceased siblings, and where he himself lies, amid winding hills near the Old Dutch Burying Ground. Incorporated in 1849 as the Tarrytown Cemetery, it did not offi-

Monument to the captors of John André, Patriots Park, Tarrytown, NY. The monument pictured dates to 1880. The statue depicts militiaman John Paulding, a principal in the capture of the British spy, who acquired a Hessian jacket while escaping from a British prison a few days earlier. Relatedly, Ichabod Crane is unnerved and undone by Brom Bones, who takes on the frightful appearance of the "ghost of a Hessian trooper, whose head had been carried away by a cannon-ball, in some nameless battle during the Revolutionary War." Washington Irving was present at the 1853 dedication of the first Captors' Monument. Photograph by Erik Weiselberg, 2021.

cially become Sleepy Hollow Cemetery (the name Irving proposed) until 1864, nearly five years after his death. In 1894, within sight of Irving's grave, on the site of a former Revolutionary War redoubt where actual veterans were buried and where Irving's fictional horseman returns every evening, the Soldiers' Monument went up.[20]

In *The Crisis of the Revolution: Being the Story of Arnold and André* (1899), William Abbatt, an amateur historian and publisher who settled in Tarrytown, obsessively marked out every step of André's ill-fated journey, identifying houses where the doomed man lodged, chairs in which he sat, windows out of which he peered, and the spring at which he watered his horse. Ghost lore continued to echo through the region: in the late nineteenth century, residents claimed to have seen André's ghost on still autumn nights, riding a madly galloping horse but going no farther south than the immense old tulip tree. While the ghost took the appearance of Irving's Headless Horseman, it was explicitly identified by locals not as one of Irving's fictions but as John André.[21]

SLEEPY HALLOWEEN

As the twentieth century opened, the focus of public awareness shifted away from Major André, loyalty, and betrayal. Henceforth, the Headless Horseman of Irving's fiction would loom as the most noteworthy symbol of the area, an embodiment of modern entertainment and consumerism.

Despite the story's Revolution-era setting and its allusive references to the capture of André, "The Legend of Sleepy Hollow" became more firmly associated with Halloween than with any celebratory ritual linked to the War for Independence. As Halloween became a national holiday geared toward children, illustrated children's books and other popular adaptations abridged and altered Irving's original text, frequently removing references to historical precedents and local traditions. Walt Disney's *Adventures of Ichabod and Mr. Toad* (1949), an animated romantic comedy narrated by Bing Crosby, featured musical numbers that completely ignored the Revolutionary War context; the social event at Van Tassel's estate became a Halloween party, with jack-o'-lanterns and ghost stories. Jack-o'-lanterns reflected a changing demographic, with the rush of Irish immigration over the course of the nineteenth century. In Ireland, carved turnips or beets were made into a lantern to hold a candle and keep the devil away; Irish immigrants used the native American pumpkin instead.[22]

This is how Irving's "Legend" became abstracted from its particular historical and material referents, encouraging audiences to forget Irving's authorial hand and disregard the story's historical context. In Chicago, the *Day Book* for October 25, 1912, announced, "'The Legend of Sleepy Hollow' amounts to 'A Good Story for Hallowe'en Parties.'"[23]

On the ground in Tarrytown, the local landmarks that appeared in Irving's tale became less important to audiences interested in a good ghost story. The wooden bridge crossing the Pocantico River near the Old Dutch Church, made famous in Irving's tale, had already been replaced twice before a stone one, built in 1912, was placed farther downstream to allow for a wider, straighter, safer roadway. Local resident William Rockefeller gifted the bridge under the condition that it be called the Washington Irving Memorial Bridge, yet the plaque today reads "Sleepy Hollow Bridge." A New York State educational road sign (probably dating to the 1960s) boldly declares it "Headless Horseman Bridge," erroneously claiming that Ichabod Crane crossed the stream at that exact spot. By the mid-twentieth century, the Headless Horseman had lost not only his head but also his Hessian identity. Historical allusions no longer figured in celebratory lore.[24]

As "The Legend of Sleepy Hollow" became relegated to the domain of entertainment, the locale assumed a working-class identity as the community of North Tarrytown. General Motors built an automobile assembly plant in North Tarrytown that turned out aircraft parts during World War II. In the postwar years it became the economic backbone of the village, producing Chevrolet automobiles in the 1970s and 1980s. But in 1995, when the plant announced that it would cease operations, residents of North Tarrytown sought a new identity and economic basis (as well as an end to misallocated federal tax dollars that had mistakenly gone to Tarrytown) by changing the village name to Sleepy Hollow. Washington Irving's tale figured prominently among the arguments offered by proponents for the name change. The *Tarrytown Daily News* acknowledged that the village had dual legacies: in the twentieth century, North Tarrytown "depended on the broad shoulders and calloused hands of working men and women—not the

Headless Horseman Bridge. "Over a deep black part of the stream, not far from the church, was formerly thrown a wooden bridge." In "The Legend of Sleepy Hollow," Irving drew upon scenes he knew well, yet this old, undated photograph of the wooden bridge—despite being known as the "Headless Horseman Bridge"—depicts a scene slightly downstream from the site where Irving's characters crossed. Courtesy of Westchester County Historical Society.

spindly frame of Irving's fictional schoolmaster, Ichabod Crane," but the paper also pointed out that "it's also a village rich in history, where Irving's scary headless horseman forever roams the American imagination."[25]

Sleepy Hollow's connections with art and history did not belong exclusively to Irving any longer. For many of the area's residents, the Disney film adaptation loomed as large as Irving's text. As one recalled, "How proud we were just after World War II when Walt Disney's beloved cartoon version danced on silver screens across America, with Bing Crosby narrating!" Not all embraced the new consumerism, however. The village historian, Theodore Hutchinson, saw the name Sleepy Hollow as a literary construction unrelated to historical reality, and he feared that "a new name could give the workaday village the synthetic aura of a Disneyland." With a sardonic touch, Hutchinson predicted the appearance of "hole-in-the-wall souvenir shops featuring plastic models of the headless horseman lovingly rendered by some artist in Hong Kong." Nonetheless, the resolution passed on December 11, 1996.[26]

Sleepy Hollow, previously just a fiction, was now real. But what heritage had the locals chosen? Each voter probably had his or her own reasons—some historical, some literary, some commercial—for their embrace of the name. The fractious process recalled both Tarrytown's contested terrain during the Revolutionary War and the fictional feud between Brom Bones and Ichabod Crane; it also echoed the drive toward self-determination and financial independence that the author of the tale himself undertook in writing "The Legend of Sleepy Hollow" in the first place. Yet instead of the ghost of a Hessian trooper, with its evocation of the terrors of the Revolutionary War, the Headless Horseman of Sleepy Hollow became the patron saint of the real village of Sleepy Hollow and of annual Halloween celebrations.

Returning, then, to the author of the *Sketch Book,* the volume in which "The Legend" is unveiled, we can recognize Irving's ability to mobilize time constructs that give the tale its adaptability. Over two centuries, very different audiences have mobilized its inner "spirit" to meet contemporary needs. What might Irving think of all this? His legend was no history lesson. The memory of John André's capture by John Paulding concealed as a Hessian in the no-man's-land appears in "The Legend" not for historical accuracy but strictly as a vehicle for Irving to tell a good yarn. As Geoffrey Crayon notes in "Stratford-on-Avon," another essay in the *Sketch Book,* "What is it to us whether these stories be true or false, so long as we can persuade ourselves into the belief of them and enjoy all the charm of the reality?"[27]

For Irving, as for successive fans of his tale, the act of storytelling has served as the ultimate form of resistance against the disruptions of historical change. In twenty-first-century Sleepy Hollow, residents and visitors alike appreciate the sight of the Headless Horseman sculpture, positioned along Broadway since 2006, chasing Ichabod without rest. And while Fox Television's *Sleepy Hollow* (2013) fantastically portrayed the Headless Horseman as one of the four horsemen of the Apocalypse, it also reintegrated the Revolutionary War history that was absent in the Disney film and other adaptations. Visitors to Sleepy Hollow come not only for Halloween events but also to visit Irving's grave site, just down the hill from the 1894 Revolutionary Soldiers' Monument overlooking ancient veterans' graves in the burial ground of the Old Dutch Church.

Between his arrival at the seventeenth-century Dutch cottage, his Sunnyside home, in 1835, and his death twenty-four years later, Washington Irving returned often to meanings yet to be extracted from the Revolutionary War. In *Wolfert's Roost* (1855), a composite of sketches he wrote for the *Knickerbocker Magazine,* he produced a mock history of Sunnyside. This included a humorous account of its Revolution-era occupant Jacob Van Tassel—a real person, a patriot militiaman born in 1744—who survived long enough that Irving met with him in 1836 at his latter-day home at 395 Greenwich Street in Manhattan.[28]

In his final years, Irving was forced by age and infirmity to choose between working on his moneymaking, crowd-pleasing Knickerbocker escapades or a historical biography of his namesake, George Washington. He chose the latter. With the help of his nephew Pierre, Irving addressed himself single-mindedly to what he regarded as the ultimate creation of his career, a five-volume *Life of George Washington* (1855–1859). Irving chose, he said, to "depict the heroes of Seventy-Six as they really were—men in cocked hats, regimental coats, and breeches, and not classical warriors, in shining armor and flowing mantles, with brows bound with laurel, and truncheons in their hands."[29]

While working on volume 2 of the *Life of Washington* in September 1855, Irving told Pierre, "I live only in the Revolution . . . I have no other existence now—can think of nothing else." His ambitious biography was well received by the nation's premier scholars as a serious work of scholarship. He followed in the tradition of Jared Sparks, who had begun collecting and reassembling Washington's wartime correspondence in the 1830s, and George Bancroft, son of a minuteman and the author of a ten-volume *History of the United States*. Both of these historians approved of Irving's work.[30]

The septuagenarian author spent time in State Department archives doing research, and he even utilized the journals of the Continental Congress. As a result, nearly half of his Washington biography covers the Revolutionary War years. Volume 4 contains an extended treatment of the capture of John André by John Paulding, Isaac Van Wart, and David Williams. It includes precise language from the lips of Paulding. Notably absent from Irving's final production, however, are the fictional figures Ichabod Crane, Brom Bones, and the Headless Horseman.[31]

NOTES

1. David Maldwyn Ellis, "The Yankee Invasion of New York, 1783–1850," *New York History* 32, no. 1 (January 1951): 3–17. Irving's Knickerbocker writings, beginning with *A History of New-York* (1809), depicted the progressive loss of a golden age, regularly personified in Irving's writings by the ahistoric, sleepy Dutch of the Hudson Valley. In doing so, Irving utilized the three English invasions that impose upon his comical and entertaining Dutch characters: the takeover of New Amsterdam in 1664 in *A History of New-York*, the Revolutionary War (1776–1783) in "Rip Van Winkle" and "The Legend of Sleepy Hollow," and the Yankee invasion of the 1790s in "The Legend." The "brave boys of Tarry Town and Sleepy Hollow" first defended the Dutch village from English interlopers in *A History of New-York*. See Washington Irving, *A History of New-York*, ed. Michael L. Black and Nancy B. Black, in *The Complete Works of Washington Irving* (Boston: Twayne, 1978), 278.

2. In a misdirection or mischaracterization typical of Irving's public explanations of his literary works, he claimed in a letter to his brother Ebenezer, "The story is a mere whimsical band to connect descriptions of scenery, customs, manners, &c." Washington Irving to Ebenezer Irving, December 29, 1819, in *Letters*, vol. 1, *1802–1823*, ed. Ralph M. Aderman, Herbert L. Kleinfeld, and Jenifer S. Banks, 572–73, in *The Complete Works of Washington Irving* (Boston: Twayne, 1978). Also in Pierre M. Irving, *The Life and Letters of Washington Irving*, 4 vols. (New York: G. P. Putnam, 1862–1864), 1:448. Far from a "mere whimsical band," however, the text is an allusive remapping of André's experience in the no-man's-land.

3. Marcius D. Raymond, *Souvenir of the Revolutionary Soldiers' Monument, Dedication at Tarrytown, NY, October 19th, 1894* (Tarrytown, NY, 1894), 87–88; Amos C. Requa, *The Family of Requa, 1678–1898*, part 2 (Peekskill, NY, 1898), 52. In "The Legend," the fictional narrator, Knickerbocker, explicitly reports that the tree "was connected with the tragical story of the unfortunate André, who had been taken prisoner hard by. . . . It was at this identical spot that the unfortunate André was captured, and under the covert of those chestnuts and vines were the sturdy yeomen concealed who surprised him." The tree stood literally in the middle of the road, rose more than one hundred feet high, and measured more than twenty-six feet around the base with a crown of 106 feet in diameter. Bolton says the "stem" was forty-one feet in length. Robert Bolton Jr., *A History of the County of Westchester*, 2 vols. (New York: Alexander S. Gould, 1848), 1:229; Henry John Steiner, "André's Tree—The Vanished Landmark," in *Sleepy Hollow Stories* (Sleepy Hollow, NY: Milestone Productions, 2020), 1–5.

4. Hessians in the Revolutionary War were not mercenaries (individual soldiers selling their services for hire) but auxiliaries (contracted troops purchased by the British crown from German princes). Of the roughly thirty thousand Hessian soldiers in service to the British crown, most came from the principality of Hesse-Kassel (16,992), although others came from Braunschweig (5,723), Hesse-Hanau (2,422), Ansbach-Bayreuth (2,353), Waldeck (1,225), and Anhalt-Zerbst (1,152). Dietmar Kügler, *Die Deutschen Truppen im Amerikanischen Unabhängigkeitskrieg, 1775–1783* (Stuttgart: Mortorbuch Verlag, 1980), 158. See also Edward Lowell, *The Hessians, and Other German Auxiliaries of Great Britain in the Revolutionary War* (New York: Harper and Brothers, 1884).

Hessian soldiers, loyal to their hereditary princes, likely believed that it was the British king's divine right to force his subjects into submission. They admired the peace and prosperity of the farms they saw in America, and after the war as many as 3,500 deserted or returned to settle. See Robert A. Selig, "Hessian Savages, Frog-Eating Frenchmen, and Virtuous Americans," in *The American Revolution: A World War*, ed. David K. Allison and Larrie D. Ferreiro, 170–86 (Washington, DC: Smithsonian Books, 2018). On American perceptions of Hessians, see Andrew Burstein, *The Original Knickerbocker: The Life of Washington Irving* (New York: Basic Books, 2007), 144–45. For a heartfelt description of empathy felt by one American soldier for the fate of his Hessian adversaries, see Joseph Plumb Martin, *A Narrative of A Revolutionary Soldier* (New York: Signet Classics, 2010), 116–17.

5. William Irving to Washington Irving, October 24, 1818, in Stanley T. Williams, *Life of Washington Irving*, 2 vols. (NY: Oxford University Press, 1935), 1:170–71.

6. According to Irving's nephew and biographer, Pierre Munroe Irving, on that evening in Birmingham, Irving and Van Wart "touched upon a waggish fiction of one Brom Bones, a wild blade, who professed to fear nothing, and boasted of having once met the devil on a return from a nocturnal frolic, and run a race with him for a bowl of milk punch." P. M. Irving, *Life and Letters*, 1:448. Though the story was outlined in Birmingham, Irving probably did not work on the manuscript itself until after October 28, 1819. See also Irving, *Letters*, 1:564; Gary Denis, *Sleepy Hollow: Birth of the Legend* (Patuxent River, MD: Gary Denis, 2015), 89–90.

7. John Paulding's ancestors came from the Netherlands at about the time the Dutch surrendered New Amsterdam to the British in 1664. James Kirke Paulding's father, William Paulding, was a member of the Provincial Congress, appointed on August 10, 1776, to be commissary of the militia and charged with raising troops in the vicinity. In 1767, William Paulding moved to Tarrytown, where he built a large frame structure at the corner of Franklin and White Streets, within three minutes' walk of a cove on the east bank of the Hudson River. Presumably, this is where Irving stayed in 1798. See Ralph M. Alderman and Wayne R. Kime, *Advocate for America: The Life of James Kirke Paulding* (Selingsgrove, PA: Susquehanna University Press, 2003), 21–25; Ernest F. Griffin, *Westchester County and Its People* (New York: Lewis Historical Publishing, 1946), 1:345; Wally Buxton, "Influential William Paulding Shaped Area History; Aided Patriots' Cause," in folder "Houses—Tarrytown, Misc. & North Tarrytown," Historical Society of Sleepy Hollow and Tarrytown; Edgar Mayhew Bacon, *Chronicles of Tarrytown and Sleepy Hollow* (New York: G. P. Putnam's Sons, 1897), 128; and J. Thomas Scharf, *History of Westchester County*, 2 vols. (Philadelphia: L. E. Preston, 1886), 2:265–66.

Henry Van Wart, Irving's brother-in-law, married Irving's sister Sarah when he worked for her father at the family hardware firm of Irving & Smith in Manhattan. Henry Van Wart's uncle on his mother's side was Samuel Youngs, who served as a guide during the war and later was a schoolteacher; some commentators have even suggested that he served as a model for Irving's Ichabod Crane character. The house of Joseph Youngs, father of Samuel and Mary, served as a patriot outpost, which was burned by British and Loyalist forces on February 3, 1780.

8. On the significance of the year 1826, see Andrew Burstein, *America's Jubilee* (New York: Knopf, 2001); and David Schuyler, *Sanctified Landscape: Writers, Artists, and the Hudson River Valley, 1820–1909* (Ithaca, NY: Cornell University Press, 2012), 100–101. Lieutenant Joseph Requa, a member of the Upper Philipsburgh Associated Company of Militia, drawn from the area just south of Tarrytown Company, served at the Battle of White Plains. Into his seventies, he fondly recalled the war at family gatherings, and "it was customary for his neighbors on the Fourth of July to come at sunrise in front of his house and salute him." Raymond, *Souvenir*, 145.

9. *American Citizen*, August 25, 1801, quoted in John A. Todd, "Greenburgh," in Scharf, *History of Westchester County*, 2:205 note 1. See also Bolton, *History of the County of Westchester*, 1:229–30; Bacon, *Chronicles of Tarrytown and Sleepy Hollow*, 103–5.

10. Robert E. Cray Jr., "Major John André and the Three Captors: Class Dynamics and Revolutionary Memory Wars in the Early Republic, 1780–1831," *Journal of the Early Republic* 17, no. 3 (Autumn 1997): 371–97; Harold Drimmer, "Major Andre's Captors: The Changing Perspective of History," *Westchester Historian* 75, no. 2 (Spring 1999): 50–55; Philip B. Secor, *Patriot John: The Man Who Saved America* (Westminster, MD: Heritage Books, 2005); *Annals of Congress*, 1817, 30:474–75.

11. William Paulding Jr., brother of James Kirke Paulding and mayor of New York, delivered the dedicatory address at the John Paulding dedication. Bolton, *History of the County*

of Westchester, 1:85–90; Secor, *Patriot John*, 149. For funeral services of Isaac Van Wart, see Bolton, *History of the County of Westchester*, 1:235–41; Sarah Comstock, "A Visit to Elmsford," in John Lockwood Romer, *Historical Sketches of the Romer, Van Tassel and Allied Families, and Tales of the Neutral Ground* (Buffalo, NY: W. C. Gay Printing, 1917), 83 (originally published in *New York Times*, July 19, 1914); "Where John André Was Captured," *Mail and Express*, October 12, 1895, in Romer, *Historical Sketches*, 74; and Louise Hutchinson and Theodore Hutchinson, *Storm's Bridge: A History of Elmsford, 1700–1976* (Elmsford, NY: Bicentennial Committee, 1980), 60–63. David Williams, who moved to Livingstonville in Schoharie County, New York, in 1805, was first buried there, but at the time of the 1876 centennial was removed to the Old Stone Fort in Schoharie, where a monument was constructed. On Williams, see C. V. S., "The Grave of David Williams, One of Andre's Captors," *Rockland County Journal*, March 15, 1879; Marcius D. Raymond, "David Williams and the Capture of André: A Paper Read before the Tarrytown Historical Society" (January 15, 1903), in *Tarrytown Argus*, supplement, March 28, 1903; and Richard C. Brown, "Three Forgotten Heroes," *American Heritage* 26, no. 5 (August 1975).

12. On the lack of monuments in the antebellum era, see Michael Kammen, *Mystic Chords of Memory* (New York: Vintage, 1993), 70–71. Washington Irving himself joined in the call for preservation of historic sites, writing a letter in 1839 to petition the state legislature to preserve George Washington's headquarters at the Hasbrouck house in Newburgh, New York. The group's efforts were unsuccessful in 1839 but succeeded in 1850, when the house was dedicated as a historic shrine, the first property preserved by any U.S. state for historic reasons. Schuyler, *Sanctified Landscape*, 104–5.

13. Todd, "Greenburgh," in Scharf, *History of Westchester County*, 2:226–27. John Romer was born in 1764 and lived with his parents in what is now called East View, three miles east of Tarrytown. In September 1780, he was sent by his mother to retrieve the pewter basin and basket in which she had prepared their lunch, but which the men had left behind at the capture site. He kept the pewter basin until the close of his life, when he gave it to his grandson, John C. L. Hamilton, who was also a grandson of Alexander Hamilton. It is now in the custody of the Historical Society of Sleepy Hollow and Tarrytown, a prominent piece in their display of paraphernalia in the Captors' Room. Romer, *Historical Sketches*, 23–24, 31–33, 44; Bolton, *History of the County of Westchester*, 1:225 note B; William Abbatt, *The Crisis of the Revolution, Being the Story of Arnold and André* (New York: William Abbatt, 1899; repr., Harrison, NY: Harbor Hill, 1976), 33; Henry John Steiner, "The Mother of Her Country," in *Sleepy Hollow Stories* (Sleepy Hollow, NY: Milestone Productions, 2020), 23–33.

14. Secor, *Patriot John*, 149; Romer, *Historical Sketches*, 29, 31–33; "Know Your Westchester: The Monument to the Captors of Maj. Andre," *Bronxville Reporter*, April 10, 1952; Arthur F. Kennell, "The Monument Story," in *Year of the Patriots, 1780–1980: In Commemoration of the Three Captors of the British Spy, Tri-Village Bicentennial, Irvington, North Tarrytown, Tarrytown* (1980), at Historical Society of Sleepy Hollow and Tarrytown.

15. As historian Matthew Dennis has demonstrated, Independence Day celebrations throughout American history resulted from various communities and groups negotiating

their identity and working out the meanings of freedom and of self-determination. The Fourth of July, Dennis states, "provides an opportunity to define, delimit, or expand—while celebrating—the American nation." Independence Day has thus become "a moment of possibility to contest or reshape such boundaries." Dennis, *Red, White, and Blue Letter Days: An American Calendar* (Ithaca, NY: Cornell University Press, 2002), 14.

16. After he was hanged at Tappan on December 2, 1780, André's body was initially buried under the gallows on the hilltop. After he was disinterred, in 1821, and removed to Westminster Abbey in London, a subsequent marker was removed by the landowner, who was frustrated by the stream of history buffs and tourists who trampled the field and stole fruit. He moved the stone down to the edge of the public road, had the grave filled in and plowed over, and planted the field. In its new location, the boulder was chipped away by souvenir hunters, so that the exact location of the hanging and grave site was lost.

John Austin Stevens, editor of *Magazine of American History*, considered the new commemoration offensive, astounded that any nation would commemorate the "memory of an enemy who sought by base and covert means to destroy its liberties." Cyrus W. Field defended himself, saying, "People here criticized me a great deal, but I thought it was proper to mark the spot where a great historical event took place."

In the following years, socialists and patriots alike physically attacked and dislodged the André monument, until through various means it came into the hands of the American Scenic and Historic Preservation Society, in 1905, which added a plaque emphasizing that the monument stood to "commemorate the fortitude of Washington," who had ordered André's execution, rather than the character of the executed spy. The tactic worked, and the monument remained unmolested. Robert E. Cray Jr., "The John André Memorial: The Politics of Memory in Gilded Age New York," *New York History* 77, no. 1 (January 1996): 10–14; Benson J. Lossing, *The Pictorial Field-Book of the Revolution*, 2 vols. (New York: Harper and Brothers, 1851), 2:204; Michael Meranze, "Major André's Exhumation," in *Mortal Remains: Death in Early America*, ed. Nancy Isenberg and Andrew Burstein (Philadelphia: University of Pennsylvania Press, 2003), 123–36.

17. Other alterations included raising the base and turning it one-quarter clockwise so that the inscription of 1853 now faced south, while a new east panel, facing the roadway, was adorned with a bas relief by Theodore Baur, depicting the scene of the capture. General Washington's words were added: "Their conduct merits our warmest esteem. They have prevented in all probability our suffering one of the severest strokes that could have been mediated against us." The sculpture was created by William Rudolf O'Donovan, who also created the life-size statues of Washington, Lincoln, and Grant. Kennell, "Monument Story."

18. "The André Anniversary," *New York Times*, September 23, 1880; "André's Captors Honored," *New York Times*, September 24, 1880; Chauncey Depew, *Centennial of the Capture of Major André* (New York, 1880), 13–14, 19; Todd, "Greenburgh," in Scharf, *History of Westchester County*, 2:227–29; "Know Your Westchester: The Monument to the Captors of Maj. André,"

Bronxville Reporter, April 10, 1952; Kennell, "Monument Story"; Drimmer, "Major André's Captors," 50–55; Cray, "John André Memorial," 20.

19. The map indicates "André first sighted here," and "Major André of the British Army taken here Sept. 23rd 1780 by Paulding, Van Wart and David Williams." Where the Old Post Road crosses the Pocantico River, the map identifies the bridge "where Ichabod Crane had his encounter with the Headless Horseman." "Tarwe-town, in the Manor of Phillipsburgh, Westchester Co., N.Y., One Hundred Years Ago" (map; Tarrytown, September 23, 1880), in *A "Centennial Souvenir": A Brief History of Tarrytown, from 1680 to September 1880, with a Map of Tarrytown as it was One Hundred Years Ago* (Tarrytown, NY: George L. Wiley & Bro., 1880). A reproduction of the map appeared in 1899 in New York Society of the Sons of the Revolution, *An Account of the Action at Tarrytown on July Fifteenth, 1781, and of its Commemoration by the Sons of the Revolution of Tarrytown on July Fifteenth, 1899* (New York: Winthrop Press, 1899).

20. Thomas G. Connors, "The Romantic Landscape: Washington Irving, Sleepy Hollow, and the Rural Cemetery Movement," in Isenberg and Burstein, *Mortal Remains,* 187–203. Local newspaper editor Marcius D. Raymond traveled to Washington, DC, to research the pension files, service records, and muster rolls, ultimately compiling a list of veterans of the area who had served in the Revolutionary War. His findings, including histories of the families and individual soldiers' exploits as well as of the celebration, was published as *Souvenir of the Revolutionary Soldiers' Monument Dedication.*

21. Jeff Canning, "William Abbatt and His Historical Work," in William Abbatt, *The Crisis of the Revolution: Being the Story of Arnold and André* (New York: William Abbatt, 1899; repr., Harrison, NY: Harbor Hill Books, 1976). Abbatt (1851–1935) was born in Manhattan. He was the editor and publisher of *The Magazine of History* from 1905 to 1922 and wrote several books on local Revolutionary War battles. For an investigation into Abbatt's fascination with André, see Judith Richardson, *Possessions: The History and Uses of Haunting in the Hudson Valley* (Cambridge, MA: Harvard University Press, 2003); and Bacon, *Chronicles of Tarrytown and Sleepy Hollow,* 102–3.

22. Lesley Pratt Bannatyne, *Halloween: An American Holiday, an American History* (Gretna, LA: Pelican, 1990), 77–78.

23. The *Chicago Day Book,* aimed at a working-class readership, was published from September 28, 1911, to July 6, 1917. It was conceived by Edward Willis Scripps as an experiment in advertisement-free newspaper publishing.

24. William Rockefeller had the dedication plaque removed at a cost of $200. *Irvington Gazette,* September 29, 1911, December 8, 1911, and June 14, 1912; "Famous Bridge Is Replaced," (Tarrytown) *Daily News,* January 27, 1940; "No 'Rockefeller' on Bridge," *New York Times,* August 8, 1912.

25. "Sleepy Hollow: North Tarrytown Set to Vote on Name Change," *Gannett Tarrytown,* December 9, 1996. One resident made an appeal for the timelessness of Washington Irving's story when he argued, "'The Legend of Sleepy Hollow,' written long before the automobile

was invented, will retain its power long after GM has gone out of business." Another agreed. "Becoming the 'Halloween capital' of the world generates interest for more than one day a year." Edward J. Burke, "Name-Change Vote Vital to Village's Future," *Tarrytown Daily News,* n.d., in folder "North Tarrytown Name Change," Historical Society of Sleepy Hollow and Tarrytown; Constance Homalya, "Restore Primacy of European Culture," letter to the editor, *Tarrytown Daily News,* December 6, 1996.

26. Patrick Munroe, "Name Change Would Establish Our Identity," *Gannett Tarrytown,* August 20, 1996; Joseph Berger, "Debate on a Name Change for Prestige and Profit," *New York Times,* October 20, 1996. The vote passed by 1,304 to 710. Sleepy Hollow Board of Trustees, minutes, December 11, 1996.

27. In her study of the uses of haunting in the Hudson Valley, Judith Richardson notes that "the specific hauntings, as well as the general atmosphere of hauntedness, that made a literary debut in Irving's writing became ingrained and valued ingredients of regional literary and vernacular culture," because they were "adaptable to the diverse social, political, and cultural conditions and needs of individuals and generations." Richardson, *Possessions,* 79–80.

28. Geoffrey Crayon [Washington Irving], "A Chronicle of Wolfert's Roost," *Knickerbocker Magazine* 13 (April 1839): 317–28, in Washington Irving, *Wolfert's Roost,* ed. Roberta Rosenberg, *The Complete Works of Washington Irving* (Boston: Twayne, 1979). Besides two chapters of the "Chronicle of Wolfert's Roost," Irving also wrote "The Legend of Sleepy Hollow" (1839), which, along with a third chapter of "Chronicle of Wolfert's Roost" (regarding his own occupancy of the cottage), was published in book form as *Wolfert's Roost* (1855). On the meeting with Van Tassel, see Irving to Abel S. Thurston, Esq., December 11, 1855, in *Letters,* vol. 4, *1846–1859,* ed. Ralph M. Aderman, Herbert L. Kleinfield, and Jenifer S. Banks, 564–65, in *The Complete Works of Washington Irving* (Boston: Twayne, 1982).

29. Washington Irving to H. T. Tuckerman, January 8, 1856, in P. M. Irving, *Life and Letters,* 4:206–7.

30. P. M. Irving, *Life and Letters,* 4:195–96.

31. Burstein, *Original Knickerbocker,* 321–23. Irving tells the story of André over the course of three chapters.

IRVING FAMILY MANUSCRIPTS

CATALINA HANNAN

Sunnyside, Washington Irving's compact, picturesque home on the banks of the Hudson River, expresses well the author's idea of labor as well as ease. A large partner desk dominates the study, its bookshelves filled—a testament to his travels and acquisitions. This room, and this house, were Irving's refuge. "Dear little Sunnyside"[1] afforded him the contentment he desired within the circle of his family, especially the numerous nieces and nephews. He was a fixture in their lives, and they in his. Along with those who stayed on for long periods were casual callers and short-term visitors, some of whom he had known his entire life, or the offspring of these old friends. The correspondence they shared forms the basis for this essay.

To place the letters in context, an introduction is necessary. Historic Hudson Valley, a nonprofit education organization, owns Sunnyside, Philipsburg Manor, Van Cortlandt Manor, and Union Church, operating tours there and at the nearby National Trust property, Kykuit. Within our library manuscript collections, which number more than three thousand, close to one thousand relate to Irving. Much of the correspondence comes from outside sources; only a portion of the letters were written by him and appear in the authoritative editions produced by Twayne Publishers from 1978 to 1982.[2]

Some pieces deserve special mention. As custodians of Washington Irving's home, we consider the three-page letter from Irving to the artist George Harvey, Irving's partner in architecture, a treasured item. "The

Cottage" was designed to Irving's specifications, in fond remembrance of places visited and places imagined, and the letter contains sketches along with explicit instructions relating to interior details for the south front bedroom at Sunnyside, then under construction. The house passed through three more generations of Irvings, and was redecorated and enlarged, so that the Harvey letter served the restoration planners in the 1940s, when Sunnyside was being converted into the historic house museum it is today.[3]

As this volume brings particular focus to the two hundredth anniversary of initial publication of the *Sketch Book of Geoffrey Crayon, Gent.*, it is of note that the Historic Hudson Valley collection includes fourteen letters from 1819. These comprise exchanges between Irving's close friend Henry Brevoort and prominent Philadelphia and New York publishers and booksellers M. Carey and Son, C. S. Van Winkle, Wells and Lilly, and Moses Thomas. The correspondence offers insight into the process of selecting quality paper for covers as well as issues about printing, binding costs, orders, pricing, and related decisions. Then there's a letter of January 1820 from Irving's protective brother Peter, who was by his side in England and subsequently joined him in Spain, to Liverpool merchant Robert Bolton. The Irving brothers were gratified that "Rip Van Winkle" had "found favour" with Bolton, writes Peter, and all the more pleased that "the sending of that vagabond into the world" had brought general satisfaction. Rip, Peter notes, "seems to be something of a general favorite."[4]

Among the manuscript items in Irving's hand that may be of interest is a partial draft of "The Guests from Gibbet-Island" (1839), a vintage Irving tale that connects directly to the "Communipaw" settlement of the early Dutch, behind the foundational story he wove into in *A History of New-York* (Knickerbocker's history) back in 1809. Other fascinating fragments in the collection are Irving's random notes on Moorish life and Revolutionary War actions, plus a sketchbook containing original drawings in pencil, along with notes done while abroad.

Irving's political-diplomatic life is well represented in the library. His official appointment, in 1830, as secretary of the American legation in London, is signed by both President Andrew Jackson and Secretary of State Martin Van Buren. Passports signed by Irving in that capacity include one on behalf of the American financier and philanthropist George Peabody.

Irving family members intermarried with prominent surnames in New York and environs. Genealogical documents and correspondence relate to the Irving/Kip/Duer clans. Letters written by (mostly female) members of the family of Judge Josiah Hoffman span some forty years. As a young man, before writing became his main occupation, Irving trained in the law office of Judge Hoffman, who served as New York State attorney general from 1795 to 1802. The future author attached himself to the Hoffman family and loved the judge's daughter Matilda (1791–1809), who is often regarded as Irving's fiancée. In popular treatments during and after his lifetime, Irving's bachelorhood has been explained (albeit less convincingly) in terms of the devastation he felt in the loss of Matilda.

In 1883, fifty-four documents and letters from people associated with Irving were bound into an enhanced three-volume commemorative edition of Pierre Munro Irving's biography of his uncle, first published in 1862. Other documents and letters derive from the estate of the prominent jurist William Duer, whose granddaughter, Anna Duer, married Irving's nephew Pierre Paris Irving. There is, too, a clerk's copy of the wedding certificate of Irving's nephew Henry Van Wart; the ceremony took place in Paris, with "Uncle Wash" in attendance as the Marquis de Lafayette gave away the bride. Of note is the diary of Susan Storrow, Irving's grandniece, who chronicles family life in the neighborhood of Sunnyside in the early 1860s, just after Washington Irving's death.

As ripe for new scholarship as the famous author is, he often adopts a guarded perspective, which family members occasionally pierce. As Irving's contemporary Jane Austen wrote in *Emma*, "It is very unfair to judge of any body's conduct, without an intimate knowledge of their situation. Nobody, who has not been in the interior of a family, can say what the difficulties of any individual of that family may be."[5] The interior view that is reflected in family documents helps acquaint us with individual lives at candid mo-

IRVING GENEALOGY

Washington Irving's Generation
(those who survived to adulthood)

- William Irving (1766–1821)
- Ann (1770–1808)
- Peter (1772–1838)
- Catharine (1774–1849)
- Ebenezer (1776–1868)
- John Treat (1778–1838)
- Sarah (1780–1849)
- Washington (1783–1859)

Children of Ebenezer Irving and Elizabeth Kip

- Pierre Paris (1806–1878)
- Sarah (1817–1900)
- Edgar (1808–1873)
- Jane (1818–1827)
- Theodore (1809–1880)
- Julia (1818–1861)
- William (1811–1854)
- Mary (1820–1868)
- Sanders (1813–1884)
- Washington (1822–1894)
- Eliza (1814–1819)
- Charlotte (1824–1911)
- Catharine (1816–1911)

ments amid different stages of life, all too often focusing on the physical as well as emotional trials that attended a time when modern medical knowledge was still in its early stages of development.

NIECES AND NEPHEWS

The gift of 205 letters from an Irving family descendant, Daniel Larkin, offers glimpses of the author from the viewpoint of various relatives. These letters extend through the end of the nineteenth century; they contain scraps of news and take us into the final years of many of the relatives whose letters are featured in the early part of the collection. The fate of Sunnyside, its owners, and domestic staff are also covered.

William ("Will") Irving (1811–1854) was the fourth son of Washington Irving's long-lived brother Ebenezer (1776–1868), the only sibling to outlive Washington. Ebenezer was a man of business, with a large family, who lived in the heart of Manhattan's financial district and regularly served as an intermediary between the author and U.S. publishers. A selection of the family's correspondence was independently printed in *Dear Will: Letters from the China Trade (1833–1836)* but contains transcription errors.[6]

Will's letters are valuable as artifacts of life in a seafaring world, showing how news traveled while also demonstrating how details of the author's career became part of a global communications network. We see how tireless Ebenezer, a widower, was in his efforts to launch his sons into the world. Pierre Paris, Edgar, Theodore, and Sanders Irving, all in their twenties, pen playful, conversational missives to their brother in China. We read their quaint expressions: when someone talks of "going to housekeeping," he means getting married—at that time understood as an event that should only take place after one had attained financial stability and established a home. Four of the nephews' teenage sisters, Catharine (Kate), Sarah, Julia, and Mary, for their part, convey news and gossip on a par with their older brothers. In 1834, we learn, Uncle Wash escorted his nieces to the prestigious Troy Female Seminary.

Manhattan in the 1830s comes alive in the younger generation's letters with each mention of social events. Theodore provides a firsthand description of Ebenezer's Bridge Street neighborhood: "I am seated in the third story room near the side window, looking out upon that small view that is left us of the green grass of the battery, and the water dancing beyond." For Will, who is by now thousands of miles from the family home at the southern tip of the bustling island, reports such as these must have been a comfort.[7]

The majority of the letters in the China collection date from 1833 to 1836, not long after Washington Irving returned from his long sojourn in Europe. Ebenezer's clan finally came to know an uncle they'd mostly engaged with through his stories. So, not surprisingly, because he was integral to their sense of life's possibilities, breathless excitement enlivens the pages of the letters. Will had sailed for Canton (today's Guangzhou) to take up an appointment facilitated by his famous uncle; the family anticipated great business ventures to emerge and financial gain for all.

When Andrew Jackson visited Manhattan early his second term, arriving at a location within walking distance of Ebenezer's No. 3 Bridge Street home, Washington Irving was part of the welcoming committee, since he was personally acquainted with the president. Irving was almost caught amid the collapse of a bridge that connected to the Battery, which was unable to support the excess of curious onlookers. "Uncle was among the number who went down to receive [the president] and came very near to being one of the number that went down with the bridge," relayed Edgar.[8]

Young Kate wrote of the arrival of the Sauk warrior Black Hawk and the balloon ascent of Charles F. Durant. Sanders Irving went off to sea in the space of a few hours, in answer to an advertisement. "You may imagine the house was in an uproar," Kate wrote, as "he saw it in papers this morning and showed it to Uncle Washington. They went out immediately after breakfast and secured the place." From South China, Will sent back shawls, fans, and precious teas. He specifically wanted to have Uncle Wash's opinion on the brew.[9]

Will failed at the China trade. He was not the first Irving to suffer a business failure. After Uncle Wash joined his brother Peter in Liverpool in 1815, it wasn't long before P. & E. Irving, the family import firm, went belly-up, which was how the youngest son's *Sketch Book* served to rescue at least two of the brothers. Reacting to Will's ill-starred venture, the Irvings once more came together, expressing a common resolve.

The younger generation's famous relative tapped his extensive personal network to help make introductions. He offered life advice to all and sundry, generally of the cautious kind. He paid for the nieces' singing lessons— "Uncle W has discovered that Kate has a delightful and uncommon voice, and she is to have the finest masters this winter." Of Ebenezer's thirteen children, Kate, born three years before publication of the *Sketch Book,* survived the longest and was able to reflect on her uncle's enduring popularity in the second decade of the twentieth century.[10]

He opened the world of letters to them all and guided the nephews toward gainful employment—when possible. In 1833, Theo informed Will that their brother Edgar "received his commission of Lieut. of Marines and will probably be married soon—Uncle Wash is with him in Baltimore and no doubt all things will be arranged." Yet two and a half years later, Theo would remind the unlucky Will, "The prospects of our family have never to my recollection been anything like bright."[11]

A vein of humor courses through the nephews' and nieces' correspondence. "Uncle" was, with affection, denoted "the Illustrious" or "the Distinguished." Having missed much of their childhood during his seventeen years in Europe, he delighted in their company, acting as chaperon at their parties, taking them along on theater and opera outings. From Kate and Sarah jointly: "Uncle is our beau wherever we go." And from Kate: "Uncle Washington has got us in the habit of dancing every evening. He dances with us with all his m[ight] . . . You do not know what a pet he has got to be [with] us all, he is very lively and is always playing [with] the children . . . we have become better acquainted [with] him that we can talk to him as much as [we can], you know we used to be very still [when he was] in the room but we are not [anymore.]"[12] In sum, at No. 3 Bridge Street, the bachelor uncle was transformed into a composite of his ably sketched characters—a man with quirky attitudes and a jolly demeanor relishing the company of the young.

No less remarkably, three of the nephews took after their accomplished uncle in pursuing literary ambitions. One (Theodore) was Ebenezer's son; one (John Treat Irving Jr., known in the family as Treat) was the son of an active New York City judge; and one (Pierre Munro) was William Irving's, who was the eldest of Washington Irving's siblings, a congressman during James Madison's presidency, and by that time deceased. "Uncle Wash" was directly encouraging of the family's writers, though without allowing any of his nephews to believe it practicable to do as he had and make literature a full-time profession.

The books they authored in the mid-1830s were part of a trend influenced, if not begun, by Washington Irving. Almost immediately after his return from Europe, Irving took to a new genre: "the Western," pushing himself to hit the trail after a scant few months back in New York. His well-received memoir of his adventures on horseback, *A Tour on the Prairies* (1835), came to life the same year as John T. Irving Jr.'s *Indian Sketches,* Pierre Munro Irving's *Astoria,* and Theodore Irving's *The Conquest of Florida.* All four books pertained, in one way or another, to the history of Indigenous tribes and colonizers. Theo dedicated his book to his uncle. Treat followed most closely in Uncle Wash's footsteps, largely replicating his path through Indian Territory (Oklahoma) and accompanying the same government official. Pierre Munro, who proved over time to be the most devoted of the nephews, went on to assist his uncle in the preparation of his five-volume biography of George Washington. After Washington Irving's death in 1859, Pierre Munro completed an authoritative "life and letters" biography.[13]

It is remarkable just how intertwined the family writing projects were in that expectant year of 1835. In January, Theo synthesized what was happening for Will: "I have been busy as a beaver of late—writing for Uncle Washington against time—he is hurrying his New work to press—it is to come out in unconnected volumes—the first will contain his tour in the West—the second not yet determined. Treat I—is about publishing his tour among the Indians—my book is in press—so I have my hands full."[14]

The peripatetic Washington Irving, before he purchased Sunnyside in 1834, spent a considerable time at Ebenezer's, making it his home base and "taking occasional trips to the country." According to niece Sarah, he was uneasy with the late breakfast hour at Judge John T. Irving's ("after eight and sometimes it is nine"), satisfying his appetite for an earlier start at Bridge Street. His presence within the household was plainly welcomed: "Uncle Wash is in good spirits, full of fun and doing a little more good every day. He has at length brought our establishment on a respectable footing—whenever anything is wanting Uncle speaks and it is got—we had a small party about a fortnight since, for which purpose he ordered a very handsome supper set—egad if he were only rich we might live like fighting cocks."[15]

NOOKS AND QUEER IDEAS

Prior to 1834, Irving had never owned a home of his own. At first called the Roost, the cottage that became Sunnyside was an approximately fifteen-acre property on the eastern bank of the Hudson, which bordered Tarrytown and the village now known as Irvington. It adjoined the property of Irving's nephew Oscar, Pierre Munro Irving's older brother. Irving completely redesigned and built onto an extant small structure, "enlarging the house pursuing its old Dutch style, and making it an inviting and comfortable nook for the family." In the new owner's fanciful thinking, it was "capable of being made a little paradise."[16]

Nephew Edgar's reaction was initially one of skepticism: "Uncle Wash has (a short time since) bought the little cottage below Oscar's," he advised Will. "You know he thought of it once before and gave it up again, but when lately on a visit there, the fit came over him and he made the purchase. I suppose he will go to the expense of putting it in order, and then give it up."

Six months later, in the spirit of cooperative enthusiasm, Ebenezer forecast to Will what Sunnyside would become: "You know that your Uncle Washington has purchased that beautiful little spot of Mr. Ferris on the bank of the river immediately in front of your cousin Oscar's—with its little old Dutch cottage. . . . We shall clear away all the old out houses fences and rubbish and have a clear green lawn. I have selected a capital spot a short distance from the house for a garden." The last owner, Benson Ferris, clerk of the Old Dutch Church, had married into the Acker (originally Ekert) family, which had held the property back in the seventeenth century.[17]

The nephews' world was not always so lovely. Assistance in gaining employment, especially having to depend on the connections of their famous relative, could be awkward, even burdensome. Ebenezer's eldest son, Pierre Paris, was a married father of three at age twenty-seven when he told Will that he had "volunteered to go out through the state to endeavor to aid in carrying into effect the resolutions of the late legislature relative to Uncle W.I.'s Life of Columbus." He was, effectively, a book promoter. "This employment was one for which from my habits of life I was far from being well fitted—but a sense of duty supported me. I made a long and laborious journey, during which I made every exertion to procure the adoption of the book by the common schools." And it is unquestionably the case that no one so shaped his fellow citizens' heroic image of Christopher Columbus as the explorer's first English-language biographer, Washington Irving.

Pierre Paris, shortly to find his vocation as a member of the clergy, went on to describe the benefits his younger brother Theo enjoyed as their uncle's frequent companion. The two were "traveling backwards and forwards between Tarrytown and New York," wrote Pierre. Alluding next to Theo's literary endeavors, he felt convinced "Uncle W's aid may turn out to be of advantage both to his reputation and pocket. . . . Under the tuition and direction of so competent an advisor as Jeffrey [sic] Crayon he will have a fair chance of improving his natural powers."[18]

That said, relations within this large family were predictably complicated. Washington Irving's aid sometimes turned to interference, and Edgar analyzed the implications. Theo, he suspected, was putting his life on hold by attaching to their bachelor uncle. "I don't think he will ever become a married man while Uncle Wash has so much sway over him. I look upon Uncle as one of the most noble men of God's creation, but he has many queer ideas, and without a man getting along in the world he is no friend to him. I am not much in favor—and I know that Theo, as great a favorite as he is, would give his right hand to be independent of him." In fact, Theo did not marry until five years had passed from the time this letter was posted. Edgar married after just one year, and despite the criticism leveled at his uncle, named his firstborn Washington.[19]

No one has as yet studied in sufficient depth the expectations placed upon the different children among several branches of Irvings, or the emotional changes brought on by the sudden addition of the long-distant author to the family hearth. The effect of Washington Irving's presence in the lives of family members—some of whom would lodge at Sunnyside for long intervals as the years went by—remains inconclusive. Antebellum-era book reviewers had a habit of nitpicking, and the most famous of the Irvings was not immune to such criticism. But while one would expect reports of the domestic life of middle-class New Yorkers in the 1830s to accentuate the positive, the record here is actually somewhat mixed.

The best illustration is a small scandal—an affair of the heart—that once again involves Theodore, in his mid-twenties at the time. He apparently offended close friends of Irving's as well as Irving himself in the wake of a "flirting" episode—the female in question is known only by her initials. Somewhat panicked, Theo poured out his anger and frustration in a letter to Will. He said he was "perfectly aware of the reason for Uncle's coldness towards me—had he acted differently I should have done likewise. When he saw that I was discouraged he, instead of increasing, as he should have done, his kindness, grew exceeding distant—this I could not brook and I mentally swore I would not speak on the subject to him again—I knew exactly upon what tenure my having his friendship lasted and that in giving up my pursuit of M.R. he and I should be twain."

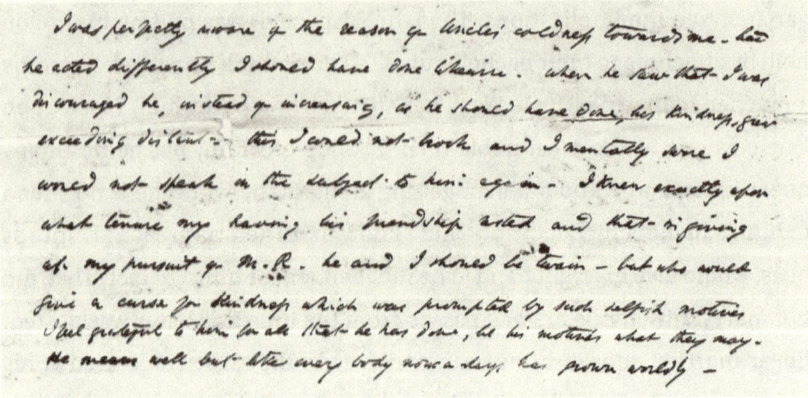

[Handwritten letter reproduction]

"I was perfectly aware of the reason for Uncle's coldness towards me." Nephew Theo Irving reveals aspects of the famous author's domestic life while providing evidence of the extended family's reliance on his good offices. Letter of Theodore Irving to William Irving, May 23, 1836. Historic Hudson Valley library and archive, W 3267.

Theo was hurt, that much is plain. Details are still somewhat lacking. "I feel grateful to him for all that he has done, be his motives what they may. He means well but like every body nowadays has grown worldly." So Theodore caused a bit of turmoil, and the uncle for whom he felt such strong emotion was being anything but helpful, anything but comforting. The meaning here of "worldly" might be something akin to "experienced," and authorized to give out life advice. No one was more "worldly" than his cosmopolitan Uncle Wash, but it was not that kind of worldliness that Theo was reacting to here.[20]

In an abode where Geoffrey Crayon took breakfast, it would seem unlikely that anyone would ever have difficulty locating a writing implement. But Kate Irving, Ebenezer's daughter, age eighteen, complains, half seriously, "I have been trying all over the house to get a pen to write with, but I can find no pen or knife and nothing but some sort of mud to write with, but I hope you will be able to make out the letters." This is what the family appears to have been about: wryly offering thoughts, some transparent, others muddy, requiring perspicacity from the researcher.[21]

Washington Irving's letters, notes, sketches, and scribblings are of inestimable value to history. Between the Twayne editions of his journals and correspondence and our own Historic Hudson Valley library and archive manuscript holdings, scholars are able to study a nineteenth-century cultural icon and better appreciate the impact he had on those who most regularly and informally surrounded him. The nephews and nieces featured in this essay are the people who knew the author's human qualities, especially in his later years, when innumerable tourists came up the Hudson to gawk at a living legend in his storybook environment.

Thanks to the efforts of publisher George P. Putnam, the collected works of Washington Irving were printed and reprinted numerous times during the second half of the nineteenth century. And while a tireless actor, Joseph Jefferson, continued playing Rip Van Winkle on stage, Treat Irving, for reasons unknown, saw to the 1888 reissue of his 1835 *Indian Sketches*. The extended Irving family had a multitude of stories to tell, and the twenty-first century should not give up looking for these and other remnants. Maybe it's idle speculation, but in my view, nothing would make Uncle Washington happier.

NOTES

1. Washington Irving to Charlotte Irving, September 20, 1842, Washington Irving Collection, Historic Hudson Valley (HHV) library and archive, Pocantico Hills, New York.

2. More documents have surfaced worldwide since the Twayne volumes came out. The Historic Hudson Valley library and archive has acquired more than twenty previously unavailable manuscript items related to Irving, including letters from his second sojourn in Spain in the early 1840s and a double-sided miniature watercolor of the floor plan of his lodgings there. The manuscripts in the collection serve the common purpose of research for scholars and genealogists, and for HHV's educational and event-based programs.

3. Washington Irving to George Harvey, October 16, 1846, HHV.

4. Moses Thomas to ——, May 1, 1819; Peter Irving to Robert Bolton, January 7, 1820, HHV.

5. Jane Austen, *Emma* (London: John Murray, 1816), vol. 1, chap. 8.

6. Daniel Irving Larkin, *Dear Will: Letters from the China Trade (1833–1836)* (privately printed, 1987). Unfortunately, only a few of Will's replies are included; the greater portion are from other family members, friends, and associates.

7. Theodore Irving to William Irving, May 26, 1834, HHV.

8. James Parton, *The Life of Andrew Jackson* (New York: Mason Brothers, 1861), 3:489; Edgar Irving to William Irving, June 14, 1833, HHV.

9. Catharine and Sanders Irving to William Irving, September 3, 1833, HHV.

10. Theodore Irving to William Irving, October 19, 1835, HHV.

11. Theodore Irving to William Irving, October 19, 1833, and May 8, 1836, HHV. Regarding the uncle's effort to secure a lieutenancy for Edgar ("I should like to have Edgar ordered to the station at Brooklyn"), see Washington Irving to Vice President Martin Van Buren, July 25, 1833, HHV.

12. Catharine and Sarah Irving to William Irving, October 22, 1834; Catharine Irving to William Irving, January 18, 1834, HHV.

13. *Astoria* was commissioned by millionaire fur trader John Jacob Astor. Pierre's job was to reside with the financier on his New York estate and prepare a chronicle of his Oregon settlement to satisfy the ego of America's wealthiest man. Washington Irving had negotiated with Astor to allow Pierre to organize the materials; all Astor required was that the famous uncle complete the writing process and place his name (rather than Pierre's) on the title page. See Andrew Burstein, *The Original Knickerbocker: The Life of Washington Irving* (New York: Basic Books, 2007), 275–78.

14. Theodore Irving to William Irving, January 15, 1835, HHV. Later in the year, Ebenezer sent a more detailed description of the trio's output: "The first no. of the 'Crayon Miscellany' being 'A Tour on the Prairies' by your Uncle Washington. Your uncle would have published something before now, but the further expectation and wish being for some article relating to our own country, he found it necessary to accommodate them—having got this work launched and thus broken the ice, we shall hear a little oftener from him—the second number is in fact prepared and will probably be published in the course of six weeks or so . . . Theodore's book is in the press and may be ready for publication in about a month or so. Your cousin John Treat I also has a work about Indians and the prairies almost ready—it is the result of an expedition he took a year since with Mr. Ellsworth the U.S. Commissioner for settling the Indians west of the Mississippi—the same gentleman your Uncle Washn. was with . . ." Ebenezer Irving to William Irving, June 1, 1835, HHV.

15. Sarah Irving to William Irving, June 19, 1833; Ebenezer Irving to William Irving, May 8, 1834; Theodore to William Irving, January 17, 1835, HHV.

16. In 1834 and 1835, Tarrytown was still part of the township of Greenburgh, not yet an incorporated village. Burstein, *Original Knickerbocker*, 279–80.

17. Edgar Irving to William Irving, November 24, 1834; Ebenezer Irving to William Irving, June 1, 1835, HHV; Burstein, *Original Knickerbocker*, 280.

18. Pierre Paris Irving to William Irving, November 25, 1833.

19. Edgar Irving to William Irving, September 3, 1833, HHV. An extensive Irving family genealogy is in Stanley T. Williams, *The Life of Washington Irving,* 2 vols. (New York: Oxford University Press, 1935), beginning at 2:241.
20. Theodore Irving to William Irving, May 23, 1836, HHV.
21. Catharine and Sarah Irving to William Irving, October 22, 1834, HHV.

AN ACTOR'S REFLECTIONS ON THE THEATRICAL IRVING

CURTIS ARMSTRONG

It has long frustrated me that Hollywood never seems to get it right when adapting Washington Irving to the screen. (Of course, whenever Hollywood *does* adapt beloved literature to screen, it's *usually* frustrating.) But in this case, the process is made more challenging in that Irving's entire reputation seems to rest on two *Sketch Book* stories: "Rip Van Winkle" and "The Legend of Sleepy Hollow." Taking nothing away from these two classics, there are other sketches in this and others of his books that are as worthy of praise, but which remain consistently unread or underappreciated after more than two centuries.

And I believe I know why that is. Those two tales are shorn of the romantic elegance of style that infuses the rest of the *Sketch Book*. There's a simplicity to the storytelling that allows them to be charmingly of their time while still touching elemental emotions in the reader. Any writer will tell you that simplicity is harder to achieve than it seems. Irving's climactic images in these stories—Old Rip awakening into an unfamiliar world, bewildered and panicked after his twenty-year sleep; Ichabod Crane, terrified, pursued by the nightmarish Headless Horseman—trigger instant recognition even in those who have never read them. The drama and humor imbued in the two tales are irresistible pluses.

These two are the only stories within of Irving's body of work to have enjoyed nearly constant appropriation and adaptation since their publication in 1819–1820. While Irving's readers would love to see more of his work adapted to stage, television, or film, we have to face the reality of how little of Irving's output is creatively transferrable to twenty-first-century media. He mainly worked in short form, and with a few notable exceptions, his work is missing the dramatic breadth, depth, visual sense, or commercial viability to appeal to studios and networks today. Many have made the attempt and failed.

"TOUGH SELL"

For forty years, even as a mere player, I have dared to dream of adapting something other than "Rip" or "Sleepy Hollow" to the silver screen. So, before I relate the history of those writers, actors, and producers who actually succeeded in adapting Irving to film or stage, I'd like to set aside any attempt at ventriloquizing a scholar's voice and explain how I tried to adapt Irving and failed.

Back in 1985, in the first flush of my Irving idolatry, while at work on a film on location in Spain, I became, bless my naive little heart, inspired. I was deep into what was already my second reading of Irving's *Life of Columbus*—I'd taken all five volumes to Spain with me, in their own suitcase. The film was *Bad Medicine,* produced by Twentieth Century Fox, based on the novel *Calling Dr. Horowitz,* by Steven Horowitz, MD, and Neil Offen. For reasons I can no longer recall, I convinced myself that this film was going to be a hit, and I was indulging in fantasies about writing screenplays myself. An adaptation of one of Washington Irving's works was high on my list, and number one on that list was not a simple American folk tale. I was going to swing for the fences.

One of the stars of *Bad Medicine* was the great actor Alan Arkin, and I became obsessed with the idea that he was the man who should play Columbus in my adaptation of Irving's *Life of Columbus.* I lost sleep over this. I still have, in my archive, a notebook with some of my notes on how this would be accomplished. I took Arkin to dinner in Madrid and pitched my idea.

I started during the appetizer course with a fairly in-depth outline of Irving's birth and early education, touched on his early international success with the *Sketch Book*. By the main course I had jumped to his discovery of Martin Fernández de Navarrete's Spanish language work on Columbus, his English-language adaptation of that, and how the film I had in mind would be different from any other ever made. The horror of the genocide of Indigenous peoples would be carefully included, and it would be historically accurate—but, yes, funny! By the time we reached dessert and coffee, I was pointing out that the four hundredth anniversary of Columbus's first voyage was fast approaching—not to mention the three hundredth anniversary of Navarrete's discovery of Columbus's journals—so the sooner we got to work on this, the better it would be.

Arkin listened patiently for I'm afraid to think how long, nodding, making the occasional mild interjection, sipping wine and eating. When I finally came to a stop and asked him what he thought, he smiled and said, "Tough sell." There was a slightly awkward pause. Then I called for the check and that was that.

A few years later, I got closer. (Needless to say, it wasn't Columbus.) In the mid-1990s, I teamed up with another would-be screenwriter, John Doolittle, to try our hands at the screenplay game. Within a few years we had enjoyed a degree of success, which in Hollywood means getting paid to write screenplays that never get read by anyone, let alone get made. At one point we were approached by the Walt Disney Company with a proposition: the company was starting a direct-to-video line (a fairly new idea at the time) and wanted to do an anthology animated feature starring their classic characters, Mickey, Donald, Goofy, Minnie, Daisy, and Pluto.

Disney had enjoyed enormous success with its adaptation of "The Legend of Sleepy Hollow" in 1949. So the company's idea was to set up Mickey Mouse and his friends on a camping trip: late at night, around a fire, each would tell a ghost story. The episode they wanted my partner and me to write was "Rip Van Winkle." Starring Goofy. I told them that it had long been a dream of mine to adapt Irving to the screen, but we hit a bump in the road right off when they told us, "Yeah, Rip Van Winkle, but with a lot of *Back to the Future* in it, though."

"*Back to the Fut—*"

"Sure. I mean, that's kind of what "Rip Van Winkle" is, right? Goes to sleep in the present, wakes up in the future, doesn't know anybody. I mean, that's scary!"

I felt strangely irritated. "Well, no," I said. "'Rip Van Winkle' isn't like *Back to the Future at all,* actually. They're two different stories. Plus, there's the whole element of social and political satire in 'Rip.' The ghostly crew of Hendrick Hudson—"

"Oh, yeah," said another executive. "Those little ghosts should be scarier."

"Have you," I said, my voice rising in pitch, "ever actually *read* "Rip Van Winkle"?!"

My partner somehow got us out of the room without me getting us fired. We did write the screenplay. They're all there, all the classic Disney characters. Goofy is an acceptable Rip, given his obvious limitations as an actor. (Not to mention his drinking problem—in Hollywood in those days it was an open secret you couldn't do anything with him after lunch.) But the day we showed up at the office to deliver the script, we found the offices locked and empty, telephones on the floor, and no sign of any of the executives who had brought us on. It turned out that this attempt at direct-to-video had failed and the executives had been laid off.

We felt a little like Rip ourselves, waking up expecting to find a bunch of highly paid gnomes playing at ninepins and being left with a rusty old flintlock instead. Our attempt at introducing a new audience to Rip Van Winkle was all for naught, though I'm happy to report that the check did clear. I'm donating my copy of the screenplay to the Historic Hudson Valley library and archive, so that future students of Irving's posthumous career can see for themselves how close we came to this disastrous adaptation actually happening.

But enough about me. Back to the all-important nineteenth century.

★ ★ ★

JOE JEFFERSON

It's pretty clear that the stream of stage adaptations of "Rip Van Winkle" began early and occurred often, by writers whose names are mostly forgotten now. Adaptations can be a habit that's both inspirational and hard to break, as Irving himself found. "Rip Van Winkle" and "The Legend of Sleepy Hollow" were adaptations themselves, from German folk sources. It was during Irving's pilgrimage to visit Walter Scott at Abbotsford that the deep well of German fairy tales and legends was revealed to him by Scott, who had found some of them useful himself. In his "Note" at the end of "Rip Van Winkle," Irving hints at his source. "The foregoing tale, one would suspect, had been suggested to Mr. Knickerbocker by a little German superstition about the Emperor Frederick der Rothbart and the Kypphauser mountain..."

"The Legend of Sleepy Hollow" appears to have come from a couple of possible sources: Robert Burns's "Tam O'Shanter" and, more significantly, from the fifth of the *Legenden von Rubezahl* in the collection of *Volkesmarchen* by Johann Karl August Musäus (1735–1787). In return, it seems, Irving's two best-known stories became oft-adapted themselves, pretty much from the get-go.

In his 1895 autobiography, Joseph Jefferson III, the American comedian given most credit for Rip Van Winkle's onstage incarnation, mentions a familiarity with three previous stage adaptations (all "bad" in his estimation) before he tried his hand at writing one himself. One was by Charles Burke, an American who failed as a businessman and became an actor as a fallback career, which one could do in the nineteenth century. Another was assembled by James Henry Hackett, who for decades toured America in a "fat suit" as Shakespeare's Falstaff. (He finally grew into the role sufficiently and was able to discard the fat suit). Then there was Frederick Henry Yates, an English actor-manager, who killed off Rip in his adaptation! He was famous for bringing a female elephant from Paris to appear at London's Adelphi Theatre.

The actor Joe Jefferson was the third of that name from a well-known theatrical family. He kept the emotionally charged character of Rip Van Winkle alive into the twentieth century, surviving long enough to appear as Rip in a silent film. *Joseph Jefferson as Rip Van Winkle*, 1871, by George Waters. Oil on canvas. Courtesy Historic Hudson Valley, Pocantico Hills, NY (SS.79.7).

Joe Jefferson joined this elite group around 1859. He learned, not long after, that the late author and avid theatergoer had seen him on stage at Laura Keene's theater in New York City, in a production of Thomas Holcroft's comedy *The Road to Ruin*. Jefferson was especially moved by Irving's comparison of the father and son actors: "I reminded him of my father 'in look, gesture, and size.'" Remarkably, Joseph Jefferson III was the third of the name to take up the same profession in early America. Irving's unexpected mention inspired Jefferson to read the *Sketch Book,* and in the process, to find in the character of Rip a perfect role for himself. He noted that all previous adaptations of "Rip Van Winkle" were in two acts; his contribution to the evolution of Rip as a theater piece was to expand the play into three acts, the middle act being focused entirely on Rip's encounter with the spirits of Hudson and his crew.

The Philadelphia-born Jefferson is one of the few nineteenth-century American actors whose name remains famous without him having assassinated a president. As was the case later with William Gillette (1853–1937) and his iconic portrayal of Sherlock Holmes, Joe Jefferson became wildly famous for one role: Rip Van Winkle. His adaptation of the story was completed and produced but was not considered wholly successful, even by him. It was only when the actor collaborated in London with Irish playwright Dionysius ("Dion") Boucicault (1822–1890) that the play became a sensation.

In his memoir, Jefferson lauded at some length Boucicault's contributions to the improvement to the play, making it one of those truly rare reading experiences—an actor's autobiography in which the subject doesn't take total credit for everything himself. Still, by most accounts—including his own—Jefferson gave a rich, nuanced, and unforgettable comedic performance as Rip. It was the making of an enduring reputation. As a result of the play's success, the story's original author and the actor-manager he'd once seen perform maintain a spiritual connection in American cultural history to this day.

Washington Irving loved the theater. Beginning in his teens, he attended plays and opera obsessively and wrote extensively on theatrical subjects, though he learned, as have many since, that if playwriting were easy, everyone would do it. His attempts at writing for the stage center on plays of the early 1820s, when Irving made an extended stay in Bohemia and Silesia, and then in Paris. His first solo attempt at a theatrical piece was *Abu Hassan,* an adaptation of Carl Maria von Weber's adaptation of Franz Carl Hiemer's adaptation of Scheherazade's "The Story of Abu Hassan, or the Sleeper Awakened" from *The 1001 Arabian Nights.* Next, he tried adapting *Der Freischutz,* or *The Marksman,* which had been adapted from an opera by, once again, von Weber, whose genius was clearly a gift that kept on giving.

In Europe around this time, Irving met up with his longtime admirer John Howard Payne (1791–1852), a Manhattanite who had debuted on the New York stage in 1809, the year of Irving's comic masterpiece *A History of New-York.* In 1823, Payne composed the sentimental standard "Home, Sweet Home" (and what's more, admitted to it). He was doing hack work in Paris, adapting French comedies for the English stage, when he persuaded Irving to collaborate with him on his adaptation of a thirty-year-old French play called *La Jeunesse de Richelieu.* Irving agreed to a partnership, provided that his name did not appear on any of the plays. When one of Payne and Irving's subsequent collaborations, *Charles the Second, or The Merry Monarch,* was produced at Covent Garden to wild acclaim, the victory was bittersweet. Owing to Irving's characteristic reticence, neither his nor Payne's name appeared on the playbill.

As for the evolution of Rip Van Winkle, the mischievous sleeper appeared as the subject of grand opera—without the opera-loving Irving's involvement. George Frederick Bristow (1825–1898), one of America's first composers in the form and an advocate for American music, completed a full-length opera based on Irving's tale, with a libretto written by John Howard Wainwright. *Rip Van Winkle,* the opera, premiered on September 22, 1855, at Niblo's Garden in New York, and closed on October 17. Irving was twenty-five miles upriver at Sunnyside at the time, but there is no mention in letters or journals from the period that he saw Bristow's opera or was even aware of it. Judging from what he wrote to friends during this period, as he was readying the second volume of his magnum opus, *The Life of George Wash-*

ington, for press, he was also feeling his age and feeling too overwhelmed to make trips into the city.

A revised version of the opera was produced in 1878. (The overture is available on compact disc on New World Records, performed by the Royal Northern Sinfonia, conducted by Rebecca Miller.) Bristow enjoyed a long and productive career as a composer of orchestral and choral music, remaining best known for his *Rip Van Winkle.*

Joseph Jefferson III and Dion Boucicault's successful stage adaptation of "Rip Van Winkle" did more than give the popular actor the role of a lifetime. It did much to keep the name of Washington Irving alive long after the author's death. In a ghostlike way, it did the same for Joe Jefferson, when a silent film version of "Rip Van Winkle" was produced in 1903. He was eighty-three when he reprised the role. The film is actually a compilation of eight short films, shot with a single camera at Jefferson's summer home in Massachusetts and directed by William Kennedy Dickson, a protégé of Thomas Edison. The "screenplay," such as it was, was credited to the triumvirate of Dickson, Jefferson, and Irving.

In 1914, a feature-length film was produced that starred the latest in the Jefferson theatrical dynasty, Joe's son Thomas. In 1921, yet another feature-length version of the story was released, again starring Thomas Jefferson, directed by Edward Ludwig, who went on to direct dozens of comedies, musicals, and adventures. That same year, Thomas Jefferson's 1914 film was reissued, leading to confusion about whether the two were the same film.

FROM BING CROSBY TO GLORIA STEINEM

So, from the mid-nineteenth century forward, by a kind of universal acclamation, it was a common assumption that Irving had written exactly two short tales that were capable of adaptation to stage, screen, television, and radio: "Rip Van Winkle" and "The Legend of Sleepy Hollow." One notable, long-running exception is the Christmas pageant that opened for the 1927 holiday season at the Ahwahnee Hotel in California's Yosemite National Park.

Based loosely—very loosely—on the several Christmas stories in Irving's *Sketch Book,* the event was originally staged by a professional pageant director, Garnet Holme; after his death in 1929, the Bracebridge Dinner was taken over by legendary photographer Ansel Adams, who continued to produce the show, save for a hiatus during World War II, until 1973. Over the decades, there have been occasional changes in the script, but none that would bring the pageant any closer to the original sketch than it was in 1929. The Bracebridge Dinner has continued to be a sellout event at Yosemite every year.

Aside from myriad small stage performances, there have been other silent film versions of "Rip Van Winkle" that are now lost. On radio, Rip was the subject of satire by radio comedy legends Fred Allen and Jack Benny, while *Your Playhouse of Favorite Stories* broadcast both stories straight, as read by the prolific actor Will Geer. On film, television, and direct-to-video, the two Irving tales leap across decades. Disney's very successful *The Adventures of Ichabod and Mr. Toad* (1949) paired a short based on Kenneth Grahame's 1908 novel *The Wind in the Willows* with the animated version of "The Legend of Sleepy Hollow," narrated by Bing Crosby (1949). This film was revived on television in the mid-1950s and remained a favorite into the twenty-first century.

In 1978, director Will Vinton retold "Rip Van Winkle" via claymation, with Will Geer returning to the character of Rip. The short was nominated for an Academy Award. In 1980, Jeff Goldblum starred in a made-for-TV version of "The Legend of Sleepy Hollow," with Meg Foster as Katrina. The two stories received dramatizations by actor and producer Shelley Duvall for two different series, *Faerie Tale Theatre* and *Tall Tales and Legends,* both on NBC. The "Rip Van Winkle" adaptation was directed for *Faerie Tale Theatre* in 1985 by Francis Ford Coppola, starring Harry Dean Stanton as Rip and Talia Shire as Dame Van Winkle. In Duvall's 1998 production of "The Legend of Sleepy Hollow" for *Tall Tales and Legends,* Ed Begley Jr. starred as Ichabod Crane, with Beverly D'Angelo as Katrina and NFL linebacker Dick Butkus as Brom Bones.

Next came Tim Burton's famously deconstructionist take on "The Legend of Sleepy Hollow," the 1999 film with Johnny Depp and Christina Ricci. *Sleepy Hollow* earned more than $200 million at the box office. Horror legend Burton expanded the story to include a marvelous and eccentric collection of locals never dreamed of by Irving, and he made one significant change: in his version, Ichabod becomes an endearing, slightly bumbling constable who is sent to Sleepy Hollow to investigate a series of grisly beheadings. (The movie was off the charts in the gore factor). *Sleepy Hollow* was imaginative, funny, and visually gorgeous, receiving an Oscar for Art Direction and Set Design (Rich Heinrich and Peter Young). But with its overemphasis on blood and butchery, Irving it was not. The following year a Hallmark feature, *The Legend of Sleepy Hollow,* starring Brent Carver, was released and marketed with the risible log line, "In the Night, No One Can Hear You Scream."

One of the most unusual adaptations of an Irving story was an episode of an animated children's television show, *Happily Ever After: Fairy Tales for Every Child,* done in 2000. The show offered weekly retellings of classic children's stories from a feminist perspective, and one of the stories picked for this treatment was "Rip Van Winkle." It is hard to imagine Rip with his nameless virago of a wife in a feminist setting. Consider, for instance, a line from the original Irving tale: "Morning, noon and night, her tongue incessantly going, and everything he said or did was sure to produce a torrent of household eloquence." But here it is, nonetheless, courtesy of the creators of *Happily Ever After.*

Vanna (Calista Flockhart) is a free-spirited young woman who falls in love with a thuggish, misogynist rock star (Tom Arnold, with Edgar Winter performing Rip's song). In marrying him, she sacrifices her dreams to serve her husband—she "lost her voice." One day, while out walking, she encounters the Blue Bird (Sandra Bernhard), who, seeing her predicament, leads her to meet the Thunder Mountain Women, voiced by a cast of A-list feminists: former NBC News anchor Linda Ellerbe, author/activist Betty Friedan, opera star Jessye Norman, and former Texas governor Ann Richards. Together, they try to encourage Vanna to stand up for herself. She tries but fails. Finally, she accepts a secret potion from her "fairy godmentor" (Maya Angelou) and gives it to her husband to drink. He falls asleep for twenty years.

When he awakes, he finds that women are in charge of everything: Vanna is CEO of her own company, which she is running with their now grown son. The story ends happily, with Rip, now "woke," working for his wife. Longtime feminist activist Gloria Steinem narrates and the multifaceted actor Robert Guillaume narrates. Carole Rosen produced the series for HBO; the episode was directed by Anthony Bell.

SPANISH ECHOES

Several other productions, decades and cultures apart, drew on one of Irving's other titles for inspiration: *Tales of the Alhambra,* first published in 1832. The Romantic collection is sometimes referred to as his "Spanish Sketch Book." Irving lodged at the Moorish palace, with the governor's consent, in the late 1820s.

In 1950, director and screenwriter Florian Rey (1894–1962) produced a popular Spanish feature, *Cuentos de la Alhambra* [*Tales of the Alhambra*], starring Carmen Sevilla. The complete film has proved difficult to find, though clips are available on the internet. Though the film is purportedly based on Irving's book, it appears that the connection is more in spirit than to the letter. Even further afield from Irving's original is the highly successful South Korean romantic series *Memories of the Alhambra* (2018), which updates the Alhambra tales, as a modern-day game-based alternate reality.

Irving connoisseurs will find two other Spanish adaptations to be of greater interest. In March 1974, the Spanish TV program *Los Libros* broadcast *Cuentos de la Alhambra de Washington Irving.* Filmed entirely in Grenada at the palatial fortress, it is an hour-long educational documentary that acts as an abbreviated version of the book, using Irving's arrival at and departure from the Alhambra as a framing device. In between, Irving (Erasmo Pascual Colmenero) meets his guide, Mateo. We see the scene at night, when Irving wanders the deserted palace alone until he is frightened back to his own room, upon which the viewer is treated to dramatized versions of several stories from the book. These tales—"The Moor's Legacy," "The Three Beautiful Princesses," and "The Governor and the Notary"—are faithful to the originals. The last story is told to Irving not by Mateo but by "the old veteran," with whom Irving shares a scene. While somewhat stagy and certainly low budget, this particular *Cuentos de la Alhambra* is a delight for any who admire the book.

Two animated films directed by Juan Bautista Berasategi take up Irving legends. The first, *Ahmed, principe de la Alhambra* (a retelling of "The Legend of Prince Ahmed al Kamel, or, the Pilgrim of Love"), came out in 1998. This was followed in 2003 by the animated film *El embrujo del sur* [*The Haunting of the South*], recounting Irving's 1829 journey to Seville and Granada. Both films were produced in Basque, Catalan, and Spanish-language versions.

Also worthy of mention is yet another *Cuentos de la Alhambra,* this film produced in 2017 by Pliski Studios by Pedro Alonso Pablos. It is an unusual adaptation of Irving, animated with the use of digital pictures and narrated by Pablos, with the female characters voiced by Rachel Mizpah. It focuses on three stories only: "The Arab Astrologer," "The Three Beautiful Princesses," and "Rose of the Alhambra." All three are scrupulously loyal to Irving's prose. The film is beautifully scored for solo guitar by Javi de las Eras. It was also adapted by Pablos as an illustrated storybook.

ECLECTICISM

The most recent major American adaptation of Irving's work takes us back to the *Sketch Book*. Twentieth Century Fox's supernatural TV series *Sleepy Hollow* (2013–2017) deserves credit, at the very least, for initiative. Created by Alex Kurtzman, Roberto Orci, Phillip Iscove, and Len Wiseman, this modern-day supernatural version of Irving reveals Ichabod Crane (English actor Tom Mison) to have been neither a pedagogue nor a constable but a Revolutionary War British expatriate soldier who worked as a double agent for George Washington. In 1781, the greatly transformed Crane beheads a mounted Hessian soldier, who doesn't die. Ichabod is knocked unconscious in the fight, and upon awakening finds himself in Sleepy Hollow 250 years later. (To my knowledge, this series is the only adaptation that features a "Sleepy Hollow"/"Rip Van Winkle" mash-up of this sort.)

Never mind the exponential expansion of Rip's twenty-year slumber being transferred to Irving's hapless pedant, because the oddity does not stop there. The reawakened Ichabod meets police lieutenant Abbie Mills (Nicole Beharie) and realizes, using Washington's Bible as a guide—stay with me here—that he and Abbie are Witnesses, and the Hessian, who has also returned, is Death and wants his head back, because if he retrieves it, the End of Days will occur.

Sleepy Hollow was greeted with enthusiasm in its first season (the show's online fans called themselves "Sleepy Heads"), but the excitement waned after a couple of seasons of erratic writing and the loss of two of the show's most popular characters. It was finally canceled after its fourth season.

Perhaps it is appropriate for an author who was above all else a teller of tales that the most consistently successful of Irving adaptations have not been big budget motion pictures or grand opera but audio recordings made of the original stories, narrated without the bells and whistles. The recordings in my personal collection include retellings by Lionel Barrymore, Boris Karloff, Will Geer, Anjelica Huston, and a more recent unabridged reading by Jonathan Kruk.

The award for most eclectic cast ever assembled to present unabridged readings goes to The Washington Irving Library from Dove Audio and Phoenix Books: six hours of unabridged Irving stories, read by Susan Anspach, Elliott Gould, John Rubinstein, Eleanor Mondale, *M*A*S*H*'s Jamie Farr, and Efrem Zimbalist Jr. You have to be of a certain age to appreciate just how utterly bizarre that collection of narrators is. Even with the addition of sound effects or musical scores, these simple retellings of Irving's tales on vinyl, tape, or CD take the listener back to the oral tradition that gave Diedrich Knickerbocker and Geoffrey Crayon their immortal tales to begin with.

So maybe we shouldn't be disappointed in the relative paucity of adaptations of Washington Irving's work. Among his contemporaries, Edgar Allen Poe, James Fenimore Cooper, and Jane Austen may surpass Irving in number and even quality of adaptations. These were authors whose work, whether in long or short form, lent themselves more easily to adaptation. It is kind of a marvel that the most memorable Irving stories have inspired as many adaptations as I've noted here. They can be enjoyed as comedies or as ghost stories by readers who may have no sense of the levels of historical satire.

In sum, "Rip Van Winkle" and "The Legend of Sleepy Hollow" have proven themselves to be short stories that contain multitudes, fit for the largest proscenium or the smallest of screens. Entire orchestras can be scored to accompany them and they can still be told to children, from memory, by firesides. Some of our greatest actors and directors have been drawn to them because of their significance to our history and culture. They are stories that never die and will, I predict, continue to challenge and inspire adapters for generations to come.

CONTRIBUTORS

CURTIS ARMSTRONG is a film and television actor, author, and Irvingiana collector. A graduate of Oakland University in Rochester, Michigan, he trained as a stage actor and has appeared (as a self-described "second banana") in such popular movies as *Risky Business* (1983), *Revenge of the Nerds* (1984), *Ray* (2004), and *Akeelah and the Bee* (2006). On the small screen, he played memorable roles in *Moonlighting* (1987–1989), *Boston Legal* (2006), *King of the Nerds* (2011–2013), *American Dad!* (2005–2019), *Supernatural* (2009–2013), and *New Girl* (2013–2018). He is the author of a memoir, *Revenge of the Nerd: The Singular Adventures of the Man Who Would Be Booger* (2017); and, with Elliott Milstein, of *A Plum Assignment: Discourses on P.G. Wodehouse and His World* (2018).

ELIZABETH L. BRADLEY is vice president of programs and engagement at Historic Hudson Valley and the author of *Knickerbocker: The Myth Behind New York* (2009). She has also edited the Penguin Classics editions of Washington Irving's *The Legend of Sleepy Hollow and Other Stories* (2014) and *A History of New York* (2008).

ANDREW BURSTEIN is the Charles P. Manship Professor of History at Louisiana State University. He is the only professional historian to have authored a complete biography of Washington Irving, *The Original Knickerbocker: The Life of Washington Irving* (2007). Among his other books on early U.S. history are *Lincoln Dreamt He Died* (2013), *Jefferson's Secrets* (2005), *The Passions of Andrew Jackson* (2003), and *Sentimental Democracy* (1999). He has coauthored two books with Nancy Isenberg, *The Problem of Democracy: The Presidents Adams Confront the Cult of Personality* (2019); and *Madison and Jefferson* (2010).

MATTHEW DENNIS is an emeritus professor of history and environmental studies at the University of Oregon. He is the author of several books, including *Seneca Possessed: Indians, Witchcraft, and Power in the Early American Republic* (2010); and *Red, White, and Blue Letter Days: An American Calendar* (2002). His next, *American Relics and the Politics of Public Memory*, is to be published shortly.

CATALINA HANNAN is a research librarian at Historic Hudson Valley. She holds degrees in history, Russian studies, and library science and has been at Historic Hudson Valley for twenty years. Apart from institutional work on the history of the Hudson Valley, she has developed a special interest in the extended family of the Irvings across the centuries.

TRACY HOFFMAN is a senior lecturer at Baylor University. She serves as President of the Washington Irving Society and has authored articles on Irving, most recently in the volume *Washington Irving and Islam: Critical Essays*.

NANCY ISENBERG is the T. Harry Williams Professor of History at Louisiana State University. She is the author of the *New York Times* best seller *White Trash: The 400-Year Untold History of Class in America* (2016) as well as *Fallen Founder: The Life of Aaron Burr* (2007); and *Sex and Citizenship in Antebellum America* (1998). She has coauthored two books with Andrew Burstein, *The Problem of Democracy: The Presidents Adams Confront the Cult of Personality* (2019); and *Madison and Jefferson* (2010).

ALEXIS McCROSSEN is professor of history at Southern Methodist University. She is the author of *Marking Modern Times: Clocks, Watches and Other*

Timekeepers in American Life (2013); and *Holy Day, Holiday: The American Sunday* (2000). Her forthcoming book is to be titled *Time's Touchstone: The New Year in American Life*.

SHIRLEY SAMUELS is professor of English and American studies at Cornell University. Among her numerous publications, she is the author of *Reading the American Novel, 1780–1865* (2012); and *Romances of the Republic: Women, the Family, and Violence in the Literature of the Early American Nation* (1996); and the editor of *Race and Vision in the Nineteenth-Century United States* (2019); *Cambridge Companion to Abraham Lincoln* (2012); *Companion to American Fiction, 1780–1865* (2004); and *The Culture of Sentiment: Race, Gender, and Sentimentality in 19th Century America* (1992).

MICHELLE SIZEMORE is associate professor of English at the University of Kentucky. She is the author of *American Enchantment: Rituals of the People in the Post-Revolutionary World* (2018).

ERIK WEISELBERG is the village historian and a social studies teacher in Irvington, New York. He is the principal historian of the ongoing project "Revolutionary Westchester 250."

INDEX

Notes: Asterisked entries refer to individual tales in the *Sketch Book*. "WI" refers to Washington Irving.

Abbatt, William, 163
Adams, John, 77–78
Addison, Joseph, 25
"The Adventure of the Mysterious Stranger," 113
The Adventures of Ichabod and Mr. Toad (1949), 138n10, 163, 199
"The Adventure of Sam, the Black Fisherman," 133
Alien Enemies Act (1798), 51
American Traveller's Guide, 27
André, Major John, 11, 55, 92, 110, 154, 156, 158–63, 166, 169n3, 172n16
Angelou, Maya, 201
"The Arab Astrologer," 202
Arkin, Alan, 191–92
Armstrong, Curtis, 12
Arnold, Benedict, 11, 55, 158
Arnold, Tom, 200
"The Art of Book-Making,"* ix, xvii, 24, 25, 33, 46
Astor, John Jacob, xiv, 188n13
Astoria (book by WI), xi, 182, 188n13
Austen, Jane, 12, 177
"The Author's Account of Himself,"* 25, 150

Back to the Future, 192–93
Bancroft, George, 168
Baym, Nina, 143
Begley, Ed, Jr., 199
Beharie, Nicole, 203
Berasategi, Juan Bautista, 202
Bernhard, Sandra, 200
Bigelow, Andrew, 25
Black Hawk (Sauk chief), 180
Blake, William, 104
Bloomer, Amelia, 151
"The Boar's Head Tavern, Eastcheap,"* 33
Bolton, Robert, 176
Boswell, James, 25
Boucicault, Dionysius, 196, 198
Bowen, Edwin W., 123
Bracebridge Hall (book by WI), xi, 2, 20, 34, 104, 132, 144
Bradley, Elizabeth, 10
Brady, Mathew, 141
Brevoort, Henry, 1, 17, 176
Briggs, Claude Dunbar, 43, 57
Briggs, Daniel, 55
Bristow, George Frederick, 197
Brown, William Wells, xvi
Bryant, William Cullen, xv
Burke, Charles, 194
Burns, Robert, 194
Burr, Aaron, xviii, 45

INDEX

Burstein, Andrew, 8, 44, 46, 92, 96n9, 97nn14–15
Burton, Tim, 200
Butkus, Dick, 199
Byron, George Gordon, Lord, xi, 21, 25

Campbell, Thomas, 21
Captain Bonneville (book by WI), xi
Carter, Nathaniel, 27
Carver, Brent, 200
Cervantes, Miguel de, 70, 142
Charles I (king), 75
Child, Lydia Maria, 37
"Christmas,"* 114
"The Christmas Dinner,"* 74
A Chronicle of the Conquest of Granada (book by WI), 20
Cole, Thomas, 93
Coleridge, Samuel Taylor, 104
Colmenero, Erasmo, 201
Colton, Calvin, 27
Columbus, Christopher, x, xv, 56, 142, 184, 192. See also *Life and Voyages of Christopher Columbus* (book by WI)
Cooper, James Fenimore, xv, 37, 48, 54, 93
Coppola, Francis Ford, 199
"The Country Church,"* 63, 65
Crayon, Geoffrey (WI persona), ix–x, xviii, 3, 5, 9, 25, 28, 34, 35, 46, 56, 63, 65, 68, 74, 89, 92, 104, 107, 109, 114, 142, 149, 166, 186, 203
Crèvecoeur, J. Hector St. Jean de, 46; and caged Black man, 51
Crosby, Bing, 163, 165, 198, 199

Dana, Richard Henry, 4
D'Angelo, Beverly, 199
Davis, Paulina Wright, 151
Defoe, Daniel, 104
Dennis, Matthew, 8, 171n15

Depp, Johnny, 200
Dickens, Charles, xii, 33, 100, 139–44
Dickson, William Kennedy, 198
Dippie, Brian, 32
Disney, Walt, 163, 165, 192, 199
"Dolph Heyliger," 132–33
Doolittle, John, 192
Douglas, Ann, 149–50
Duer, Anna, 177
Duer, William, 177
Dunbar, Jesse, 57
Durant, Charles F., 180
Duvall, Shelley, 199

Eagleman, David, 115
Edison, Thomas, 198
Ellerbe, Linda, 200
"English Writers on America,"* 33

Ferguson, Robert A., 151
Ferris, Benson, 184
Field, Cyrus W., 160–61
Flockhart, Calista, 200
Foster, Meg, 199
Franklin, Benjamin, 84
Friedan, Betty, 200
Fritzsche, Peter, 100, 115
Fugitive Slave Act (1850), 125

Geer, Will, 199, 203
George III (king), 45, 56, 75, 88
"The German Student," xviii
Gillette, William, 196
Goldblum, Jeff, 199
Goldsmith, Oliver, xii, 142
Goodfriend, Joyce, 129
"The Governor and the Notary," 202
Grahame, Kenneth, 199
"Guests from Gibbet-Island," 134–35, 176
Guillaume, Robert, 201

INDEX

Hackett, James Henry, 194
Hailwood, Mark, 103
Halleck, Fitz Greene, xv
Hamilton, Alexander, xviii, 57, 132, 160
Hamilton, James Alexander, 160
Hamilton (musical), 45, 46
Hannan, Catalina, 11
Harvey, George, 175–76
Hawthorne, Nathaniel, 2, 27, 42, 57
Hedges, William L., 3
Henry IV, Part II (Shakespeare), 85
Hiemer, Franz Carl, 197
Historic Hudson Valley (library and archive), 11, 175, 176, 186, 187, 193
A History of New-York (book by WI): xi, xvi, xvii, 13, 20, 36, 56, 68, 78, 84, 87, 126–29, 176
Hoffman, Josiah, 177
Hoffman, Matilda, 177
Hoffman, Tracy, 10
Holcroft, Thomas, 195
Holme, Garnet, 199
Horowitz, Steven, 191
Horsman, Reginald, 30
Houston, Sam, xviii, 140
Hudson, Hendrick, 90, 108
Hugo, Victor, 100
Hutchinson, Theodore, 165–66

"The Inn Kitchen,"* 22
Irving, Catherine ("Kate"), 179, 180–81, 186
Irving, Ebenezer, 179–81, 183, 186
Irving, Edgar, 179, 180, 184–85
Irving, John Treat (WI's brother), 182, 183
Irving, John Treat, Jr. (WI's nephew), 182, 187
Irving, Julia (WI's niece), 179
Irving, Julia Paulding (WI's sister-in-law), 158
Irving, Mary, 179

Irving, Oscar, 183–84
Irving, Peter, 176, 181
Irving, Pierre Munro, 12, 141, 167, 177, 182, 183
Irving, Pierre Paris, 177, 179, 184
Irving, Sanders, 179, 180
Irving, Sarah, 179, 181, 183
Irving, Theodore, 179, 181, 182, 184–86
Irving, Washington: American Revolution evoked by, 11, 36, 42, 55–58, 83–84, 88, 90–92, 108, 154–63, 166–68, 176, 202–3; Blacks in stories by, 10, 55, 77, 123–37; and Christmas, xi, xv, 10, 13, 74, 106, 107, 114, 136, 144, 198; class elements in stories by, 3, 4, 7–8, 44, 49–51, 63–81, 104; and copyright, 20–21; depictions of women, 10, 44, 47, 54, 63, 65–67, 71, 78, 107, 137, 146, 147, 149, 150, 155, 200; and Dutch culture, xi, xvi, 6, 48, 59, 66, 77–79, 90, 125–29, 133, 135, 145–47, 164, 176, 183–84; and English tradition, xii, 5, 6, 14, 21–36, 46, 59, 63, 66, 103–5, 109, 111–12, 114, 116, 147, 155; family relationships of, ix, xiv, 9, 11–12, 20, 42, 44–45, 124, 141, 175–88; featured on postage stamp, xi; Gothic elements in writings of, 44, 47–58, 63, 73–74, 76, 92, 99, 108, 110, 113, 114, 132, 136, 163; and Halloween, 13, 154–55, 163–64, 167; horses in stories by, 7, 8, 62–80, 110, 127; interrogates memory, x, 3, 5, 7, 8, 37, 43, 55–56, 58–59, 63, 86, 97n15, 115, 128, *130,* 155, 166; libraries and, ix–x, 26, 44, 46–47, 52, 109; love of theater, xviii, 22, 181, 195–97; Native Americans in stories by, xiii, xiv, 6, 7, 10, 31–32, 42, 48–50, 69, 126, 182; on nature of history, xvii, xix, 2, 6, 7, 8, 14, 21, 24–25, 29, 30–34, 56, 58–59, 84–86, 89–92, 112–14, 126–29, 166–67; on nature of time, xiv, xvi–xx, 8–9, 24, 83, 85–87, 90–92, 99–115; as New Yorker, ix, 6, 11, 43, 46, 79,

Irving, Washington (*continued*)
123–24, 132, 136, 141, 148, 180, 197–98; reputation of, ix–xii, xv–xvii, 1–5, 12, 14, 20–21, 34, 82, 123, 136, 143–44, 154; sentimentalism in stories by, 2–4, 26, 28, 30, 31, 70, 92, 114–15; Spain in life and writings of, xi, xvi, 5, 12, 56, 114, 115, 141, 142, 176, 191, 192, 201–2

Irving, William (WI's brother), 158, 182

Irving, William (WI's nephew), 179–82, 184, 186

Irvington (NY), 160, 183

Isenberg, Nancy, 7

Jackson, Andrew, xviii, 177, 180

James, Henry, 28

James I (king), 25–27

Jefferson, Joseph, II, 12

Jefferson, Joseph, III, 12, 13, 139, 148, 187, 194–96, 198

Jefferson, Thomas, xvi, xviii, 48

Jefferson, Thomas (son of Joseph III), 198

"John Bull,"* 31, 53

Keene, Laura, 195

Kidd, Captain William, 134

Knickerbocker, Diedrich (WI persona), xv, xvii, xviii, 36, 37, 56, 57, 84, 86–89, 92, 96n10, 123, 125–28, 130–31, 133–34, 136–37, 142, 146, 167, 169n3, 194, 203

Knickerbocker Magazine, xv, 136

"Knickerbocker's History." See *A History of New-York* (book by WI)

Knyphausen, Wilhelm von, 156

Lafayette, Marquis de, 8, 82–84, 92–94, 158, 177

Landes, David, 103

Larkin, Daniel, 179

Laurens, John, 57

"The Legend of Prince Ahmed al Kamel," 202

"Legend of Sleepy Hollow,"* xi, 4, 7, 8, 11, 13, 37, 45–46, 53–56, 58, 85, 107–10, 157–58, 161–66, 168, 190, 192, 194, 198, 199; enslaved characters in, 55, 77, 129–31, 137; equine element in, 62, 70–72, 76–80. *See also* Sleepy Hollow entries

Levasseur, Auguste, 93

Life and Voyages of Christopher Columbus (book by WI), 184, 191

Life of George Washington (book by WI), 167, 168, 182, 197–98

"Little Britain,"* 77, 103, 107, 111–12

Longfellow, Henry Wadsworth, 27–28

Lowell, Francis Cabot, 115

Ludwig, Edward, 198

Madison, James, xviii, 45, 182

Mandiville, James, 131

Mather, Cotton, 54, 131

Mattingly, Carol, 150–51

McCarter, Pete Kyle, 2

McCree, J. Woodrow, 2, 4

McCrossen, Alexis, 8

Melville, Herman, 2, 44

A Midsummer Night's Dream (Shakespeare), 148

Mison, Tom, 202

Mitchell, Donald Grant, 43, 59n3

"The Money-Diggers," 133–34

Mooney, Katherine, 62

Moore, Thomas, 143, 145

"The Moor's Legacy," 202

Mott, Lucretia, 150

Murray, John, xi, 20–21

Musäus, Johann Karl August, 194

"The Mutability of Literature,"* 33, 46–47, 112

Navarrete, Martin Fernández de, 192

Offen, Neil, 191
Osborn, Matthew Warner, 151

Pablos, Pedro Alonso, 202
Paulding, James Kirke, xv, 125, 158, 159
Paulding, John, 92, 154, 156, 158–59, 161, 166, 168
Payne, John Howard, 197
Pepys, Samuel, 104
"Philip of Pokanoket,"* 7, 31, 42, 52–54, 96n6
Poe, Edgar Allan, 46
Pourtalès, Albert Alexandre de, 69
"The Pride of the Village,"* 66–67
Prown, Jules, 91
Putnam, George P., 27, 187

Ramsay, David, 89
Renwick, James, 25
Rey, Florian, 201
Ricci, Christina, 200
Richards, Ann, 200
Richardson Samuel, 104
Ricketts, John Bill, 75
"Rip Van Winkle,"* xi, xiii, xix, 4, 6, 7, 10, 13, 24, 37, 43–47, 53, 58, 76, 82, 84–93, 108, 110–11, 115, 140–51, 176, 190, 192–94, 196; adapted to opera, 197–98; on radio, 199; as silent film, 195, 198–99; as staged play, 12, 13, 194–96; on TV, 198–99
Rockefeller, William, 164
Romer, John, 159
"Roscoe,"* 33, 109, 111
Rosen, Carole, 201
"Rose of the Alhambra," 202
"A Royal Poet,"* 6, 25–27, 112, 121
Rubin-Dorsky, Jeffrey, 3, 148–49

"Rural Funerals,"* 66, 114–15
"Rural Life in England,"* 35

Salmagundi (periodical by WI et al.), 4
Samuels, Shirley, 6–7
Schuyler, David, 158
Schuyler family, 132
Scott, Sir Walter, xii, 21, 70, 194
Sedgwick, Catharine, 37, 50
Serling, Rod, 13
Sevilla, Carmen, 201
Seymour, Horatio, 160
Shakespeare, William, 29, 85, 107, 115, 135, 136, 194
Shelley, Mary Wollstonecraft, 95n4, 140, 143
Sherman, Stuart, 103
Shire, Talia, 199
Sizemore, Michelle, xix, 5–6
The Sketch Book of Geoffrey Crayon, Gent. (book by WI), ix, 1, 3, 4, 6, 9, 20, 43–45, 48, 50–54, 56, 59, 62, 82, 100, 104, 106, 111, 114, 139, 143, 150, 157, 166, 176, 181, 196, 199; Bracebridge Hall sketches in, 10, 24, 74–76, 111, 112; English motifs in, xi, 24–27, 31, 33–34, 36, 56, 59, 107, 147; publication history of, xi, 21, 140, 144–45, 190; as travel writing, 21–22, 24–25, 27. *See also individual tales by title.*
Sleepy Hollow, Village of, xii, 11, 155, 164–66
Sleepy Hollow (1999 film), 200
Sleepy Hollow (TV show), 167, 202
Sleepy Hollow Cemetery, 161–62, 167
Sparks, Jared, 168
"The Spectre Bridegroom,"* 9, 71–74, 99, 107–9, 115
"The Stage-Coach,"* 67
Stanton, Elizabeth Cady, 151
Stanton, Harry Dean, 199
Steinem, Gloria, 201

INDEX

Sterne, Laurence, 104
Storrow, Susan, 177
Stowe, Harriet Beecher, 27
Stowe, William, 24
"Stratford-on-Avon,"* 6, 29, 35, 77, 107, 166
Stuyvesant, Peter, 128–29
Sullivan, General John, 53
Sunnyside (WI's home), xi, 5, 34–37, 114, 125, 160, 167, 175–76, 179, 183–85, 197

Tales of a Traveller (book by WI), xi, 20, 113, 132, 133
Tales of the Alhambra (book by WI), xi, 20, 114, 201–2
Tallmadge, Benjamin, 159, 160
Tarrytown (NY), xiii, 11, 35, 53, 55, 92, 154, 155, 157–64, 183
Taylor, Bayard, 27
The Tempest (Shakespeare), 135–36
Teuton, Christopher, 32
Thompson, E. P., 103
Thompson, James, 53
Thoreau, Henry David, 86, 90
"The Three Beautiful Princesses," 202
Tilden, Samuel J., 161
A Tour on the Prairies (book by WI), xi, 8, 69, 182, 188n14
"Traits of Indian Character,"* 31–32, 48, 51, 54; speech of Logan in, 40n22, 48, 60n10
Trollope, Frances, 33
Trumbull, John, 75
Tuckerman, Henry, 27
Turner, Edith, 28
Turner, Victor, 28
Twayne Publishers, 2–3, 175
The Twilight Zone, 13

Van Buren, Martin, xviii, 79, 177
Van Cortlandt, Pierre, 131
Van Tassel, Jacob, 167
Van Wart, Alexander, 161
Van Wart, Henry (WI's brother-in-law), 157–58, 170n7
Van Wart, Henry (WI's nephew), 177
Van Wart, Isaac, 92, 154, 159, 161, 168
Van Wart, Sarah (Irving), 157
Vinton, Will, 199
von Weber, Carl Maria, 197
"The Voyage,"* 9, 19, 109, 150

Wainwright, John Howard, 197
Warner, Michael, 136
Washington, George, xiii, 6, 8, 45, 75–76, 82–84, 89, 136, 167, 202. See also *Life of George Washington* (book by WI)
Washington Irving Society, 139–40
Weems, Mason Locke, 89
Weiselberg, Erik, 11
"Westminster Abbey,"* 9, 24, 29, 63, 109, 111, 115
Williams, David, 92, 154, 168
Williams, Stanley, 1–2
Winter, Edgar, 200
Wolfe, Theodore, 35–36
"Wolfert's Roost" (1839 tale by WI), 36, 41n32
Wolfert's Roost (1855 book by WI), 136, 167, 174n32
Wordsworth, William, 104

Yates, Frederick Henry, 194

www.ingramcontent.com/pod-product-compliance
Lightning Source LLC
Chambersburg PA
CBHW020812230426
43666CB00007B/969